Idol of the West

*The Fabulous Career of
Rollin Mallory Daggett*

FRANCIS PHELPS
WEISENBURGER

SYRACUSE UNIVERSITY PRESS

To my daughter

BETTY WEISENBURGER WECKESSER

whose great-grandmother was the
Betsey Daggett Carter of this story

Acknowledgments

IN INVESTIGATING MATERIAL RELATING TO THE CAREER OF ROLLIN MALLORY Daggett, I have made two trips to the Library of Congress and two to the Pacific Coast and am indebted to many people for friendly and helpful cooperation. First of all, I am grateful for the use of genealogical materials and family papers placed at my disposal by my sister-in-law, Miss Maude M. Carter, of Defiance, Ohio, and for significant letters in the possession of Mrs. Welles Bedford of Van Nuys, California, and William E. Carter of Lakewood, Ohio. In reconstructing the boyhood life of Daggett, I found the old files of the Defiance *Democrat* very useful and am indebted to Gordon Dix and Homer Schutt of the Defiance *Crescent-News* for placing them at my disposal. Church records were made available to me by the very cooperative Rev. Edward B. Welsh, Synod Room, College of Wooster Library, Wooster, Ohio. Much research in contemporary newspapers and in manuscript collections at the Ohio State Museum, Columbus, Ohio, was done with pleasure through the cooperation of Mrs. Elizabeth Martin, Mrs. Marion Bates, George Kirk, and Kenneth Duckett. At the Ohio State University Library, George P. Schoyer, Jane Gatliff, and Ruth M. Erlandson were most helpful. Mr. Watts Marchman of the Hayes Memorial Library, Fremont, Ohio, placed at my disposal interesting letters from Daggett to Hayes. I am also deeply indebted to Dr. George Hammond and Dr. John Barr Tompkins of the Bancroft Library, University of California, Berkeley; Frederick Anderson of the Mark Twain Collection, University of California, Berkeley; Herbert C. Schutz of the Huntington Library, San Marino, California; James de T. Abajian of the California Historical Society, San Francisco; Mrs. Clara Beatty of the Nevada Historical Society, Reno; the librarians of the University of Nevada, Reno; the Society of the California Pioneers, San Francisco; and the Pennsylvania Historical Society, Philadelphia. In Washington, D.C., Dr. E. Taylor Parks of the Department of State and the efficient staff members of the Manuscript Division, Library of Congress, and the National Archives gave most considerate attention to my research. Two grants from the Ohio State University and helpful typing services provided by the Ohio State University College of Arts and Sciences were very useful.

FRANCIS P. WEISENBURGER

Columbus, Ohio
April 1965

Contents

Introduction

The world of Rollin Mallory Daggett was one of kaleidoscopic change. When he was born in 1831, the population of the whole country was about thirteen million; when he died in 1901, the total was six times that number. During his boyhood years in northern New York and northwestern Ohio, the primitiveness of pioneer life persisted; at the time of his death, the entire nation was settled; the frontier had passed forever. As a youth he saw the Mexican War end with the acquisition of the Mexican Cession, including California and Nevada, where he would spend much of his mature life. Later he saw civil war temporarily tear the union asunder. Even in his own family sympathies were divided: his closest kinfolk in Ohio were ardent Democrats of Copperhead leanings, while he was a vociferous Radical Republican.

Tremendous economic expansion in the decades after 1840 led to the rise of cities, the rapid progress of manufacturing, and the steady advance of population toward the Pacific. Daggett participated in this westward movement; in his active years he took part in the bustling life of the West Coast metropolis, San Francisco, and the amazing development of the rich Comstock Lode of Nevada. The passing of the frontier at home led to expansion of American commercial interests in the Pacific and Caribbean. In the closing years of his life the United States hoisted its flag over the Philippines, Puerto Rico, Hawaii, and part of Samoa. Daggett shared significantly in this mood of expansion as United States Minister to Hawaii for three highly important years before annexation.

Daggett was not a great man, but he packed his three score years and ten with thrilling adventure. His career illustrates the Horatio Alger legend: although of humble background he was alert to his opportunities, daring in his pursuit of them, and resourceful in turning difficulties into achievements. In 1850, a young man of nineteen, he

1

went through one exciting encounter after another as he wandered to the gold fields of California. In the mining regions he experienced disappointments and cruel hardships until he made a "strike" of precious metal. With the capital provided by his good fortune he and a partner established the *Golden Era* in San Francisco. With Daggett and other authors such as Bret Harte writing for it, the *Era* became the most notable literary journal in California history.

For about nine years Daggett was a familiar and influential figure in San Francisco's journalistic world. Toward the end of this time, having sold his interest in the *Era,* he published the San Francisco *Mirror,* but his ardent pro-Union sentiments in the transitional period of 1860/61 made him unpopular and detracted from the sales of the paper. In 1862 he left California for the alluring Comstock Mining region of Nevada but only after he had virtually driven the leading Presbyterian minister of San Francisco from his pulpit because the clergyman avoided vocal political alignment. At Virginia City, in Nevada, Daggett became a successful broker specializing in mining stocks and then a member of the extraordinary group of reporters, including Mark Twain, that made up the staff of the widely known *Territorial Enterprise.* He was a member of the Territorial Council and for many years Clerk of the United States District Court in Nevada. He maintained a continuing connection with the *Enterprise,* writing many perceptive editorials and at times serving as editor-in-chief. For almost twenty years he was a leader in the community, an enthusiastic patron of its saloons, restaurants, and theatres, a celebrated local literary man who could be relied upon to offer an original sentimental poem or a stirring oration on any special occasion, and an unfailing supporter of Radical Republican political principles. He became the trusted friend of politicians and mining tycoons and served from 1879 to 1881 as lone Congressman from Nevada. In Washington he often convulsed fellow Congressmen in the cloak rooms with his unconventional humor. President Chester A. Arthur appointed him United States Minister to Hawaii, where he served ably from 1882 to 1885. The native King Kalakaua became his close friend, collaborating with him on a volume about the legends of the Hawaiian Kingdom. Daggett had previously written a novel, *Braxton's Bar,* concerning the California Gold Rush. He eventually retired to a fruit ranch near Vacaville, California, but continued to contribute to San Francisco newspapers and the *Overland Monthly.* He spent the last three years of his life in San Francisco, where he died in 1901. Although born in New York State and reared in Ohio, Daggett was essentially a Westerner, having cast his lot with the Far West as a youth of nineteen. In 1877, returning from one of his trips to the East, he felt renewed admiration for the rugged individualism and brisk enthusiasm of his adopted region. He believed that men of the East were "of a most common mold; that the Western man, as he talks with them, grows hourly more and more in love with the men of the West." While the libraries and cultural institutions of the East are worthy of sincere appreciation, Daggett continued, "no man who has been here through the years can go back there and live."[1]

Like the West, Daggett was often rough, crude, and even violent, but like the San Francisco he knew intimately, he had a high degree of sensitive sophistication, enabling him to acquire a wide acquaintance with history, literature, and the arts. Like the West, he was democratic. He hated sham, and he found common ground with men of every station. Yet he loved the company of the privileged few. He was a close friend of Mark Twain, John W. Mackay, the wealthiest "Silver King" of the Comstock, and King Kalakaua, long monarch of the Hawaiian Islands.

About five feet eight in height, in his younger days Daggett was so spare that he could have gone "through an Alderman's thumb ring," but he gradually became heavier. Associates later declared that at two hundred pounds he had no more form than a "sack of apples," and one friend asserted that Daggett's physique reminded one of a hippopotamus. His swarthy complexion, keen black eyes, and black hair, falling with the straightness of an Indian's locks, seemed to give support to the belief, apparently false, that he was part Iroquois.[2] Some thought that he looked like Stephen A. Douglas at the height of his career. In 1878 a friend commented on his "calm, secretive, self-contained" qualities, his tireless energy, amazing endurance, and vengefulness. The same friend was impressed with his marked features, particularly the "heavy scar just above the eye," about which Daggett would never comment. To this associate, Daggett was a person "at whom you will look twice in a crowd, and mentally mark as a man to be heard from."[3]

To a fellow journalist, Daggett was one who "dearly loved a fight" but "in moments of peace" was gentle as a dove. Daggett's foes "dreaded him for his incisive, vitriolic excoriations," while his friends "loved him for his warm heart and his charming manners." This same journalist, recalling that an able observer once referred to Daggett as the "Mirabeau of the Press," suggested that he was more, "the Cyrano de Bergerac of Nevada journalism."[4]

Another prominent western journalist was struck by Daggett's "strange personal magnetism" accompanied by the "heartiest and jolliest" of personal qualities, his unfailing "journalistic judgment," and his exquisite taste in words, which enabled him to combine in a single sentence "the cynical bitterness of Carlyle with the majestic organ-roll of Macaulay's prose." This associate observed that his pen was "like a mighty trip hammer, which . . . can, at will, strike a blow which seems like a caress, and the next moment hurl hundred-ton blows, one after another with the quickness of lightning, and filling all the air around with fire." In his tender moods, Daggett could "set thoughts to words which the angels might set to music to sing on state occasions."[5]

Little wonder that Nevada's most important historian of the last generation has confirmed the estimate of many of Daggett's old Virginia City friends: he was "the Comstock bard and the glory of the town."[6] Bernard De Voto has said that when Daggett died, in 1901, he had become "a complete idol of the West!"[7]

I

Early Years in
New York and Ohio

It was February 22, 1831, and patriots throughout the nation were celebrating Washington's birthday. The bitter chill of winter hung on in the upper reaches of New York State, where it often seemed that after five months of winter came three more months of cold weather. In the Gardner Daggett home at Richville, in St. Lawrence County, which borders on the river of that name, there was excitement not uncommon in households where large families were accepted as an inevitable part of nature. A son, Rollin Mallory, was ushered into the world with the tested procedures which frequent use had made almost routine but without the elaborate ritual of the modern hospital. Certainly a special joy came to the six older sisters, as they welcomed a baby brother.

Rollin was born into a family which had been moving westward in rather easy stages, as many other families participated in the "Yankee Exodus" from the rock-bound coastal area. His grandfather Gideon served in the Revolutionary Army from New Hampshire. His father spent much of his early life in Vermont, marrying Eunice White in 1811.

The White family also illustrated the gradual westward movement of population. The family was descended from John White, who had located at Salem, Massachusetts, in 1638, but by the time of the appearance of the fifth generation in America, a part of the family was residing at Leominster in north-central Massachusetts, a few miles southeast of Fitchburg. Gardner Daggett's bride was one of eleven children of Luke White, born in Leominster in December 1757, and Eunice White, a cousin. The couple raised their family in Heath, Massachusetts, a village sixty miles west of Leominster and only a few miles from the Vermont border.[1]

5

The western and northern pull of population to fill less settled areas drew Gardner and his wife to Poultney, Vermont, sixty miles north of Massachusetts and close to the New York border. But this area, too, had rocky farms, protracted winters, and the New England disease, "consumption," so they continued their westward trek. In some New England areas dislike of high taxes and rebellion against the austerity of Puritan theology and morality spurred westward migration. But most New Englanders on the move sought an easier and more abundant livelihood.

The Daggetts had followed this movement from New England, locating in Richville, a village founded in 1804 in the northernmost tier of New York counties.[2] Here winter temperatures and snowfall equaled and even outdid those in much of New England. Often the bitter cold penetrated the thin walls of the houses, keeping the men busy piling wood in the fireplaces for warmth. Much of the land was densely wooded, so fuel was plentiful. Long months of winter, additional periods of uncertain weather, and a restricted growing season made for a rugged existence. The year 1816, when the Daggetts still lived in New England, was remarkable, being essentially without any of the usual warmth of summer. Frost had visited St. Lawrence County during every month of the year, killing all the crops but potatoes, which, with milk, kept the people alive. In ordinary winters layer after layer of snow sometimes accumulated to a depth of five feet, making it necessary to dig canyon-like paths to the outbuildings and sometimes to the homes of neighbors. The more prosperous citizens in the community kept sheep to provide their families with homespun clothing.[3]

In the Richville neighborhood, many people were former New Englanders who enjoyed intimate social relations. The Rich, Stoddard, Phelps, Blackman, Goddard, Daggett, and other families discussed the possibility of participating in another wave of western migration.[4] New Englanders and Yorkers had long been moving into the Western Reserve of Ohio. Now word began to be spread that canal building was soon to help develop northwestern Ohio, where the old Black Swamp had deterred settlement. By this time, moreover, the gradual draining of the swamp, with the resulting fertile farmland, seemed only a matter of time.[5]

Life in St. Lawrence County was demanding, and animated interest must have characterized family conversation about the allure of the Lake Erie Country. In June 1834 two of the members of the New England families in the De Kalb-Richville neighborhood, Amos Stoddard and his nephew Edwin Phelps, left for the western country.

By late summer they were in Defiance, in the northwestern part of Ohio, where Stoddard joined another émigré from St. Lawrence County, Sylvester Blackman, in operating a hotel.

On a return visit to Richville in 1835, Stoddard, a widower, married Sophronia Daggett, Gardner's daughter. The newly married couple and the Blackman family, accompanied by another Richville youth, William A. Brown, arrived in Defiance on June 5, 1835.[6] Thus, northwestern Ohio came to have a special attraction for the Daggetts Sophronia left behind in St. Lawrence County.

During a visit to Richville two years later, Sophronia probably induced her father to go with her on her return to Defiance. The death of Gardner's wife in June 1833, and two years later, of his father-in-law, Luke White, a widower for more than a decade, may have encouraged him to consider moving to the Ohio country. A nephew, William K. Daggett, Jr., moreover, had gone west in 1835 and was carrying the mail between Fort Wayne, Indiana, and the mouth of the Maumee (Toledo). Perhaps young William had accompanied Gardner's brother Gideon, who migrated to Andersonville, Indiana. Even Gardner's aging father, Gideon, a Revolutionary veteran, had joined in the move to the Hoosier state, where he died in August 1838.[7]

In July 1837 Gardner wrote from Defiance to his daughter Betsey in Richville that the trip cost him only seven dollars. He was vibrantly enthusiastic about the prospects of the new location, reporting that Sophronia's health was better than in New York State, that the land far exceeded his expectation—"better crops of corn, wheat, and potatoes" he had never seen, and that Defiance was "one of the pleasantest situated towns in the country." He found that, in spite of the Panic of 1837 and complaints of hard times, cash was as plentiful in the Defiance area as he had ever known it "in the best of times" and that he was making $1.50 a day for his work. He indicated that he would start back to Richville in four weeks and that the family should be prepared to move to Ohio "as soon as convenient." His closing injunction was, "Rollin, be a good boy and you shall see Defiance. Harriet and Esther likewise. Write me the same day you receive this."[8]

It was indeed a major undertaking to leave one's settled home and move eight hundred miles to the West. But the allure was compelling, for life in St. Lawrence County was indeed circumscribed. The movements of the Daggett family in the years preceding the move were severely limited. Long after the family had moved to Ohio, they often recalled events from St. Lawrence County days as happening during the year "Betsey went to Potsdam," a village in the same county forty miles to the northeast, or other similar excursions.[9]

Yet "stakes were pulled up" later in 1837 when the Daggetts undertook the migration to Ohio. Accompanying Daggett were his six children, his brother William, and the latter's four daughters. Except insofar as the youngsters restricted the activities of the travelers, the trip as far as Cleveland was probably similar in detail to that taken by Amos Stoddard and his nephew three years before. Then passage had been secured on the *Coburg*, a Canadian side-wheel steamer on the St. Lawrence River. Persons traveling first class had staterooms and had their meals with the officers of the boat. Second-class passengers had berths off the cabins, and meals were served in the family style of an old-fashioned country hotel, with the seat at the head of the table carrying with it the responsibility of carving the meat for the others. Steerage accommodations were also available for those not concerned with comfort in travel. After crossing Lake Ontario, the boat docked at Queenstown (later Queenston), a Canadian village six miles north of Niagara Falls. The travelers took time to enjoy "a fine view of the lake and surrounding country, which was then an almost unbroken wilderness." A stage took travelers from Queenstown to Niagara Falls, where accommodations were available at the old Clifton House. After viewing the massive falls from the Canadian side, the travelers of 1834 went to the Lundy's Lane battlefield of the War of 1812 where they witnessed a parade of a Scotch-Canadian regiment of nearly a thousand men, all at least six feet tall, dressed in tartan uniforms. Then a stage carried them from the Falls to Black Rock, where they recrossed the river by ferry. There horse cars running on wooden rails furnished transit to Buffalo. Passage was then taken on a large steamer, the *New York*, crowded with over seven hundred passengers. At Dunkirk and Erie large quantities of wood were taken on (coal was not used at the time). After the ship left Erie, Pennsylvania, a fierce gale blew so tempestuously that seasickness became general, with so many persons having to "heave up" the contents of their stomachs that all over the boat "there wasn't a decent place to sit down." They stopped at Cleveland for half a day, where they dined at a small wooden hotel on Superior Street kept by a pioneer family, the Scovills.[10]

The Daggetts disembarked at Toledo, were Gardner Daggett had landed on his trip from New York state earlier in the year. Toledo, destined to be the metropolis of northwestern Ohio, was incorporated as a village in 1836, after earlier attempts to build a town there had failed.[11] In 1837 the boundary dispute between Ohio and Michigan Territory that involved the Toledo area ended with the admission of Michigan as a state. Toledo was then a rather crude community with little business or cash. Joshua R. Giddings, later a noted antislavery Congressman, there on legal business in April 1837, complained that no meeting house was to be found and no preaching on Sunday but instead "a bustle of business" in the hotel barroom.[12]

With the assistance of William K. Daggett, Jr., the Daggett family pushed on up the valley to Defiance, near which Sophronia's husband was already engaged in business. William, Gardner Daggett's nephew, as a carrier of the United States mails, operated the only conveyance between Toledo and Fort Wayne. The family crowded into the big mail wagon with its two large seats and four horses to pull the load. At the end of the first day they reached Napoleon, then a hamlet of only three houses, forty miles up the Maumee River. After traveling sixteen miles more the next day, they arrived at their destination.

Located at the juncture of the Maumee River and its chief tributary, the Auglaize, Defiance was a natural center of trade. Here Anthony Wayne in 1794 built his chief fort, of which he reputedly exclaimed, "I defy the English, Indians and all the devils in hell to take it." To this, it is said, General Charles Scott replied, "Then call it Fort Defiance."[13] Later, during the War of 1812, General James Winchester established a fortification about a long city block from the site of Fort Defiance.

After the war some soldiers settled in the area. A number of French-Canadian families located there, and gradually other people came to the vicinity. Yet as late as 1830, a pioneer judge who traveled from Findlay to Defiance commented that the trip was through an "unbroken wilderness of some sixty miles" with an intervening settlement of Tahwa Indians, who cheered lustily as the visitors passed.[14]

Defiance had been laid out in November 1822 by Benjamin Leavell of Piqua and Horatio G. Phillips of Dayton. After 1830 new settlers arrived in increasing numbers. A pioneer who located in the community in August 1834 described the wonderfully beautiful appearance of the town as one approached with "no bridge to mar the view, nor anything unpleasant in sight." The larger trees in the town were Indian apple tress, while beyond the village was a dense forest of hickories and oaks.[15] In June 1837 the leading Cincinnati newspaper carried an advertisement for the sale of four hundred village lots in Defiance, a place whose commercial advantages and consequent future importance seemed "obvious."[16]

Ann Daggett Snook, Rollin's cousin, later recalled that when they reached Defiance, which had no sidewalks, the mud was a foot deep. Indians, more numerous in the vicinity than whites, lived in the woods outside the village. They generally went into town to trade their deer- and bearskins for things they wanted at Evans' store. The old squaws wore leggings and wrapped themselves in blankets. Their hair hung over their faces and strung down their backs, as they rode horseback with papooses often strapped behind their shoulders.[17]

Gardner Daggett, on his initial visit to Defiance, considered buying a lot at Independence, a hamlet two miles down the Maumee. But Brunersburg on Bean Creek (Tiffin River) two miles northwest of Defiance had a sawmill and a gristmill and for a time threatened to surpass Defiance in size and importance, so the Daggetts took up residence there. In the new Brunersburg home were just the father, a nineteen-year-old daughter Betsey, four younger daughters, Esther, Harriet, Eunice, and Diane, and little six-year-old Rollin Mallory.

Young Rollin's relations with his father were not always harmonious. In mature years he told an associate that in boyhood he had owned a pet pig: "I loved that pig better than a brother, and when time to butcher I implored my father to spare him. But my father would not, and added hatred to grief by compelling me to kill my pet. Do you know how it impressed me? When my father died I did not shed a tear, not a d——d tear."[18]

Perhaps the father, having known the brutal realities of pioneer life, felt impelled to use extreme measures to thwart excessive sentimentality in the boy. On occasion the father showed real affection for his family. Perhaps, on the other hand, Rollin was exhibiting in his attitude toward his father some of the complex aspects of his personality which many people noted at a later time. At any rate, the father died in 1843, when the boy was only eleven years of age.[19] Left an orphan, Rollin found strength and comfort from his sister Betsey, a vigorous person of seasoned Yankee fiber. Even in her elderly years she maintained that when one was weary it was often necessary to "work up" one's strength through labor.

When Rollin was a boy of eight, Betsey had married William Carter, whose family, like the Daggetts, had migrated from New York State to Ohio. Born in Columbus, Chenango County, New York, in December 1812, Carter as a lad of six had come west with his parents, his brothers, and sisters. They settled on a farm in the Firelands section of the Western Reserve in what later became Erie County. Soon after reaching his majority, Carter left the paternal home to make a place for himself in the workaday world. He headed west for Perrysburg, near Fort Meigs, which was the head of navigation for sailing vessels on the Maumee. Here young Carter sold several loads of lumber brought from the abundant virgin forests of northwestern

Ohio. On a trip to Defiance in 1834, Carter was so attracted to the bustling village that he returned the next year. Speculation was then rampant in the development of nearby Brunersburg. Carter invested in a toll bridge across Bean Creek and for a time conducted a country store. Speculators plotted various village sites, but the projects were ill-fated. The bridge in which Carter had invested was carried away by a freshet, and the store was not remunerative, so he left Brunersburg for Defiance. But 1839 brought brighter prospects: he married Betsey and was elected constable.[20]

Thus, another person joined the family circle of which Rollin Daggett was a part. Rollin's new brother-in-law soon began to read law in the office of Curtis Bates, who had served as a member of the Ohio Legislature. After being admitted to the bar in July 1841, Carter began to practice law in Defiance. A canal contract case early gave him considerable legal reputation, and he prospered as a western loan agent for eastern companies. A man of few words, he had acquired a habit of reading much in history and the classics. His influence on the growing boy was great indeed.[21] Not long after being admitted to the bar, Carter was elected Mayor of Defiance, serving for three terms, beginning in 1846.[22]

Carter was an active Democrat, and his young brother-in-law must have listened with animated interest to discussions of the annexation of Texas and the coming war with Mexico. The household surely was saturated with political excitement when in August Governor Marcus Morton of Massachusetts gave a Democratic speech on the tariff in Defiance. A month later, David Tod and William Sawyer, Democratic candidates for governor and congressman, participated in a parade and a political meeting. Following Polk's election as president in 1844, Carter presided at a Democratic county meeting which gave enthusiastic support to the new administration, and he was active in other Democratic meetings during 1845. Rollin's uncle, William K. Daggett, who had settled in nearby Paulding County, where he was sheriff, as well as hotel and stable manager at the thriving canal community of Junction, was also a leading Democratic politician of the area.[23]

Rollin's boyish imagination must have been stirred by expansionist views. At the Democratic state convention in Columbus on January 8, 1846, one delegate exclaimed, "California—The rising star of California—may it soon rise to a full refulgence in the galaxy of the American firmament." Another, from Seneca County, demanded "the whole American continent—Destined to become one great and united people."[24]

In Ohio militia service had come to be considered a nuisance, and its musters and parades became subjects of ridicule. In 1842 an effort to assemble militia officers of Ohio met hopeless indifference. With the declaration of war, five Whig congressmen from Ohio voted nay, and numerous Whigs lamented the coming of the conflict.[25] The editor of the *Ohio State Journal* condemned Polk for "bringing us into this conflict" but promised, "Ohio will do her share in the war and will rally about the unfurled flag." Considerable war fever developed in the state, and patriotic demonstrations were arranged to stimulate enlistments. Much tension developed in many communities as William Bebb, the Whig candidate for governor, "dwelt on the injustice of the present war brought upon us as the first fruits of the iniquitous annexation of Texas and behest of the Southern slave power and servility of Locofocoism."[26] Bebb was elected governor in October, and in his inaugural address on December 16, 1846, he concluded his comments on the war with the query, "Where is the man who does not know and feel that this Mexican War is a Presidential War?"[27] In February 1847 Senator Thomas Corwin of Lebanon, Ohio, went further in his startling speech on the Senate floor, expressing warm sympathy for the Mexican people, who, in his view, were the victims of American aggression.[28]

Inevitably the citizenry largely supported the war. Colonel William Sawyer, a one-time blacksmith, now Democratic Congressman from the Defiance district, sent to Defiance a pamphlet intended to show the justice of the war, in view of the "wanton murder and robbery" by Mexican authorities. The local Democratic paper asserted that this was "proof" in regard to the war "that should seal the lips of the most brawling Whig in the state."[29] Soon a company raised in the area left for the war front, citizens of the locality presenting Lieutenant James W. Wiley with a sword, as the men proceeded by canal to Cincinnati. Later word came that the Defiance boys had displayed bravery at Churubusco and elsewhere.[30]

But in 1848 the war ended with the treaty of Guadalupe Hidalgo and the granting to the United States of the so-called Mexican Cession, including California. With the opening of new territory a spirit of adventure swept the country and captivated young Rollin. Two years later he would go to Califonia and Nevada, a region ever afterwards to be his home.

During these years life in Defiance had its rugged aspects. By the census of 1840 it was still a small village with only 944 people in the whole township. Unlike the sprawling city of today, with its numerous industries and considerable local trade, it was then confined to

a small area close to the Maumee and Auglaize Rivers. The young
Carter couple with Rollin soon settled on lower Jefferson Street in the
residential section and later in what is now the heart of the business
district.[31] Life in a pioneer section was always taxing. In Defiance,
which was on the edge of the Black Swamp, special difficulties existed.
The experience of a prospective settler in the area illustrates the problems encountered. In the spring of 1841 David Hockman sought to
reach his destination in the present Henry County, immediately east
of the Defiance area, from the present Ottawa in Putnam County, thirty
miles southeast of Defiance, by taking a short cut of eighteen miles
through the swamp. For two days Hockman wandered through the
dark, pathless woods, following the course the water seemed to follow.
His team pulled a lightly loaded wagon through the water, which
varied in depth from two inches to over a foot. At the end of the second day, provisions were running low, and Hockman's stepsister, who
was with him, was almost distracted with fear. At midnight two pioneer settlers who had noticed the wagon tracks furnished help, making
it possible for them to reach their destination through the valley of a
flooded creek, which in places had water up to their waists.[32]

Agues, fevers, and other ailments abounded in this unhealthful
area. Mosquitoes were a major annoyance; horses had to be blanketed
with their heads wrapped for protection in the summer season, in
spite of the hot temperatures. Pioneers themselves had to work with
their heads covered and their hands shielded by buckskin mittens. In
the village of Defiance the situation was less burdensome, but cholera
and other diseases were such scourges that death took in infancy seven
of Betsey and William's eleven children.

In Defiance, as elsewhere, pioneer conditions often made support
of an established minister difficult. In 1836, under the Plan of Union
between the Congregational and Presbyterian churches, Rev. Benjamin
Woodbury, a Congregational home missionary, started calling upon
persons interested in establishing a church. In November 1837 the
Reverend William B. Stowe of the Home Missionary Society began his
ministry at Defiance at a salary of five hundred dollars in cash and
grain (at the market price). Practically all of the congregation organized as the First Presbyterian Church were of New England stock,
many of them recent arrivals from New York State. Among the charter
members were Betsey and Eunice Daggett.[33] In March 1839 Mr. Stowe
closed his ministry because of ill health, and was succeeded in July
1841 by Rev. Edwin R. Tucker of Massachusetts.

Betsey Daggett Carter was a spirited soul who found it difficult
to accept the Puritan demand that the faithful must forsake all worldly

pleasures which might entice one from fellowship with one's Maker.
Church membership was a serious commitment, and the church elders
in Defiance carefully scrutinized the conduct of its members. In 1846
they interviewed a daughter of a prominent family of the congregation, who finally acknowledged that "it was not consistent with the
character of a Christian to be found at places of social dancing and
amusement." Later she confessed to attending a public ball and requested dismissal from the church. Two years thereafter the Session of
the congregation excommunicated a female member for attending
places regarded as sinful by the church. The officers also refused a
letter certifying good standing to a divorcee who sought to transfer her
membership to another congregation. Betsey may have attended a
public ball and incurred the displeasure of the church officers, who
excommunicated her. But she asked forgiveness, secured reinstate-
ment, and remained an active member of the congregation until her
death in 1914.[34] Two-thirds of a century after her excommunication,
when a young granddaughter and her playmates diverted themselves
by "putting on a play" in the family home, she drove them outside
with the rebuke, "No theatricals in my house!"

As Betsey Carter took a motherly concern for Rollin, it is likely
that she undertook his religious instruction. At a time when the "respectable" element in a community, whether church members or not,
commonly attended divine services, Rollin must have heard Mr.
Tucker, a moderate Calvinist, preach on various occasions. Some of
the pastor's sermons indicated that he looked upon the time-honored
Calvinistic doctrine of predestination not as a harsh creed but as the
logical, Bible-based corollary of the belief that God is the Supreme
Ruler.

Rollin was to embrace a much more worldly approach to life than
that countenanced by Tucker and the church elders, although he later
would react occasionally with authentic Puritan severity against what
he deemed the powers of evil.

The line of demarcation between the Divine Plan and Man's responsibility, according to Tucker, was shrouded in mystery beyond mortal ken. For him God was not only just but good, and those
who followed Him could rely on constant assurance of His protecting
care, as they found themselves secure in the "hollow of His hand."
Tucker asserted that only one's own "unwillingness to come" kept
individuals from being "admitted to all the Privileges of the Sons of
God."[35] Such faith, according to this Ohio preacher, would become
evident in transformed lives. Tucker denied the allegation of some
that God's forgiveness of sin was an inducement to sinfulness to be

followed by a show of repentance. Drawing an analogy from everyday life, he suggested that when a person expressed a high regard for a fellow man, the latter was apt to be very careful of his acts lest he become unworthy of such regard and lose it. Tucker believed that a similar attitude characterized those who had received God's offer of love.[36] Yet Tucker also emphasized the wrath of God to be visited upon those who resisted divine grace.

To make his warning more forceful, on the first Sunday of a new year the preacher resorted to local statistics for the year just ended: "Sixteen persons have been called from this immediate vicinity into the Eternal world of Death and burial is as it were a momentary lifting of the veil which is between us and the Eternal World—an invitation to look into that far future whither we all trend."[37] Tucker indicated that all around one could be seen sin and even cruelty, wantonness, and bestiality, but Christ beckoned his followers to "cut off a Right Hand, pluck out a Right Eye, rather be put to Death the most ignominious" than follow the path of sin.[38]

During this period some of the pioneers of the Ohio country were finding in Methodist camp meetings and revivals the emotional outlet and warm fellowship they craved. Methodists at this time were quite as insistent as Presbyterians in disavowing worldliness. In Ohio, through exhortation, preaching, and even legal compulsion, their evangelical leaders sought to subdue the crudities, sensuality, corruption, and materialism of a backwoods society.[39] In Defiance there had long been an energetic group of Methodists, and Esther, a sister of Rollin and Betsey, became one of their enthusiastic leaders. Even half a century later, Esther sometimes expounded so enthusiastically and protractedly at Methodist meetings that the preacher in charge would have to insist that she bring her testimonial to a close and "sit down."[40]

In Defiance Rollin had the limited schooling available in an Ohio pioneer community. When he was fourteen the local paper declared the district school to be in "miserable condition."[41] But, as a ward of his brother-in-law William, who was a leading lawyer of the town, he probably had some associations with "Mr. McCord's Select School," which each year gave a public exhibition which the Defiance *Democrat* termed "highly creditable."[42] On such occasions the superior students presented essays and evidence of proficiency in reading, writing, spelling, and arithmetic, to the delight of relatives and friends.

During the summers Rollin indulged in boyish activities, including "the sublime pleasure of robbing melon patches and peach orchards." On winter evenings the youth of the community enjoyed the "charming and healthful pastime" of sleigh ride parties to Langton's Tavern, a stagecoach stop three miles north of Defiance, and here on summer evenings there was lively dancing.[43]

Rollin was always an alert, observant individual. He was doubtless on hand on such occasions as when fire threatened the home of Squire Edwin Phelps and was put out with a minimum of damage, through efforts of local citizens.[44] Probably he joined other residents of the community in viewing the "magnificent" painting of Christ raising Lazarus, a copy of the original by Benjamin West that was then on tour and was exhibited at the Methodist Church. Certainly he shared in the excitement that pervaded the community when the Maumee overflowed its banks in January 1847, inundating much of the village and carrying away half of the bridge that joined the north side of the community with the main portion of the town.[45]

A gala event in the village was always the Fourth of July celebration, which was ushered in by the firing of guns and "soul-stirring" music by the Defiance band. Various Sunday Schools of the town assembled at their places of meeting and then marched to the Methodist Church. There a prayer, the reading of the Declaration of Independence, and speeches by prominent citizens constituted the program. Then dinner was served in a grove near Fort Defiance. In the evening the gayer set participated in a cotillion at the Defiance Exchange, followed by supper.[46]

Pioneers continued to move into this part of Ohio, the last to feel the transforming hand of new settlers. Toward mid-century many new buildings sprang up: a gristmill, a sawmill, two warehouses, many dwellings, and shops. As an indication of the increased activity in the area, the United States Land Office moved there from Upper Sandusky, Ohio, opening on May 1, 1849.[47] But, as Defiance grew, there grew also the appeal of another section of the country yet untamed. Visions of wealth and adventure in the Far West appeared in the dreams of young and old.

II

Off for California!

In January 1848 James Wilson Marshall, while constructing a sawmill at Coloma on the American River in California, noticed flecks of yellow metal in the stream. He tried unsuccessfully to keep the thrilling discovery a secret, lest others seek a share in the hidden wealth.[1] Soon journalists sent the news to the farthest reaches of the land. As early as September 1848, the Cincinnati *Enquirer* and the Cleveland *Herald* reported to interested Ohioans that the discovery of gold had turned everybody in California "topsy-turvy."[2]

Rollin must have learned the news with unrepressed excitement. In January 1849 "Gold Hunters" organized a company in Defiance, and in February at least eighteen men left for the West via New Orleans and Chagres.[3] They reached Port Lavaca, Texas, after a "horrible time" in crossing the Gulf of Mexico from New Orleans on the steamboat *Palmetto*. Cholera brought death to some on the ship, and the waters were extremely rough. At that time they wanted to buy mules, but the price was twenty to seventy-five dollars each. The trip westward was to be via El Paso.[4]

With the departure of these men the Defiance *Democrat*, of which Samuel Yearick was the proprietor, lost a journeyman printer, and Rollin took his place. On the *Democrat* he learned a trade that kept him in touch with the literate world of his day and paved the way for many of his accomplishments. His independent spirit took him later in 1849 from Defiance by the route of the Miami and Erie Canal to follow his trade at Piqua, a town of thirty-two hundred inhabitants in the Miami River Valley, about twenty-seven miles north of Dayton, Ohio.[5]

Piqua was only eighty miles from Cincinnati, then the "Queen City of the West," larger than any other western community except New Orleans, in many respects a southern city. Cincinnati's preeminence at that time is indicated by its population, twice that of the next four largest Ohio cities combined (Cleveland, Columbus, Dayton, and Zanesville). Naturally a printer in a small Ohio town scanned the newspapers of the neighboring metropolis for exciting news of the world, and especially of California, which was drawing youthful adventurers and more mature fortune seekers from all parts of the country.

By early 1849 Cincinnati stores were advertising Colton's *Map of the United States, Mexico, and California,* "showing the Routes of the United States Mail Steamers to California, and a Plan of the Gold Regions." Stores offered "California Pilot Bread," which supposedly would keep twelve months, and cheese which would not spoil in the warmest climate and would last for two to four years. Corn meal and flour, reputed to "keep sweet for one year in any climate," were also available.[6] Blankets, gold sifters, cooking equipment, revolving pistols, hunting knives, pocket compasses, spyglasses, and percussion caps were also for sale. For various ailments Dr. Myers' Sarsaparilla and Dr. Bragg's Queen Vegetable Sugar Coated Pills could be secured, and the agent of the Knox Insurance Company offered life insurance for those taking the overland route.[7] By April 1849 the editor of the *Ohio Statesman* in Columbus was estimating that at least twenty thousand Ohioans would make their way to California during the year. *Cist's Weekly Advertiser* of Cincinnati placed the number at ten thousand.

As in the case of those going from other states, Ohioans took various routes. Those going via Panama, the quickest route, generally endured fewer hardships. This route involved taking a steamer from New York to Panama, crossing the isthmus, and boarding a steamer at Panama City for San Francisco, the whole trip sometimes taking only thirty-three to thirty-five days. Until the building of the transcontinental railroad, mail and express shipments were often carried this way. The number of passengers using the Panama route was relatively small, but it was preferred by merchants, politicians, army and naval officers, and other persons of means.[8]

The long sea route had disadvantages. The voyage involved the possibility of running out of coal, broken machinery, desertion by the crew, or even a drunken master of the ship; the cost was high, $230 to $410, depending on accommodations; tropical fevers threatened as the passage across the isthmus was made by native canoes and mules; and there were delays on the Pacific Coast in securing passage from Panama to San Francisco. A less expensive route was by ship to the Gulf of Mexico, across Mexico, and then northward to San Francisco by water. Diseases and bandits, however, menaced this venture. This was the route taken by a large company organized under the leadership of Lieutenant Colonel Webb of the 16th United States Infantry. The company, financed by many wealthy New Yorkers, was to carry on trade, purchase gold dust, and use Indians to mine gold, and was entrusted with government dispatches to California. The federal authorities agreed to provide men with arms, camp equipment, and transportation from New Orleans to the Rio Grande. The company, which included William Henry Harrison, grandson of "Tippecanoe," left Cincinnati aboard the steamer *John Quincy Adams* for Cairo, Illinois, and New Orleans. From there they sailed for the Rio Grande. However, misfortune overtook them at Clay Davis' Rancho on that river. A Mexican robbed a son of Audubon, the eminent ornithologist, of twelve thousand dollars in gold, and cholera took the lives of eight of the men, including young Harrison.[9]

In many respects the Cape Horn route was the safest, but this required four to eight months with attendant boredom and fatigue. One venture from Ohio that used this route was that of the sailing vessel *Eureka*, which left Cleveland in September 1849, going via Lake Erie, the Welland Canal, Lake Ontario, and the St. Lawrence to the ocean, and then, by the Cape Horn route, to California. Forty-seven Ohioans, including some from Cleveland and at least a dozen other communities, were on board.[10]

The most strenuous but most popular routes were those overland across the western plains. The southern trail traversed Texas to Sante Fe, where the adventurer might proceed via the Gila-Colorado junction and the Imperial Valley, reaching Los Angeles by way of San Gorgonis or Warner's Pass. On the other hand, he might use the Spanish Trail from Sante Fe to San Bernardino. The California-Oregon Trail passed through the Platte River Valley and then crossed the Rockies at South Pass, reaching Fort Hall on the Snake River. From here the California Trail went by way of Salt Lake and the Humboldt and Truckee Rivers on to Sacramento. From Fort Hall the Oregon Trail proceeded to the Columbia River, from which area a journey southward took one to California.[11]

The southern overland route was less popular because of terrible storms, horrible roads, dangerous fords, cold winds, desert sands, and a shortage of provisions for men and grass for animals. D. C. Horton, a Cincinnatian, made the trip in four months but suffered greatly in crossing the desert just as he reached California. There he reported, "The desert is 65 miles across, without grass or water, except one boiling spring of salt water which animals would not drink. It is a sea of land, and we were two days making five miles, having to unload and pack our things upon our backs, and carry them a mile."[12] Another argonaut termed the "great desert" a "dread to all emigrants," one which was "nothing but sand and earth strongly mixed with alkali . . . with occasionally a bunch of wild sage." The road through the desert was "strewn with dead and starving oxen, mules and horses, but principally oxen."[13]

For those taking the northern route, there were similar hazards. A young Cincinnatian recounted that in crossing the desert before reaching the Carson River, eight out of thirty men in their party were left exhausted in the desert, but several recovered when water was brought back to them. After the plains and desert, two miles above the sea in the Sierra mountains, one struggled in immense fields of snow and saw the road lined with broken and abandoned wagons.[14] An Ohioan who had reached Yuba City by December 1849 had taken the trail through Oregon rather than the Donner Pass into California, but he too encountered the hardships of being soaking wet for a week, living on salt meat and hard bread, and standing guard "over a lot of worn out oxen to prevent a pack of hungry Indians from eating them."[15]

Such hardships did not quell the enthusiasm with which Ohioans of nearly all classes of society and age groups continued to yearn to try their luck in California. Earlier, the excitement in the opening months of 1849 had even prompted Wilson Shannon, Governor of Ohio (1838-40, 1842-44) and United States Minister to Mexico, to lead a party to the coast.[16] Ohio businessmen now sold the fortune hunters huge quantities of a wide variety of supplies and equipment and even safes and houses, the latter built by Cincinnati carpenters and transported by way of Cape Horn.

In Piqua, where Daggett had located in 1849, during the following winter advertisements appeared in the *Register* that included:

> I am for California! ! ! Offers for sale Tavern, house with lot with shop, horses, buggy and harness, 80 A. of land, etc. by Thomas M. Beamer, Fletcher, Ohio, Dec. 22, 1849.
>
>   To be sold before March 1, or in case of failure to do that, rented, for I start for California, if I never get there.[17]

Daggett was caught up in the enthusiasm, and in January 1850, although he believed that he was doing well as a printer, he was maturing his own plans to join others in "taking an unlimited company of men" from Piqua to California, starting in late March or early April by the "Northern Overland Route." The terms from Piqua to Sacramento were to be only a hundred dollars for each man, all expenses paid. Daggett claimed that this was the "cheapest yet offered," and sought by advertisement in the Piqua *Enquirer* and personal correspondence to recruit a company. The advertisement suggested that a company of fifty men with Sacramento as the objective was desirable, and the editor of the paper indicated that Daggett was a responsible man who would make good his promises.[18] The venture at best would be hazardous, but at home one also faced harrowing dangers. The year 1849 saw a devastating epidemic of cholera. In August the Defiance churches held a fast day in an effort to obtain divine help.[19]

Daggett had much of the imp in his make-up. When word of his project reached Defiance, the home town paper commented: "Boys in our office have a hearty laugh over Rol's proposition, which is nothing more than a hoax. Daggett was a devil in this office last year, and a devil of a devil he was."[20]

Rollin realized, as did others, that it was desirable to start west as soon as the snows passed, so as to reach one's destination before summer. Soon numerous companies were setting forth from Ohio. A group of eight, for example, left Newark toward the end of March. At about the same time the "Delaware Mutual Protection Company" left Delaware, Ohio, the company of about seventy being divided into messes of four or five.[21]

Although Rollin's hopes for a larger company did not materialize, he set forth with like-minded companions to seek his fortune, equipped through the generosity of his brother-in-law in Defiance. His first setback occurred in Independence, Missouri, where he was robbed of practically all he had, but, undismayed, he continued toward the coast.[22] In a later semifictional autobiographical account, Daggett described a journey with twenty-three others who left Independence, Missouri, bound for California. He relates that "the love of adventure and romance was the ruling passion" of his existence, his one regret being "that of leaving, forever, perhaps," home ties in the Ohio area. According to the story, the company then traveled through the reservations of the Pawnees, Delawares, Potawatamies, Ottawas, and other Indian tribes in a wholly peaceful way. Within a few miles of Fort Laramie, Daggett noted that some of the company were dissatisfied with the way in which he scoured the country in every direction from morn till night, hunting buffalo and otherwise engaging himself so as to anger the Indians and jeopardize the company. Finally he wrote that he wished no longer to be a burden to the company "but to leave the train and alone with my trusty rifle on my shoulder, and the sun as my guide, find my way to the Pacific, or any other place that chance might lead me." So, on the morning after the arrival of the company at Horse Creek, near Scott's Bluff, "just as the sun began to gild the broad plains on which we were encamped," he left his comrades sleeping soundly in their tents. Taking only a rifle, ammunition, a pair of saddlebags in which he packed a blanket, a Bible, two quires of paper, writing materials, and three or four days' provisions, with matches and trinkets, he set off on foot toward the West.[23] With neither compass nor map, he traced on it the rivers and mountains, as he recalled them, on a sheet of paper and then marked the route he planned to follow.

Reluctantly leaving the Platte River, the only landmark he knew in the wilderness, he walked about twenty-five miles the first day and arrived in sight of what may have been a part of the Wind River range. Crossing the mountain, he followed a small tributary of the North Platte and at length reached the Laramie Plains, where wild horses and antelopes abounded. Traveling for one and a half days to the southwest he reached the foothills of the Green Mountains, where he encountered many wild goats and panthers. Crossing the mountains, he met handsome Indians, resembling the Sioux. They were friendly and seemed much interested in his gun, pistol, calico shirt, and the brass buttons on his coat. They treated him kindly, giving him dried elk and venison and a kind of cake made of dried barley. He gave them a few pins, needles, and a calico shirt, which he tore into about fifty pieces and divided among them.

Subsequently he followed the Colorado River for five days through an almost continuous canyon. At the mouth of one of its larger tributaries, he encountered the largest trees he had seen since leaving Kansas, and a couple of days later he came to an Indian camp in a large valley. The Indians there were short and dark-skinned with sloping foreheads and strange features. Next morning he resumed his journey, traveling down the Colorado for six days and camping each night by the side of the river until he reached the Grand River, a fork of the larger stream.

Then, going westward through a beautiful valley, he encountered groups of wild horses. Soon arid land came into view, and at length Daggett saw buildings of stone and adobe; he had reached the land of the Moquis, or Hopi, Indians. Among these Pueblo Indians of Arizona he seems to have remained for a time, learning the language and lore of the people. This became the basis for a series of literary sketches which he published some years afterwards, "Lost in the Wilderness."[24] Daggett surely had a very retentive memory and a lively imagination, so the stories may well be a remarkable blending of truth and fiction. In 1854 the *Golden Era,* of which Daggett was coeditor, gave the following description of the Moquis. They have occupied a few villages near the boundary line between Utah and New Mexico, not many miles from the Colorado. The land which they claim as their own, is an oasis in the waste which surrounds it. They were a peculiar people, and sought no intercourse with neighboring tribes, but seemed to desire to be left to brook in seclusion over some national misfortune. The arts of war were imperfectly retained by them, and consequently their little property was often almost entirely sacrificed to the cupidity of their more warlike neighbors. It is supposed that they were a remnant of a tribe of Aztecs.[25]

Eventually going northward, he fell in with another immigrant train, in which cholera was taking its ghastly toll. In the party were a man, his wife, and their three children, the eldest child only nine. The man had two ox teams, but the driver of one died, so Daggett took over the dead man's responsibility for a day or two. Near old Fort Hall tragedy struck again, as the father succumbed to the terrible plague. Next night the wife, on her deathbed, asked Daggett to promise that if he and the children survived, he would see that the youngsters were taken to the home of friends in Sacramento. It was soon Daggett's grim task to bury the mother. Afterward, selecting the strongest oxen and hitching them to the lightest wagon, he set out again, with a milch cow tied to the wagon. Fortunately Daggett was able to take the children safely to Sacramento.[26]

William Mitchell, another Piqua, Ohio, man, wrote his impressions of Sacramento at about the time Daggett arrived there:

Sacramento city is growing right up. I never saw any place grow equal to it in my life. The buildings are mere shells, and a great many of them canvass with wooden fronts, canvass roofs, etc. But those buildings now have shingle roofs, and I believe there are three or four brick buildings going up. A great many kinds of business are overdone. There is any amount of eatables, and a great many to eat them, and flocks of poor, penniless people coming both ways, every day to help. Quite a few have arrived over the Plains, and they are coming every day. The report is that those coming over the Plains must suffer 50 per cent more than last year.[27]

Mitchell, who may have known of Daggett's plan, expressed fear that "those who started from Piqua will suffer very much." Mitchell's own party had tried prospecting at Auburn but had found that they were a little too late for the "dry diggings" and entirely too early for the wet or river diggings, so they had tried carpentering at Sacramento for twelve dollars a day, boarding in their own tent. But the weather was warm and the work hard, so they tried mining, with little success, in the Oregon Canyon neighborhood. Mitchell had then returned to carpentering in Sacramento, although his father and brother had tried mining again near Georgetown. Mitchell asserted that thousands would leave to return to the East at once if they had the means. He declared, "I thought that I had considerable nerve and perseverance, but I found that I have not a grain to spare." He himself had lost eleven pounds in seven days due to dysentery, but he believed that much of the prevalent illness was avoidable. He wrote: "Those who get sick are generally in fault themselves. They come here after a long voyage by Sea or Land as hungry as wolves, and, if they have any money, pay two or three dollars for a large watermelon or muskmelon, or eat a quarter of mutton, ½ bushel of cucumbers or a parcel of rare fried steak which would make any man sick."[28]

Daggett did not remain in Sacramento but started for the gold fields. Little is known in accurate detail of his mining career, although under the pseudonym "Blunderbuss" Daggett later wrote extensive "Mining Recollections of '49-'50" for publication. Here, as elsewhere, with his lively imagination Daggett probably embroidered upon his experience. In the recollections he is often very specific in regard to dates, but he always liked to give the impression that he was an original "forty-niner," although he did not go to California until 1850. Even the *Biographical Directory of the American Congress* states that he went west in 1849. But these recollections probably indicate something of the atmosphere and the trials of his mining years, if not entirely true in details.

In one of his accounts Daggett recalls standing on the morning of September 23, 1850, near K and Fifth Streets in Sacramento with a pair of red blankets strapped across his shoulders. Around him were many immigrant wagons. He was wondering how he would invest his last quarter. He decided that potatoes would give him the most nourishment for the money, and sought them at J and Front Streets. The merchant, apparently thinking he wished to buy in quantity, gave him a huge specimen to cut and examine. Daggett told him that he would buy from him if from anyone and bolted down the potato. Then, going to a bakery, he bought a loaf of bread, ate a third of it, and stowed the rest in his blankets. That night, seeking rest under a tree near Daylor's Ranch, he was besieged by ants and soaked by rain. Later, arriving in the mining country, he found that no hands were needed, but he was allowed to work the claim while others were at dinner. He washed eighteen pans of dirt and got seven dollars in gold.

Next day, moving on two miles, he found a miner with whom he formed a successful partnership.

Daggett also related his early experiences at Brown's Bar, about twenty-five miles above the junction of the north branch of the Yuba River with the southern and middle forks, and on the north fork of Dry Creek, about ten miles northeast of Drytown, where supplies had to be obtained. Later, believing that gold existed on the east slope of the Sierra Nevada Mountains, he joined a party leaving Murderer's Bar on the American River for the headwaters of the Carson, Walker, and Truckee Rivers. There they found beautiful scenery and many fish but no gold. After thrilling experiences with the Indians, they returned to Placerville. In another account Daggett told of wandering on foot over the San Joaquin Plains and (according to the story) of having narrowly escaped death as myriads of wild cattle pursued him. Later, as the tale related, he remained in Stockton for a couple of weeks and then again returned to the mines, planning to reach the Stanislaus River about twenty miles above the city. Running into two other prospectors, he induced them to accompany him to the Toulumme, and this time the three of them narrowly escaped a stampede of wild cattle.[29]

In the mining communities Daggett saw hundreds of miners who, regardless of background, commonly wore a red or gray flannel shirt, old trousers, high boots pulled over the trouser legs, and a dilapidated slouch hat. Living in a crude shelter, the miner looked to Sunday as a time when, after a strenuous week of labor, there was time for conviviality and obtaining supplies. Drink, vice, and gambling beckoned, but most miners were not dissipated and wanton.[30]

After Daggett's retirement from active life many years later, he was one of two writers to contribute a series of "True Tales of the Old West." He wrote:

> My success as a gold miner was never bewildering. I could always find gold in paying quantities; that is, I never found it difficult to secure a location where I could gather from half an ounce to two ounces of gold dust per day of remarkably energetic and persistent labor; but I was not among those who were continually stumbling upon nuggets as large as a man's head, or dropping upon pockets and crevices from which small fortunes were panned between successive Sundays, and frequently in less time.[31]

According to this account Daggett and two other men diverted about fifteen hundred feet of the South Yuba, below the mouth of Rush Creek, or five or six miles from Nevada City and about the same distance from Grass Valley, to form a flume, or inclined trough, where they could work over the gold deposits. In the general area were many mining camps—Nevada City, Rough and Ready, Boston Ravine, Frenchman's Bar, Jones' Bar, and many others.[32] The flume in which Daggett was involved was constructed under contract by a visionary old mechanic known as "Deacon Locke," who erected a sawmill at the lower end of the bar, solely to provide lumber for the single undertaking. So much time, however, was consumed in building the mill that the waters of the river were not diverted from the bed until the first week of November. The draining pumps had scarcely been placed in operation before the aqueduct of sawed lumber was torn into fragments by the seasonal floods. Reacting characteristically to this cruel disappointment, Daggett in his wrath threw his water shovels, crowbars, wheelbarrows, and other tools into the raging river, his anger increased by the knowledge that others several hundred yards below had taken out a fortune in nuggets. During the ensuing year Daggett apparently made a fortunate "find" in the gold fields of the area. By December 1852 he was ready to begin an important business enterprise in San Francisco.

III

San Francisco
Journalist

ACCORDING TO ONE OF DAGGETT'S "TRUE TALES," PUBLISHED IN THE
Overland Monthly, he was still an eager miner in the South Yuba gold
fields in July 1852 but some months later was in San Francisco, on one
occasion being the guest of a friend at a French restaurant.[1] In spite
of the title, the account may be partly fictional. With capital available
from success in mining, Daggett located in the Golden Gate city in
the fall of that year. For a time he worked there as a printer for
Loren Pickering, later a well-known newspaperman. But by December
19, Daggett and his coeditor, J. Macdonough Foard, had brought out
the first issue of the *Golden Era,* which has been termed the "most
important journal ever published on the Pacific slope."[2]

Foard was born about 1828 in Cecil County, Maryland, and came
as a youth to California in 1849. It has been claimed that he was a
descendant of Commodore Thomas Macdonough, famed for his victory
at Plattsburg on Lake Champlain during the War of 1812, but this is
in error.[3] Foard had fierce blue-gray eyes and in later life an iron-gray
mustache; he looked more like a Frenchman than an American.[4]

The abilities of Daggett and Foard complemented each other, and
a distinguished historian of California has asserted that Daggett's
"principal fame is as co-founder" of the *Golden Era.* The times were
propitious for such a journal. This was "evidenced by the long queues
at the San Francisco post office, by the special fees readily collectible
for delivery of letters at the mines, by the popular excitement whenever a steamer entered Golden Gate, and by the high prices current
for eastern newspapers which were part of the incidental baggage of
the argonauts."[5]

In the first issue of the *Golden Era,* a weekly, appeared an explanation of purpose. Admitting that a large number of journals of

"almost every size, price, and character" were coming from the presses of California, the editors declared that it was obvious "that there was still room for another—a Good Family Paper; calculated for circulation in every parlor and miner's cabin; that would be found of interest to the merchant, the farmer and the mechanic; untainted with politics, and unbiased by religious prejudices. To supply this deficiency we today present the first number of *The Golden Era.*" Then they extended an invitation, which over the years proved remarkably productive:

> The Literati of California—Another great feature in the publication of the *Golden Era* is the opportunity offered a host of our fair poulation, who possess literary attainments of a high order, but have heretofore been deprived of a medium through which to give their productions to the world. As an earnest of their willingness to contribute to our columns we have already received several original romances and poetical effusions which in the course of a week or two will be laid before our readers. The favors of male contributors are also coming in upon us, many of them bearing the impress of the scholar and author. To all of whom we offer our acknowledgments, with the assurance that the columns of the *Golden Era* will ever be open to their productions.[6]

The *Golden Era* was a literary weekly rather than a newspaper. Bret Harte, Mark Twain, Joaquin Miller, Charles Warren Stoddard, Fitz Hugh Ludlow, Orpheus C. Kerr, and "Ada Clare" all wrote for it at one time or another. Bret Harte's earliest published work to be preserved, "The Valentine," appeared in the *Golden Era* in 1857. Occasionally Foard received a poem or little sketch from Harte, which he would publish anonymously and which attracted considerable attention. Harte's first prose work of consequence, "A Trip Up the Coast," appeared in the *Golden Era.*[7]

But the unique asset of the journal was its human sympathy. According to one writer:

> It has always met its readers half way, and, in fact, been more of a chronicler of people than events; human nature rather than the face of nature; thoughts and feelings rather than lakes and mountains; making, indeed, the old files of the *Golden Era* a sort of book of fate in which may be read the beginning of the career of many of our California celebrities before they dreamed of greatness or had it thrust upon them.[8]

It emphasized colorful aspects of mining life and stimulating dramatic criticism. The drama department was the first in any paper in California and became such a power that all the theatrical stars, upon reaching San Francisco, rushed to the *Era* office to secure recognition, and the establishment became a resort for the celebrities of the day.

At first the proprietors hired type at thirty-five cents a thousand ems for each issue, but soon afterwards they raised money enough to purchase a printing office of their own. Costs were high in a mining state, and they had to pay $22.00 a ream for paper (by 1893 a ream cost $5.00 or $6.00), and $1.25 per thousand ems for composition. By 1893 this labor cost forty cents.

The crowning glory of the paper was a highly decorative masthead with the title printed with letters carved out of quartz. The novel type weighed over eight pounds and carried seventeen pennyweight of gold to the pound. Within a month its city circulation alone was two thousand copies, and the owners tried to secure extensive subscription lists in the mining areas. Contemporary newspapers in San Francisco such as the *Evening Journal* and the *Transcript* praised it for its excellent typographical features, judicious selections, and sprightly editorials.

Its chatty approach was very appealing, as when it related that within a week, in at least six cases, miners on their way back home had been "roped in" by gamblers and in most cases had lost five hundred to two thousand dollars each, in many instances necessitating their return to the mines. The *Golden Era* admonished: "Keep from the gambling houses; for if you do not gamble your money off, you are liable to have it picked from your pockets."[9]

News items were often of dramatic occurrences, such as that concerning the first legal execution in San Francisco, the hanging of a Spaniard, Forni, for the murder of one Rodriguez. Poetry, fiction, news summaries, editorials, and advertisements shared the columns of the four-page journal. Writers using pseudonyms like "Vide Poche," "Dow, Jr.," and "Cadiz-Orion," made their contributions. As the journal surpassed its rivals, contributions such as the "Wild West" sketches by Alonzo Delano ("Old Block"), poems by John R. Ridge ("Yellow Bird"), and learned treatises on such themes as the progress of civilization during the previous quarter of a century by John S. Hittell appeared.

Daggett thought Elbridge Gerry Paige ("Dow, Jr.") whose "Short Patent Sermons" first were published in the New York *Sunday Mercury* and then were reprinted in the *Golden Era*, was "of rare literary abilities; but unsteady habits wrecked him in the prime of life." "Dow's

Sermons" were short essays, "combinations of philosophy and humor, and were characterized by abrupt descents from the sublime to the ridiculous."

Delano, to Daggett, was a "thoroughly lovable man," whose *bright* sketches of mining life over the name "Old Block" were "breezy and full of quiet humor, and a dull line could scarcely be found in any of them."

John R. Ridge, an educated half-caste Cherokee, had left the tribe because of bitter factional warfare. He died in the prime of life, but Daggett recalled that "he loved nature and his soul was full of tenderness and song. The great waters of the ocean awed him, and we sometimes strolled along the open beach . . . to listen to the voices of the waves."[10]

The holidays of 1852/53 brought forth moralizing editorials with a distinct Daggett flavor. In one of them he expounded:

> "Old Fifty-two" having passed his allotted time on earth, was quietly hobbled off the "stage of time. . . ."
>
> If during the gone year one may have been deficient in the discharge of his duties in any relation of social or domestic life, the silent monitor again awakes him to the necessity of repairing his error and restoring the harmony he may have disturbed or destroyed. And, indeed, if there were no divine precept on this subject, the experience of man, in every age and clime, proves beyond question that by such a course only can worldly happiness be secured. It is the law of our being that we must live at peace with all men, even for the sake of our own peace and tranquillity.[11]

He opposed prohibiting business on the Sabbath, writing:

> For some time past an effort has been making in the city by some of our well-meaning people to suspend all business on the Sabbath, and which has been at length rewarded by the passage of an ordinance to this effect by the City Council. Now, there is none who would hail such a reform with a heartier good will than we would, whenever the majority of our citizens demand it; but at the present time, considering that a large portion of our inhabitants is made up of different religious opinions such a definite action by this body is premature, and if enforced will lead to unnatural results.[12]

Yet moral reform had many facets, and the *Golden Era* deprecated horse-racing, especially on Sunday, as an "uncivilized evil," which should be avoided, "if not in reverence for the ordinance" of God, at least through reverence for the law of the state. This prompted the California *Christian Advocate* to express "no little grief" at having the *Golden Era* hawked in the city on the Day of Rest, but rejoicing in its stand against Sunday horse racing, expressed the hope that it would change its date of issue.[13]

With an eye for the picturesque, Daggett left Foard to manage the paper, while he donned a red shirt and top boots and went to the mining camps to secure subscriptions. From these places he sent back intimate pictures of the communities, the contributions being signed "R.M.D." These letters proved highly popular as Daggett, an old miner himself, gave a graphic description and a vivid narrative regarding life in the mining community. In the first letter, written late in February from Grass Valley, he described the journey by stage through January floods. At one point the stage became "completely stuck in a mudhole," so the passengers alighted, put their "shoulders to the wheel," and raised the vehicle to solid ground. Daggett reported that at Grass Valley, the first mining settlement in Nevada county, miners were doing better than for eighteen months previous and that at Boston Ravine, a mile west of Grass Valley, eight quartz mills were in operation.[14] A week later, on March 2, Daggett reached Nevada City. There he found life monotonous except for an occasional dogfight. The miners seemed to be doing well, but he did not see how the prosperity could continue, for the diggings had been thoroughly worked. Nevada City was a place of considerable small-scale gambling, and he paid his respects to the participants: "Nevada is well stocked with the most contemptible of all classes of humanity—would-be gamblers—a hermaphroditic gang of degenerate scrubs, too lazy to work, with not sufficient brains to make a living by gambling, but who assume all the airs of this fraternity, and take to mining when driven to it by starvation or lack of credit."[15]

Soon he was at the mining camp called Yankee Jim's, twenty miles southeast of Nevada City. Daggett reported that it had burned down twice since it was established eighteen months before but had come to be a compact, substantial village which deserved to be known by a name less "rowdyish and poetic" than the one which it had acquired. From there Daggett proceeded almost due south a few miles to Georgetown, which he recalled as one of the earliest mining communities, once surrounded by very rich gulches, most of which had been depleted of treasure. Life was monotonous in the community except for an occasional rough-and-tumble fight. Then he moved on to Coloma, at that time the county seat of El Dorado county, where Marshall's mill had led to the discovery of gold in 1848. During this period disap-

pointments in the mining fields led to an exodus from the area, with
some people on foot and others driving mule-drawn vehicles piled
with "household and kitchen furniture."[16]

Proceeding southward to Placerville, he avoided the main road,
traveling instead over a beautiful trail. At that time Placerville had
come to be the third largest city in California. Traveling farther southward through Hangtown and Drytown, in the oldest mining areas
of the state, he reached Jackson on March 27, where a musical presentation by the "Sable Harmonists" was enlivened by the report that
a celebrated bandit, Joaquin, had been seen in the vicinity of Placerville.

Many of the miners were literate, disciplined individuals and
welcomed an opportunity to subscribe to the *Golden Era*. Within a
month Daggett secured eleven hundred subscriptions in nine mining
centers. Daggett carried back to San Francisco a complimentary report
of the "character of our Miners," as the *Golden Era* explained: "They
sit around the fire at night, and as they smoke their pipes, unfold to
each other the wealth of their minds, experience, and secret aspirations, with unreserved confidence. Their mutual enlightenment, by
free exchange of knowledge and sentiment must create a general intelligence, which can be found in no other place."[17]

In May Daggett wrote to his beloved sister in Ohio, apologizing
for his long neglect of their correspondence and promising to do better
in the future. He was sending the *Golden Era* to her regularly and
asked her opinion of it, which he said "would be inestimable." He
asserted: "The *Era* is quite a favorite in our young State, and its
reception has been flattering, and I calculate on making it *the* paper
of California. But not too far ahead—for a fire, you know—and such
fires as we have in this country often leave many perfectly destitute.
But I must run my chances."[18]

By October 1853 the circulation of the *Era* outside of San Francisco was twenty-four hundred. But the editors sought to improve
their prospects further and in the late spring of 1854, Daggett again
visited the northern mining camps with obvious pleasure, reporting:
"Well, here I am again, piled in among miners, grizzlies, long toms and
a rough portion of the country as ever mortal coaxed himself into
. . . enjoying to the fullest extent the pure mountain air clear cool
water and enchanting scenery for which this part of the country is
celebrated."[19]

Writing from the "Headwaters of the North Fork of the Con-
summes" on May 24, he reported on his visit to once-bustling Drytown,
now almost abandoned because the value of the diggings seemed

negligible. He commented on new undertakings near the Mountain House (about twenty-five miles southeast of Sacramento), which appeared to be the most important of recent years.

Anti-Chinese feeling, caused partly by frequent Chinese wars, had developed to the point of favoring the "total expulsion of the entire Chinese population from the mining districts." In his report the next day from Jackson, Daggett described the gathering of two thousand Chinese from the surrounding area for a showdown battle in a struggle that had been waxing in magnitude for a year throughout California between two political factions of the "Celestials," known as the "Cantons" and the "Hong Kongs." A rich San Francisco merchant had offered a large sum of money to county officials to suppress the disturbances, and up to that point the officers had prevented violence.

During the month of July Daggett visited many other communities. He was charmed by Georgetown, "one of the most beautifully located mining towns in the state" but was repelled by the "homely and fogyish appearance of Coloma." Heat in that region could be oppressive; writing from Yankee Jim's, Daggett engaged in the rhetorical outbursts he loved:

> The weather today is quite comfortable; a strong breeze is whistling through the tops of the pines. . . . To say that the weather since the first of the month has been warm, is to convey no idea of the intensity of the heat. It has been hot—suffocatingly, wretchedly hot—the sun hanging in the horizon like a huge ball of fire, casting its fiercest rays in every penetrable corner, without a cloud to obscure its flaming visage, or a breath of air to counteract its scorching beams.[20]

Here, as farther south, the crying need was for a larger water supply.

Daggett's series of fictional letters written by "Miles Quinton" from the "Land of the Moqui" in New Mexico to a friend "Frank" was especially successful. The series, which started in October 1853, involved adventures in the canyons and valleys of the Colorado River area, experiences with wild sheep, and warfare between Indian tribes.[21] In the story Quinton became intimately associated with the Moqui during a full year's residence among them, cementing his friendship by marrying the chief's daughter. He described the wars of the Moqui with the Navajos, explained the religious views and customs of the Moqui, and wrote of ancient Moqui traditions revealed to him by an old chief. Ultimately fever, drought, grasshoppers, and smallpox brought decimation of the Moqui tribe.[22]

Under the pseudonym "Blunderbuss" Daggett wrote stories of

mining life, such as "Salting a Claim," and one dealing with "Dancing
Bill," a sailor who deserted from a whaler and who could "dance
longer, stronger, and heartier than any man I ever saw." Another
was a human interest story of a timid six-foot-six miner from Iowa,
who was too bashful to propose to an interested widow. Next year
a melodramatic account of a Sacramento gambler in the years 1850-54,
appeared as "Lucky Bill, the Thimble-Rigger." An additional contribution was "The Blacksmith of Fenton, California: Gold and Kentucky
Aristocracy," a six-chapter novelette presented in two issues of the
Era in September 1858. The story was that of Jared Morse, a blacksmith, whose father Thomas had migrated in 1828 from Virginia to a
small village in Kentucky when Jared was two years old. Jared went
to California, made a strike in the gold fields, and returned to Kentucky
to marry the girl of his choice, Cornelia, the daughter of a judge whom
Jared rescued from the brink of bankruptcy.[23] In describing the
intimacies of mining camp relationships, Daggett probably drew on
his own experiences:

> We mined together, slept in the same bed of pine leaves and
> drank our muddy coffee from the same basin. Among mining com-
> panions of early times, little private history remained untold. As
> they sat night after night around the camp-fire or cabin hearth,
> gradually they unbosomed to each other the secrets of the heart,
> until each became as familiar with the affairs of his associate as
> though he were a brother.[24]

Later, from time to time, under the same pseudonym Daggett
wrote other stories, such as a tale of San Francisco, "A Restaurant
Acquaintance: How Mark Hilton Found a Wife," and "The Trapper's
Wooing," a story of the romance between the widow of a settler killed
in an Indian attack in the Humboldt River Valley and her rescuer.
Another dealt with the amours of a San Francisco matron who finally
secured an Indiana divorce and married an earnest, prosperous
mechanic. "Fee, the Conjurer" is an account of a learned Chinaman
who offended his emperor and a secret drawn from his familiarity
with the court at Peking.[25]

Daggett also wrote under the pseudonym "Korn Kob," using
devices of spelling and alliteration that in later years were part of
the humorous appeal of Artemus Ward and Petroleum V. Nasby.[26]
"Korn Kob's First Rehearsal," appearing in March 1855, was followed
by "Korn Kob in the Orchestra Box" and "Lucky Ball, the Thimble
Rigger," describing the experiences of a Sacramento gambler. A later
one, which developed the theme of Korn Kob's expecting a fortune

from Germany, included: "Magnanimus Surs": Irite with mi kote opn, and my hare standin out like the splints of a hickery shrub-broom." Another included: "Exolted Surs: . . . Gen. Kornwallis was of the Kob phamily, and ode the terminashun of 'wallis' to the marriage of his grate-grandfather, Sur Pectur Korn Kob, to the half-sister of Wallis, the Skotch hero. Lord Kobden is also of our phamily." One discussed with mock erudition the influence of the peanut since antiquity and included the following: "Rephulgent Surs: Disappointed ambishun has killed more people than wor or bad whisky. I kan prove it, but won't; for if my word isn't good for the assershun, let the disrespecktful raskle who disputes it prove it otherwise." Another contained the salutation, "Stoopenjus Sirs," with the comment: "I have been 'layin-lo' lately. I haven't sed mutch, I havn't writ mutch and havn't dun mutch but lay round and studdy up for mi nu lokle dramy." Later a letter beginning "Triumfant Sirs" dealt with an account of a benefit tendered Korn Kob by the leading citizens of the community. By 1858 "Korn Kob" had engaged in a fight with the "Kandy Man of Kla strete," due to hostility evoked by Korn Kob's selling "pee-knuts" three cups for a bit. The result was that Korn Kob left California for the Atlantic states as a dishwasher on the *Stevens*.[27]

In the summer of 1857, "with a view of contributing our mite to the development of the literary talent of the State, and at the same time, we are free to admit, securing for the *Era* an increasing popularity equal in value to the extent of the hazard," the *Era* offered two hundred dollars for the best story contributed, with one hundred dollars and fifty dollars for second and third winners. The judges were Joseph R. Prefontaine, J. E. Lawrence, and E. G. Paige, who announced the awards late in November. First prize went to "Dolly Dashwood" for "Madeline, the Heartless"; second prize, to Edward Pollack for "Logan Forney: A Tale of the Mountains"; and third prize, to Walter Camden for "The Golden Cross." The stories were published in the *Era* during December 1857 and January and February of 1858.[28]

One of the contributors, Edward Pollack, died within a year of softening of the brain, induced by alcoholism. The *Era* commented that in reality "he was a poet, in feeling and action—a restless, dreaming, improvident poet, seeking for what he could never possess." Yet, it added, among his prose works were "a number of imaginative pieces of genuine merit."[29]

The San Francisco theater had been associated with amateur presentations by military companies during the Mexican War. But, with the prosperity accompanying the Gold Rush, crude platforms gave way to well-equipped, luxurious theaters.[30] Early in 1853, when Edwin Booth made his first appearance in an important role in *The American Fireman,* the *Era* reported: "He has a fine figure and an excellent voice, and promises a high rank in the profession." The *Era* declared that in the role of Richard III he far exceeded "any former one we have ever witnessed in this country, save . . . his lamented sire."[31]

Thus, spirited dramatic criticism became an important feature of the *Golden Era.* In September 1853 it denounced the poor plays current in San Francisco: "Theater-goers have been at the mercy of a combination of ingrates who have become fattened upon the people's generosity and indulgence, and who value a reputation no farther than it will serve their avariciousness. People should know the difference between a company of high-minded artists, whose aim is the elevation of the drama, and a clique of grasping Shylocks, whose sole object is gain."[32]

But praise could be dispensed with vigorous enthusiasm, as a month later when it was stated that Vinson and Beatty, managers of the "neat, comfortable, and cozy Olympic Theatre," showed that a theater "conducted on liberal principles" would be supported in San Francisco. Vinson, moreover, was complimented on his local services to drama in the city and for his personal able delineation of the character of old men.[33] With the coming of the New Year, the *Era* was exuberant about dramatic attractions:

> At the "Metropolitan" we have Murdock—glorious Murdock; and Mrs. Sinclair—talented and generous—who stand forth as the standardbearers, while Mrs. Woodward, the Booths . . . and a host of others close the column in bright array.
> And at the "American," the scene of a thousand dramatic triumphs—we find Mrs. Baker, the incomparable artiste, the gem of the social circle.[34]

When *Uncle Tom's Cabin* was presented at the American Theater, the *Era* declared Charles Robert Thorne, who played Uncle Tom, the "honest, faithful old slave designed by the authoress," and every shade of the perfect plantation "nigger gall" was observed in Mrs. Thorne (Maria Ann Mestayer) as Topsy. It was stated that Backus Minstrels, performing at San Francisco Hall, offered burlesques which were "ridiculously rich" in the delineation of stereotyped Southern Negro characters.

The dramatic season of 1854 was particularly attractive in San Francisco. The *Era* commented that "California at present can boast of being the center of theatrical attractions of the whole Union." When the famous Laura Keene appeared in April at the "Metropolitan" she "was laboring under the chilling effects of an arduous sea voyage," and did not make as good an impression as she did later in Sacramento. But she soon returned to San Francisco to appear at the "American" in *Masks and Faces* and *Antony and Cleopatra*. In the meantime, these dramatic presentations were "the all-absorbing theme . . . in the store, the saloon or in the street," as crowds thronged the theater, and "both high and lowly" gave complimentary appraisals.[35]

While the Bateman Children, who followed Miss Keene, were well received, the dramatic reporter for the *Era* (possibly Daggett) was not "carried away" by the performance, for he had been prepared "for something wonderful" but found the girls to be "precocious children" rather than the "finished artistes" many represented them to be. Kate, the older and more beautiful of the sisters, he found more "mechanical" in her acting than her sister Ellen.[36]

Year after year, the great, the near great, and those of lesser stature appeared in San Francisco and were appraised by the *Era*. In 1859, when John Drew was appearing at the Lyceum in *Knight of Arva*, the journal reported that large audiences deemed him a great hit and that he had an able supporting cast.

A series, "San Francisco Without Doors," and another, "San Francisco Within Doors," each written in a style that suggests Daggett was the author, depicted the "secret" life of the city.

> The elegant and polished Parisian, whose *toute ensemble* stamps him as one conversant with the "first society" . . . is rudely jostled in his afternoon walk on the fashionable side of Montgomery or Stockton streets, by the half brutalized Kanaka, who with a blanket carelessly thrown over his shoulder, wanders about, amazed at the tokens he beholds on every side of princely wealth and embodied art. John Chinaman, bending beneath his enormous double load, is pushed from the side by the reckless son of Neptune, who looks on with a self satisfied expression, while his victim picks himself and his load out of the gutter, and hurls at his assailant a volley of Chinese phrases that do not sound like blessings.[37]

The *Era* beckoned its readers to climb to the pleasant summit of Telegraph Hill on a hot summer day. There one would observe a group of sailors watching the ships of every nation in the bay, for "natural beauties have no charms for the son of Neptune; he views all objects with a nautical eye." One would also note a gentleman in black who

proved to be "a servant of the church. He has come hither that his
overtasked mind may be benefited by breathing the pure fresh air,
and perhaps to con over his next Sunday's sermon." Also observed
were two or three men talking about titles and land claims, idle men
basking in the sun, and two or three legislators "sharpening their ap-
petites previous to taking dinner at the Union or Wilson's Exchange."[38]

Not in the same series but in similar vein was a sketch of the
northwestern section of San Francisco at night:

> The rattling boards echo to the tread of outcasts from every clime
> and nation. There is music everywhere, and of every kind. . . . As
> the night grows late, the place begins to wear a look of decided
> dissipation. The haunts of vice and sin are overflowing, the neigh-
> borhood actually *seethes.*—Voices are heard singing, or rather
> shouting, in a variety of foreign tongues, songs in honor of Mars
> and Bacchus. Gambling in spite of the law, is a common avoca-
> tion. The Chinese form a conspicuous element. The houses are
> "open to the public" on every side, and the most filthy and dis-
> gusting practices are openly carried on, without so much as a
> nod from the authorities. Mexicans, Chinese and Jamaicans crowd
> the dens to which they nightly resort, and no doubt many an
> unwary stranger has disappeared forever from the sight of the
> world, after a night passed in some of these vile resorts, where he
> has indulged too deeply in draught, while losing his money at
> play.[39]

In "San Francisco Within Doors," one is taken to a gambling
establishment, where in each room twenty to fifty persons congregate
about a faro table. Here a wholesale commission merchant sits with
a judge, the latter with his head waddling right and left, under his
load of cocktails, looking like a picture of anything but that of justice.
Occasionally a feeling of shame will steal over him as he for a moment
recollects the position which he occupies in society, but he banishes
it with a snatch of bawdy song or another glass of brandy. Then there
is a man "with bloated face and seedy apparel silently waiting the
turning of the cards," for he has lost his money. Five years earlier he
was a minister of the Gospel in the Atlantic States, but "he left behind
him that which he thought would be useless in California—his con-
science. Sentiments of piety which he once uttered with reverence,
he now burlesques for the amusement of the crowd, and sacred
anthems are turned to vulgar doggerels which he sings with mock
solemnity." Look still further, and you will see a Representative in our
State Legislature. He who should lend his voice in purging such a

vice from the land is giving it his countenance and support. His salary has been sacrificed, and in drunken desperation he holds himself in readiness to pledge his vote to him who will pay him the most for it.[40]

Another issue dealt with San Francisco Employment Agencies or "Intelligence Offices," generally considered to be honorable and even philanthropic but often associated with great abuses. The offices collected five dollars from an unemployed man and then sent him to an employer who took care that the workman would not stay long, for the latter is "treated as though he were not human, and leaves the next day without even demanding his pay." It appears that once the fee had been collected "it matters but little what sort of situation they give in return; they are not satisfied with the legitimate results of the business honestly conducted, but seek to fatten on the misery and want of their fellowmen."[41]

San Francisco in the 1850's was a lawless city. A section known as Happy Valley was inhabited by ex-convicts from Australia, referred to as the "Sydney Ducks." Many men and women were bestial in their behavior, and children south of Market Street acquired debauched and criminal habits in an area where "Tar Flat Hoodlums" carried on. In the "Barbary Coast" section, vile criminals from all over the world congregated, their victims often being thrown into the bay. Gambling places, such as "El Dorado" on Kearny Street, were packed every night with men of every description. Brazen prostitutes walked the streets. A notorious Rose Cooper hired a band to present two concerts a week from the balcony of her palace of vice. Then "the girls" would mingle with the crowd and invite "the boys" inside.[42]

In such a crude, boisterous society Daggett's puritanical training prompted him often to write articles in the *Golden Era* demanding a return to the old virtues. In December 1853 the San Francisco City Council was commended for its attempt to deal with the numerous houses of ill fame. The *Era* commented that the suppression of such "vile dens" would be "the work of a generation" but that their confinement to a certain portion of the city would enable them to be "avoided by those" who so desired.[43]

The journal heartily endorsed an effort on the part of the California legislature to suppress gambling:

> There was a time with us when gamblers and their supporters composed a very large proportion of our population—when a large part of the taxable property of the State was in the hands of these men. To subject their property to taxation, it became necessary to acknowledge the profession of gambling a lawful one, and

as such entitled to protection. . . . These days are now passed,
and we have no longer a plea for acknowledging as lawful a
crime which necessity once compelled us to approve. It should
be totally suppressed. . . . We shall be well satisfied, however,
should the first effort prove successful in removing gambling
from the public streets, and in compelling the sharper to practice
his arts within closed doors.[44]

With severe moralism, the *Era* denounced the "drones" of California
society: "We have no patience with Jeremy Diddlers particularly those
of the gentlemanly class, whose dainty hands refuse to earn the food
which their luxury-loving mouths never refuse to eat. These dandy
idlers seem to be under the hallucination that they are too good to
work; that they are made for ornament rather than use . . . that the
world owes them a living in return for their condescending to be
born."[45] In a similar vein, the *Era* expounded: "If you want your
talents appreciated, get rich. That tells the tale in a nut shell. . . . Extravagance, fashion, and cheating throng our streets and jostle against
honest toil. . . . Riches are coveted, sought for, and worshipped by the
millions. Honesty and truth, merit and talent, are sold for a mess of
pottage."[46]

The *Era* also took a lively interest in religious matters. In his
mature years Daggett was to embrace the doctrines of the Swedish
mystic and philosopher, Emanuel Swedenborg, but in 1854 the *Era*
approached his doctrines with mixed reactions. It asserted that Swedenborg was a poet by nature and that his doctrines had appealed to
many, but his ideas of marriage are such that might "appeal to a
Bluebeard."[47] As the Swedenborgians were establishing a new church
at Santa Clara, the *Era* commented: "All the isms and ridiculous new
fangled notions of the day appear to be taking refuge in California."[48]

Ferdinand C. Ewer, a profoundly serious forty-niner of Unitarian-
Quaker antecedents, created a considerable stir in California literary
and religious circles with his articles in the *Pioneer*, a literary magazine he and William H. Brooks founded in January 1854.[49] As a youth
Ewer joined the Episcopal Church, but he emerged from Harvard an
infidel. His imaginative articles in the *Pioneer* called "The Eventful
Nights of August 20th and 21st" purporting to be the account of the
death of a John F. Lane, and of messages spiritually communicated
by him to the writer, were accepted seriously by prominent spiri-
tualists over the country.[50] The *Era* commented that the Ewer paper
involved "some singular statements concerning the modern spiritual
theory, which must . . . stagger even the spirit-rappers themselves."[51]

The *Era* soon secured and published a continuation of the story in an October 1854 issue.[52] Daggett later seemed to believe that Ewer was personally influenced by supernatural forces at this time.[53] Afterward, Ewer returned to religion, and in April 1857 was ordained a priest of the Episcopal Church in San Francisco.[54]

The *Era* contained numerous articles denouncing the claims of Spiritualism. One entitled "Spiritualism: A New Phase of the Malady" included the following comment:

> Seriously, it seems strange that in the nineteenth century, and in a country famous for its schools of learning, and liberal cast of thought, such a pernicious species of tom-foolery should have met with any degree of progress. We look back with wonder to the days of witches and witch-burning, yet mentally tolerate a fanatical theory equally absurd, and far more wide-spread and pernicious. The witch-burners destroyed the body only; the spiritualists sap the foundations of society by alienating the mental vision, and rendering life a worthless burden.[55]

The *Era* was often extremely critical of institutional religion but attacked with tigerlike ferocity any assaults upon basic religious assumptions. It sharply denounced congregations that were not worshiping fellowships but organizations for snobbish sociability. Austerity, the *Era* declared, had yielded to "the luxuriously furnished pew"; the Bible was "mounted and bedizened with gilt and gaudy colors"; congregational singing had been replaced by music rendered by "a few attaches"; while "gaping and yawning" auditors listened to the eloquence or eccentricity of a good-looking, bland preacher with a musical voice who praised "the beauties of virtue rather than the deformities of sin."[56]

In like vein the journal sharply criticized the large salaries paid prominent New York ministers, commenting:

> The first idea of many a wealthy father is to select a respectable as well as a profitable *profession* for his son, and thus it happens that the pulpit is often filled by young men, mere tyros, who have a very limited idea of the responsibility of such a position, and who receive the ovations of their congregations as so many tributes to their personal accomplishments. The result is precisely the same as in the case of the successful actor, whose airs and assumptions it is perfectly refreshing to witness.[57]

When John S. Hittell, a frequent contributor to the *Era*, wrote a book on the *Evidences Against Christianity* (San Francisco, 1856), which was later expanded into a much larger work by a New York publisher, the *Era* commented, "John, we judge, is making some noise in the East."[58] And when W. A. D. Ewing planned a *Biography of Ten Preachers* derogatory of organized religion, the *Era* published a typical Daggett rejoinder:

> Let it alone, Mr. Ewing.
>
> Yes, let Christianity alone, unless you have a good word to to say in its favor. We have read your prospectus of the proposed *Biography of Ten Preachers* and find nothing in it to commend and much to condemn. . . . You would root from the heart every religious sentiment, and fill the world with skepticism and infidelity. You would banish from the human mind every faith in the existence of a Supreme God, and substitute the forbidding opinions of a gloomy and misanthropic philosophy. Should you succeed in completely overthrowing the Christian religion as you sincerely hope, what then? A nation without a religion is like a nation without government, and the absence of the former is more to be deplored in a people than the loss of the latter.[59]

On the other hand, the *Era* opposed Bible reading in the public schools:

> Persons who take no interest in religious bickerings are supporters of Common Schools, and, although willing that their children should be educated in almost any religious faith, and that they should be made familiar with the moral precepts taught in that Book of Books, they have a right to say whether our Public School system shall be destroyed by religious enthusiasts in attempting to subvert them to their own purposes.[60]

On local issues the *Era* often expressed itself emphatically. In 1854, for example, it approved the indignation of many citizens against the "unmerciful prices" projected by the San Francisco Gas Company. But when the business was not a natural public utility monopoly, as it was not in the case of combinations controlling the river traffic in the San Francisco area, the *Era* termed the situation an unavoidable evil resulting from ruinous competition and one which would eventually correct itself.[61]

The journal took a rather uncompromising attitude toward the Chinese, declaring that in San Francisco they were generally "supremely stupid, consummately lazy, the greatest liars in existence" and inclined "to steal and pilfer," so that the sooner they left the better it would be for the city.[62] When 780 Chinese reportedly arrived on one vessel in April 1854, the *Era* again commented that they were destructive of the "peace, virtue, and simplicity" of the community, so that San Franciscans owed it as a duty to the state and to their children to work for the end of such immigration. Correspondents wrote indignantly of the increasing number of Chinese in the mines. The *Era* replied that unless laws were soon passed to stop this immigration "the free-born and enlightened American" would take matters into his own hands against "the servile and degenerate" Chinese.[63]

The *Era's* attitude toward the Indians of California was somewhat less harsh. Since Indians could not live in harmony with the whites, said the *Era*, the only solution was to remove them from their native hills, place them in a valley removed from the whites, and teach them the elements of civilization. The *Era* elaborated: "Let the money now expended by the government in fattening, at the expense of the Indians, the rascally agents who pretend to distribute among them its favors, be set apart for domesticating them, and in five years the work will be happily effected."[64]

Yet the *Era* had little patience with racial prejudice associated with the Know-Nothing Movement, calling it a "cabalistic force," about which the world could only sense that it was a "shrewd expedient to obtain a share in the loaves and fishes."[65] Know-Nothingism continued as a bitter political issue in San Francisco during 1855. Indeed, the *Era* admitted that the revival of the possibility of lynch law in California out of lax moral conditions was due to the fact that the immigration of the preceding years had been made up of "the very dregs and off-scourings of European society, mingled with the worst of our own." The *Era* believed that only a radical change in the laws could prevent crime but that judicious administration of existing laws could mitigate the situation.[66]

In view of Daggett's diplomatic service in Hawaii more than a quarter of a century later, the *Era's* attitude toward possible annexation of the Kingdom to the United States is especially interesting. The *Era* favored annexation if both countries were willing, for the United States, it felt, more than any outside nation had contributed to the greatness of the islands. It commented:

King Kamehameha is certainly the most fortunate of savage monarchs. . . . He has . . . earned a fair title to an honorable mention in the world's history. The great danger now . . . is from the great influx of foreigners which can hardly fail to follow its annexation to the United States. Among them will be many unprincipled characters. . . . Speculators will make inroads, and the

din and bustle of an active people will usurp and drive away
forever the romantic quietude which has brooded from time im-
memorial over the lovely bays and islets of that land of poetry
and prayer.[67]

The strong spirit of local self-government in California found
expression in the *Era's* emphatic endorsement of the Kansas-Nebraska
Bill, which, it said, "does nothing more than declare the general principles deducible from the legislation of 1850, that this exiciting question may be settled by the people themselves. . . . The settlement
of the question in this manner must disarm the slavery agitation of its
most dangerous tendencies, and in fact leave little room for agitation
except of a purely local character."[68]

For about a year after its founding the *Era* suffered financial difficulties, having many a bout with the sheriff to keep him from putting
a lock on the door. But, as has been indicated, the various attractive
features of the paper and Daggett's personal energetic efforts to obtain
subscriptions in the mining camps brought success. By February 1853
a special edition for circulation in the Atlantic states, Europe, and
the Pacific Islands, was being issued. Artistic engravings, copies of
which sold for as much as twenty-five cents each, were among the
attractions included in the various issues. These included San Francisco scenes such as the east side of Montgomery Street, between
Sacramento and California streets, with its various two-, three-, and
four-story buildings.[69] With increasing prosperity in the spring of
1954, the *Era* offices were moved to 124 Sacramento Street, near Montgomery. For a time a Mr. McCombe had assisted in publishing the
paper; then in May 1854 Manuel M. Noah, eldest son of the well-
known deceased New York journalist of the same name, became one
of the editors and proprietors. The new connection was of short duration, ending on August 5, 1854.[70]

An element in the success of the *Era* was its efficient method of
circulation. Each Sunday morning, special carriers took the papers
to subscribers in forty-three interior towns and by sundown to at
least seventy-five mountain and valley villages. To other places it was
dispatched by mail and express. Daggett, moreover, continued to
journey to mining communities to secure subscriptions. Occasionally
advertisers had to be warned not to make payments to an unauthorized
agent.[71]

After the termination of Noah's connection with the *Era*, "Colonel"
Joseph E. Lawrence joined Foard and Daggett in their publishing

efforts. Lawrence, of Long Island ancestry, had been a newspaperman in California since 1849. Bland and urbane, he was known for his "personal beauty" and neatness of dress.[72]

In September 1856 the publication offices were again moved, this time to 151 Clay Street, below Montgomery. During this period the *Era*, both in size and circulation, was the largest journal published in California. In size it was then surpassed by only two newspapers in the United States, both published in New York City, the *Sunday Dispatch* and the *Journal of Commerce*. Because of its leadership in circulation, the San Francisco post office year after year awarded it the advertising of uncalled-for letters.[73]

Early in 1857 Lawrence disposed of his interests in the *Era*. By June James Brooks had joined Daggett and Foard as publishers, with Foard and Daggett as editors. By this time Daggett appears to have surrendered his role as traveling subscription agent to a Mr. A. Ellis. In April 1860 Daggett severed his long connection with the *Era*, disposing of his interest to Lawrence. Later in the month the journal carried the heading, "Brooks, Lawrence, and Foard, Proprietors." By June Foard, intent on other journalistic and political ventures, disposed of his interests to Lawrence and Brooks. One element in the retirement of Daggett and Foard from the *Era* may have been the increased competition in San Francisco, where forty-five periodicals sought patronage in a city of eighty thousand people. This ratio appeared larger than that of any other city in the world.[74] Foard later stated his belief that the *Era* had declined with the introduction of women writers, for "they killed it, with their namby-pamby schoolgirl trash." It lived on, however, until 1893, when, having moved to San Diego and been stripped of its "old free and easy ways," it came to an end, and its facilities were taken over by the *Western Journal of Education*.[75]

The decade of the 1850's had been exciting for Daggett. Beneath his aggressive, self-confident attitude, however, he often revealed to his intimates the need for love and affection. He wrote with deep feeling to his sisters back in Ohio, sending them copies of the *Golden Era* to keep them in touch with his progress and imploring them to reply more often than they did. His beloved sister Betsey was taxed with family responsibilities and, unlike her brother, did not find excitement in writing.

As Daggett acquired economic stability with the prosperity of the *Era*, he remembered nostalgically the warm affection of his old Ohio home. Writing to Betsey in May 1853, he unburdened himself:

I received a very pretty little letter from Emma [Betsey's daughter] for which I am truly grateful. Tell her that I very often think of her and should be extremely happy to have her write often. For it is certainly a great treat to note down in the book of memory an occasional guileless train of thought from so pure a source, unadulterated by the selfishness of business or unbridled by the tone of care. Such epistles have a strong tendency to revive the recollections of bygone days and bring me back once more to the thoughtless hours of youth.[76]

In the summer of 1857 Daggett had experienced his first illness in California, and he considered, somewhat facetiously, that his long period of good health spoke well "not only for the climate but for the regularity and consistency" of his own habits. As he gradually recovered from "Influenza Fever, a most tormenting disease," he longed for the old-time warmth of family affection, but the only sister who had written within six months was Esther Gleason, whose Methodist enthusiasms prompted her to emphasize her concern for the soul of her brother. As a result, he was led to protest:

Esther writes to me as though she was attempting to reform a state prison convict, or one whose crimes had carried him to the verge of perdition. Religious lectures are good—very good—superlatively good—*in the pulpit*—but damnably out of place in a private letter between two adults with fixed opinions. I write a little petulantly, perhaps, but her last letter . . . was monopolized almost exclusively by religious matters. . . . Among all my sisters I have not received within the past six months an aggregate of four letters. There certainly seems to be a studied and understood silence all around.[77]

This entreaty apparently stimulated the sisters to letter-writing, for soon letters from Betsey and Diane came on the same mail. Diane indicated that she was compiling a family history. Daggett was thereby stimulated to write his uncle William in Paulding County, Ohio, to secure all possible data on the family, information he believed would be of "equal moment and interest" to the uncle's family and to the other relatives. He then asked Betsey for the names and addresses of their uncles, aunts, and cousins, and for news about the old neighborhood. In one letter he paid a heartfelt tribute to the dear sister who had nurtured his boyhood: "To forget *you*, would be to cease to remember father, mother, sisters,—all—you, who have been to me all that a mother could, and who are so closely associated with every event of my earlier life."

Once again he sent condolences, as death had taken another babe from his sister's household. But he rejoiced that his sister and her husband on their twentieth wedding anniversary were moving into a big new house. Regarding the new home, he suggested: "When you move into it, I may pay you a brief visit, just to admire the magnificent potato patch with which you will doubtless surround it." At the same time Daggett had, in his impish way, encouraged the old home village gossips to be deceived into believing that he was interested in a home town girl, but he privately assured Betsey that the purpose of his visit to Defiance would "*not* be matrimony," whatever the appearances might indicate.[78]

By June 1860 Daggett and Foard had disposed of the *Golden Era.* Daggett, still a bachelor and only twenty-nine years of age, was eager for a new venture. During the next month, the partners began publication (with a Mr. Rutherford) of the San Francisco *Daily Evening Mirror.* With Daggett and Foard as the editors, the early issues stressed news and poems and minimized editorial comment. A contemporary paper, the *Calaveras Chronicle,* said that the *Mirror* was "the cheapest and best family daily paper in the State, and by far the most elegant. . . . It is a credit to the art preservation of all arts, and an honor to the good taste of the people of the State." The *Mirror,* commenting on its own merits, said that its literary departments were "perhaps less deserving of note than . . . its deserts as a *news* journal," containing "more of new intelligence divested of trash and verbiage, than any other journal printed in San Francisco."[79]

The *Mirror* endeavored to appeal by offering short articles of human, often melodramatic, interest. One of these involved an account of the execution in the county of a James Whitford for the murder of a man named Sheridan, with a pathetic description of the passionate kissing of a crucifix by Whitford during the final moments before the death trap was sprung. The *Mirror* commented that "so long as the present law regarding capital punishment blots the statute book— however repugnant and abhorrent the task—*someone* must be the instrument of bloodthirsty justice." But when word came from Nevada of the sentencing of a man named Carr for murdering one named Tennessee, the newspaper suggested that while this was apparently the first legal execution in Nevada Territory, it was not "for want of individuals who needed hanging."[80] Another feature article, probably written by Daggett, recalled a striking episode of just a year previous, the historic duel between two political rivals, David C. Broderick, whom Daggett warmly admired, and David S. Terry.[81]

Up to this time journalism in California had decidedly followed

Democratic political patterns. Horace Greeley, on a trip to the Pacific Coast in 1859 had found only one decidedly Republican paper, the San Francisco *Times,* among twenty daily papers in California.[82] This period was one of extreme bitterness, associated with the presidential campaign of 1860, followed by the secessionist movement in the South. The new *Mirror* was vehemently Republican, but, like many other Republican papers of the time in other parts of the country, denied the possibility of secession: "We are weary of reading and hearing so much meaningless talk of disunion. It is a shallow artifice of demagogues, who underestimate popular intelligence. We do not know of any party, or of any formidable body of men in any portion of the republic who propose any such measure, or who would not rebuke any such proposition as treasonable."[83]

After South Carolina manifested its secessionist trend, the *Mirror* termed this as "somewhat alarming" but "probably exaggerated." It insisted that "the storm, however threatening will blow over. . . . We are dealing with a controversy now which must be adjusted by concession and friendly conference, not by fire and sword."[84] As late as December 12, the *Mirror* stated that, in spite of inflammatory utterances, the fire-eaters of both sections were yielding to conservative principles. Buchanan's annual message of December 1860, however, was deemed illogical and contradictory in denying the right of secession but also the right of the federal government to prevent it.[85]

The influential San Francisco *Herald,* too, a strong Douglas Democratic paper, hoped that the Union might be preserved by an understanding consideration of the problems of the South and of their demands. It was especially bitter against Greeley's New York *Tribune* and in March 1861 advocated "appeals to reason and not to the sword; to patriotism and not to cannon; to every noble impulse of the soul, and not to coercion" as the means of restoring brotherly spirit between the North and the South.[86] But after Fort Sumter the *Herald* declared that it was "heartsick" over the "madness" that ruled in the East, where the first shot had been fired in "an internecine war" of unpredictable duration.[87]

Before Sumter the San Francisco *Bulletin* and the *Alta* expressed strong Southern sympathies and were branded "Hessian" and "Secessionist" papers by the *Herald.* The San Francisco *Times* had long been the pioneering Republican paper of the area, but the *Mirror* entered the field during the campaign of 1860, hoping that it would share in the spoils of victory. The *Times* failed to receive patronage from the new Lincoln administration during the summer of 1861 and became somewhat disgruntled. The *Mirror* thereupon became increasingly aggressive in demanding money and men from the California legislature for support of the war. When the *Herald* strongly criticized what it deemed the corrupt actions of members of the Lincoln administration, the *Mirror* declared that cabinet members were a vital part of the government and that it was essentially treasonable to doubt their capacity, integrity, or wisdom. In autumn 1861 political sentiment became even more bitter. The *Herald* complained that the *Mirror* had "the unparalleled impudence to denominate all as traitors who do not fall down and worship with loud hosannas the Chicago platform and its promulgators." John R. Ridge, a literary man of distinction, resigned as editor of the *Herald,* apparently unable to endure the personal maligning involved. He protested that he was proud to have "opposed as well the sectionalism of the North as the mad ultraism of the South."[88]

Daggett loved a scrap and with Ridge capitulating to the virulence of the *Mirror's* attacks, he turned his attention to the pastor of one of San Francisco's leading churches. The task of a minister, like that of an editor, was at this time extremely difficult. Some parishioners wished the churches to be forthright in their support of recruiting for the Union army.[89] Rev. William Anderson Scott, a native of Nashville, Tennessee, and a graduate of Princeton Theological Seminary, had been the pastor of Calvary Presbyterian Church, a leading congregation of the city, since its organization in 1854. A cultivated gentleman and a vigorous civic leader, in 1856 during the reign of a vigilance committee that had arisen against corruption in local government, he preached a powerful sermon, "A Discourse for the Times," taking a very conservative stand against its proceedings and in favor of conventional "law and order." In 1858 he received the highest honor in his denomination, being chosen moderator of the General Assembly of the Old School Presbyterian Church.

California had long had a large, influential element with Southern sympathies. Many Californians, because of the relatively short affiliation of their native state with the American Union, had not developed a deep devotion to it. After the formation of the Confederacy, Mr. Scott changed the form of prayer at his services, calling on God's blessing on the president "of these American states," instead of only on the United States president. His avoidance of active commitment in political matters and his Southern background were factors in his voting no on some resolutions of loyalty offered in a meeting of the Presbytery. He "continued to serve the congregation with great zeal, fidelity, and earnestness," but papers like the *Mirror,* with their uncompromising views, made his course difficult, so he submitted his resignation, dated July 1, 1861. But the congregation refused to accept it.[90]

For some time Daggett considered that Scott had expressed disloyal sentiments from the pulpit and assailed him so severely that a son of the minister threatened to chastise him publicly. From then on Daggett constantly carried an old-fashioned horse pistol in one of the pockets of his long frock coat.[91] The dispute reached a climax on Sunday, September 2, 1861, when Unionists placed a United States flag atop the Calvary Church with flags flying from each lamppost in front of the building, while within a window opposite dangled an effigy of "Dr. Scott, the reverend traitor." A large crowd surged into the church, filling it to capacity. On this occasion Scott made no reference to more than one president. After the service he reached his carriage safely but was attacked on the way home.[92]

Probably Daggett had not been wholly fair to the minister, who on September 23 renewed his request to terminate the pastorate. A week later over three hundred members of this prominent congregation, without a single dissenting voice, while accepting Scott's renewed request to resign, expressed their unlimited confidence in him and emphatically denied that he was disloyal to the government and asserted that he had never introduced politics into the pulpit. Even Governor John G. Downey of California wrote to Scott of his sincere regret that he was leaving, saying in part, "I beg you will carry with you the assurances of my high appreciation of your merits, both as a citizen and distinguished minister of the Gospel."[93]

Daggett seems to have been very aggressive in other charges, as when the *Mirror* accused Archibald McAllister of being a Secessionist Democrat who had just been elected to office by fraudulent practices. McAllister at once categorically denied these charges. At about the same time, a bitter controversy developed between Daggett and Calvin B. McDonald, a rival newspaperman. Encountering each other one day in Montgomery Street, the hostile editors engaged in a savage scuffle that became a rough-and-tumble, clawing fight. In the fierce struggle Daggett's horse pistol flew out of his pocket and exploded on the sidewalk, terrifying bystanders. But the affray ended suddenly as each participant, who in the fury of the fight had been stripped almost naked, hurriedly sought refuge in nearby stores. Daggett always claimed the victory, insisting that McDonald was forced to remain in hiding until the crowd took up a collection to buy him a new suit of clothes.[94]

As issues of the war came to dominate the political scene, competition between the many papers became unbearable. Late in January

1862 the old rivals combined as the *Daily Herald and Mirror*. Daggett announced that he found his retirement a necessity, as he was reaping no benefit from the change. He would not retain any voice in the control of the new paper.[95] His able, energetic, sometimes brilliant, and occasionally irresponsible career as a San Francisco editor was over.

IV

Daggett and the
Territorial Enterprise

In 1861 Daggett resided at 659 Clay Street in San Francisco, but highly competitive journalism had turned the odds against him, and by early 1862 he was "out of business, out of money, out at the elbows." But he had irrepressible vitality, quenchless courage, and the invaluable experience of a decade in California. Turning to Foard, his old partner, he said, "By ———, I am going to do something. I am going to make money; and, after this, it will be my fault if it doesn't stick."[1] So in 1862 he joined the trek to the Comstock Lode, the fabulous silver deposit in the Virginia City of Nevada Territory.

Other than early Mormon outposts in the region, withdrawn in 1857 because of the hostility of the United States, only scattered miners and settlers had ventured into the vicinity before 1859, when rich silver deposits were discovered in the Washoe region. Just when two Irishmen, Peter O'Riley and Patrick McLaughlin, had made a strike in the Six Mile Canyon, the boastful and rapacious Henry "Old Pancake" Comstock came into camp on a scrawny mule. The two men indiscreetly told the newcomer of their find, whereupon Comstock successfully pressed for a share. Later, after receiving a favorable assayer's report from California, the three men could no longer keep their find secret, and the rush was on.

Adventurers, miners, gamblers, swindlers, professional men, and others soon swarmed the area to scoop up ore from open cuts or from shallow shafts with a minimum of equipment, or to share in the growth of the region by fair means or foul. Drawn there, like many others, by the business opportunities, with Warren F. Myers Daggett established a brokerage house in Virginia City in 1862, which soon prospered.

Daggett's convivial nature made him an attractive candidate for political office. Defeated in his bid for the Nevada Territorial Assembly in September 1862, a year later Daggett was elected to the Nevada Territorial Council,[2] where he found expression for his vigorous, even violent, Unionist sentiments. Southern sentiment in Nevada was so strong that after the first battle of Bull Run, in the summer of 1861, Confederate sympathizers were openly jubilant. In 1863 Virginia City was a refuge for some Secessionists and Copperheads from Missouri and California.[3]

As a member of the Council, Daggett spoke often, introducing various petitions and bills dealing with taxes, assessments, proceedings in civil cases, and incorporation matters. He made a strenuous but vain effort to transfer the capital from Carson City to Virginia.

Among Daggett's associates was the first and only territorial governor of Nevada (1861-64), James W. Nye, a native of New York State, who was one of the first two senators from the State of Nevada. Popularly known as the old "Gray Eagle," Nye, a ready debater, was reelected to the Senate in 1867 as a Radical Republican. Other political associates were fellow Council members, the youthful Alexander Baldwin and William M. Stewart. Like Daggett a native of New York State who had spent his childhood in Ohio, Stewart later became a United States Senator.

In Virginia City Daggett once again engaged in journalism, beginning in 1862 to spend part of his time as a reporter for the *Territorial Enterprise,* a paper whose staff was to add luster to the history of the American newspaper. The paper had been founded in Genoa, Nevada, in December 1858. Less than a year later it moved to Carson City, and in 1860 to Virginia City. In March 1861 Joseph T. Goodman and Dennis E. McCarthy became active partners in its management. Originally a weekly, it now became a daily. Both Goodman and McCarthy had worked with Daggett on the *Golden Era.* Now McCarthy ran the press room and Goodman was in charge of editorial work on the *Enterprise,* which soon gained a national reputation.[4] It reveled in human interest stories and gossip of the town, and it pleased the populace by its belligerence toward the financial and cultural overlordship exercised by San Francisco over Nevada. The local miners were well paid, and many were bachelors with much leisure and so were willing to pay two dollars a month for a subscription. In an opulent community, advertisers eagerly sought its services.

One day in August 1862, Daggett used to describe in a favorite story, a dusty, disreputable looking young man who came into the newspaper office identified himself as Samuel Clemens and announced that he was the new reporter. Daggett commented: "He had been

living on alkali water and whang leather, with only a sufficient supply
of the former for drinking purposes, for several months, and you
may imagine his appearance when I first saw him."[5] Daggett's story
apparently carried his customary romantic embellishments, because
recent scholarship has shown that Clemens was still in Esmeralda on
September 9 and could hardly have reported for duty in Virginia City
before the second week in September.[6]

In 1861 Samuel Clemens served briefly with a group of Confederate Rangers in Missouri. Apparently deciding to detach himself
from a cause that no longer commanded his loyalty, Clemens, with his
brother Orion, newly appointed Secretary of Nevada Territory, left
for the West, arriving at Carson City in August 1861. In the Esmeralda
mining district to the southwest, he sought his fortune. Apparently on
days spent in camp, possibly when the weather prevented him from
working his claims, he wrote burlesque sketches under the pen name
"Josh" and sent them to the *Enterprise.*

One of his first sketches to win renown reported a speech by
George Turner, Chief Justice of the Nevada Supreme Court, who became known as "the shallowest, most egotistical and mercenary occu-
pant of the Supreme bench." Referring to Turner as "Mr. Personal
Pronoun," Clemens wrote a "scorching exposition of Turner's vanity,
egotism and emptiness," as Joseph Goodman, editor of the *Enterprise,*
termed it. Clemens was encouraged to write several more pieces for
the *Enterprise,* and after contributing a highly humorous account of
a fictitious Fourth of July speech, he was given a permanent place
on the paper. Daggett later recalled how Goodman had been looking
for someone to take the place of William Wright (known by his pseudonym, Dan De Quille), a feature writer, while the latter was on
vacation in the East, and after reading the Fourth of July sketch, he
passed it over to Daggett with the comment, "That man is worth
cultivating. That is the sort of thing we want."[7]

The atmosphere of the *Enterprise* office was "like that of a fraternity house without a house mother." Most of the young men were
in their twenties (Daggett was thirty-one in 1862), and the place was
a bachelor's paradise. They played billiards and went to the theatre,
they smoked cigars and imbibed a special "reporter's cobbler;" and
they were presented with "feet" of mining property which they could
dispose of for enough cash to finance vacations in San Francisco.[8]

In the early days the *Enterprise* was located in a shaky one-story
frame building on the northeast corner of Sutton and A Streets. Com-
positors, editors, pressmen, and all other hands worked together in
one room. In a shed on the north side of the building, bunks, one

above the other as on a ship, provided sleeping quarters for all except "Joe," the Chinese cook. The sleeping area also served as the kitchen and dining room, for the proprietors lodged and fed all employees. When Clemens came to Virginia City, Dan De Quille was about ready to leave for an extended vacation, but when he returned, Clemens and he roomed together. Their careers and pranks were closely entwined until Clemens' departure from the Comstock.[9] The two men sought luxury unavailable to most other employees and shared a parlor-bed-room suit on the third floor of the Daggett-Myers Building at 25 B Street, which housed the city library, too. Owned by Daggett and W. F. Myers, Daggett's brokerage partner, it survived when many of the flimsy structures on the lower levels of the town burned in the great fire of August 1863. The *Enterprise* offices later were moved to what became their permanent location in the heart of the business community on C Street.

Clemens developed a close association with Daggett, too. Daggett became one of Clemens' "staunchest friends." It was Daggett who introduced him around the *Enterprise* office, calling to Steve Gillis through the window between the editorial and composing rooms, "You're wanted!" As Steve came running, Daggett relieved him by saying that there was "no trouble"; he just wanted to make him "acquainted with Sam Clemens."[10]

Life among these journalistic cronies was informal indeed. When Clemens was in Carson City in January 1864 reporting the legislative proceedings, he told of receiving his old "carpet sack" at last, containing "two shirts and six champagne bottles," along with a "garrote collar" and a note from Dan De Quille. One of the shirts was marked "R. M. Daggett," so he perceived that Dan "had been foraging again."[11] The measure of truth in any statement of some of the men is dubious; Clemens and Daggett especially were given to jokes and hoaxes.[12]

The numerous *Enterprise* reporters made big wages and sometimes would give a favorite journalistic friend a gold-headed cane. Clemens complained that everyone except him seemed to be remembered. A few days later Steve Gillis and a friend noticed a beautiful pipe in a shop window but found upon inquiry that it was merely an imitation meerschaum, priced at $1.50. Deciding to buy it, they had engraved on the tinsel mounting, "To Mark Twain from his friends," and had it attractively wrapped. All of the office coterie except Clemens knew of the hoax. De Quille informed Clemens that a presentation was to take place, and the latter spent some time preparing an acceptance speech. At the ceremony Clemens kept ordering sparkling Moselle (at $5.00 a bottle) until six bottles had been consumed. A few days later, told that the pipe was not genuine, he was rather irritable until assured that a real meerschaum, costing $45.00, was coming his way.[13]

When there was a dearth of news or when exuberant spirits knew no bounds, Clemens or one of the others would stimulate excitement through a hoax which often would be readily accepted and circulated by the undiscriminating in the other newspaper offices. Gullibility often led them to bitter irritation. Clemens had been on the *Enterprise* only a short time when he presented an elaborate yarn about the discovery of a "Petrified Man" near Gravelly Ford. Another was a tale of an ordinarily mild and affable man who, in a mad rage, killed his wife and seven children in the "Bloody Massacre" of Empire City.[14]

In 1864 the Virginia City coterie projected a new literary magazine after the manner of the *Golden Era*. Daggett, Tom Fitch, Dan De Quille, and others were to be among the contributors, and Daggett was represented in the first number. Four issues of the *Weekly Occidental* appeared, the first on March 6, 1865, but no copy of any issue has been found.[15]

Clemens decided to leave Virginia City in May 1864. Seven years later, in *Roughing It*, he indicated that it was his intention to go east with two associates to aid in selling a silver mine just discovered. Almost incidentally he mentioned that certain editorials he had written for the *Enterprise* had left Joe Goodman with six duels to fight, but he added no further comment. Forty years later, in his *Autobiography*, Clemens omitted mention of the mine project and presented an involved story of the necessity for his quick departure from Nevada because of the danger of falling into the arms of the law because he challenged James L. Laird to a duel. In this account, Daggett spurred him on to challenge Laird, the proprietor of the Virginia *Union*, and Daggett wrote for him a challenge filled with "a stream of unsavory epithets." When Laird did not respond, Clemens reported that Daggett kept on, penning one more challenge after another. Clemens published a similar account in 1873.[16] The story gained wide acceptance. Scholars have shown that the story of the duel was "clearly fictitious" and involved a dispute which "did not develop beyond the state of high-flown insult."[17] Yet exciting imaginary narratives die hard, and unconvincing efforts have been made to rehabilitate Clemens' "tall tale."[18]

In 1868 Clemens, by this time a lecturer of distinction, was warmly welcomed on his return to Virginia City. Coming to talk on the "Voyage of the Quaker City," he was greeted by a "crowded and delighted audience" that experienced "the greatest treat of the season." He communicated with his audience as if he were holding a conversation with some old friends and acquaintances in a parlor and exhibited a whole "menagerie of curious characters," such as the "old Doctor with his hard medical Latin." Conrad Wiegand, a prosperous Comstock assayer, presented Clemens with a beautiful, highly polished silver brick, valued at forty dollars, inscribed, "Mark Twain—Matthew, V:41—Pilgrim."

Clemens did not forget Daggett and his other cronies. In February 1869 he wrote to them from Titusville, Pennsylvania, that he had been lecturing in New York, New Jersey, and six other states and would soon conclude "the long, wearisome winter siege." He expressed uncertainty as to whether he would go on tour the next season, for he would be married to a "rich and handsome" Elmira, New York, girl. He concluded: "I shall lecture in San Francisco in April or May. Come down, boys. I can't go to Virginia having killed myself twice there already in the lecture business."[19]

In view of the phenomenal way in which Clemens "sold" his own exceptional talents to the public, a certain irrepressible jealousy on the part of Clemens' old cronies, many of whom themselves possessed extraordinary talents, was unavoidable. Not unlikely Daggett himself penned the appraisal of Clemens that appeared in the *Enterprise* in October 1875. Clemens was termed "a writer of sterling and spontaneous humor," but the observation was made that "humor is an inspiration, and not a talent and any effort to cultivate it destroys it." Clemens, however, was already under compulsion "to sustain a world wide notoriety, and in endeavoring to do so" had fallen into the common error of writing too much. *Roughing It* was "ridiculous hodge podge"; *The Gilded Age* included "strained humor and feeble situations"; and now his *Sketches, New and Old* would not advance his reputation.[20]

In 1878 the *Enterprise* observed that Clemens was taking charge of the Hartford *Courant* and that, although a humorist was always tempted to write too much, Clemens would probably resist the temptation. Then a note of reminiscing, apparently from Daggett's pen, followed:

> He always avoided work as he would a pestilence; but, when finally goaded to it by a sense of duty or any other impulse, he finished his task without stopping. The brightest paragraphs "Mark" ever penned were written for the local columns of this journal, while he was a part of the dreamy, reckless and adventurous throng whose tents were pitched almost a generation ago along the Comstock.[21]

Clemens replied to "My Dear Daggett" from Hartford on January 24 that the report that he would take over editorial command of the *Courant* was without foundation and that apparently the report, first published in the New York *Sun*, grew out of the fact that, for his own convenience, his home had been connected with the *Courant* by telephone. As to the statement that a humorist tended to write too much but that Clemens had not been so afflicted on the *Enterprise*, Clemens commented:

> You say a thing which I can indorse without overstepping the bounds of modesty. I am not so indolent as I was in those days; still, my habit of avoiding the indiscretion of too much labor is pretty firm and trustworthy yet . . . I always liked newspaper work; I would like it yet; but not as a steady diet.[22]

Next to Clemens, the most outstanding of Daggett's Virginia City associates was Clemens' old roommate, Dan De Quille.[23] Born of Quaker parents in Knox County, Ohio, in 1829, as a youth he traveled with his family to take up a homestead claim near West Liberty, Iowa. In 1857 he prospected in California from Nevada County to Mariposa County and later in the Mono Lake region,[24] three years later joining the miner's invasion of Nevada and becoming prospector at Silver City. Invited to become one of the staff of the *Enterprise*, he remained with it, except for brief intervals, until 1893. A contemporary described him as "a bright-minded, sweet-tempered, loyal, unaffected philosopher with a love for the lode and a faith in it that neither years nor disappointment can quench." Quaker-like in disposition, he was known—unlike Daggett—for his mild temper and demeanor.[25]

For years he was a keen but sympathetic reporter of men and events, combining the roles of news gatherer and commentator. For variety, like other Comstock journalists, he sometimes engaged in deliberate hoaxes. He excelled "when writing close to human subjects— Chinese, Frenchmen, Irishmen, Piutes, prospectors, roughs, bummers, muckers, and those sallow, slovenly poor whites from the Mississippi Valley whom the early West called Pikes."[26] For over thirty years his local columns in the *Enterprise* included sketches, dialogues, monologues, and anecdotes packed with human interest. Sooner or later he commented on almost every aspect of Virginia City life: street fights, excursions to Steamboat Springs, the shortage of stove wood, April Fool pranks, the hazards of employment in the deep mines, fires, the crowd awaiting an eclipse of the sun, and similar accounts of daily living. He contributed to numerous San Francisco publications, including the *Golden Era, Overland Monthly,* and the *San Franciscan.* At times there was friction on the *Enterprise,* and for a period De Quille served as local reporter on the nearby Gold Hill *News.* In 1875, after being back on the *Enterprise* for a long time, he left for Hartford, Connecticut, to secure Clemens' help in preparing a volume of local sketches of the Comstock region. The two old friends spent a joyous spring together in Clemens' luxurious home.[27]

Their sketches appeared as a *History of the Big Bonanza,* brought out by Clemens' publishing firm in 1876. Today it is still a rich source of information on the economic and social aspects of life on the Comstock. By February 1876 De Quille was again writing his "locals" for the *Enterprise.* Occasionally a new story would appear. His "Chisp," in three chapters, was published early in 1876.[28]

By 1893 the *Enterprise* went the way of the declining fortunes of the Comstock, but De Quille remained in Nevada until after the defeat of Bryan in 1896. In the meantime, he had been writing for San Francisco publications and the Salt Lake City *Tribune* in order to eke out a living. By this time he was worn out from bouts with alcoholism and plagued with rheumatism. Taking notice of his friend's pathetic plight, John Mackay, the silver magnate, gave instructions that any Virginia City debts of De Quille's should be paid, that he should be provided with two of the best suits in town, and that a companion should be employed to accompany him back to his family in Iowa. This was done, and Mackay supplied a weekly allowance, equal to his salary on the paper (sixty dollars a week), for the rest of his life. A year later De Quille wrote that he was living like a fighting cock, doing nothing but swinging in a hammock under a shade tree in the midst of his children and grandchildren. He was drinking fruit punch to help his rheumatism and was looking forward to a visit next winter to the home of a friend in Kentucky who promised him baked possum and sweet potatoes. He never made the trip, for he died at West Branch, Iowa, on March 16, 1898.[29]

Like Clemens, De Quille dealt with hoaxes, burlesques, tall stories, and vivid antecdotes. Joseph Goodman thought him the equal of Clemens "in every respect, except the commercial instinct necessary for marketing his remarkable talent." Although his name is missing from many standard encyclopaedias of American literature, De Quille remains "for the social historian the chief diarist of an extinct but extraordinary way of life, the civilization of bonanza days in silver-land."[30]

During Daggett's years on the *Enterprise,* he associated with other men of talent. A central figure was Joseph T. Goodman, who, like

Daggett, was a native of New York State. Born at Masonville, Dalaware County, in September 1838, he had gone to California as a mere lad in the 1850's. "A poet of imagination, a scholar, a dramatic critic, a playwright," he wrote leading articles with "the charm of entire freedom from every restriction save his own judgment of what ought to be said." Boundless in his enthusiasms, he found the *Enterprise* a safety valve for his vigorous ideas rather than a daily responsibility.[31] A "handsome, charming, *bon vivant* bohemian," he was connected with the paper from 1861 to 1874, having part or complete ownership during that period. Daggett knew him well, for Goodman had learned his profession on the *Golden Era*. In the early years of the *Enterprise*, at Virginia City, Goodman was the editorial writer; De Quille, local reporter and mining editor; Dennis McCarthy, foreman of the print shop; and Denis Driscoll, bookkeeper. Goodman entered the belligerent atmosphere of the community when a bitter feud developed in 1863 between Tom Fitch of the Virginia City *Union* and the *Enterprise*. A duel took place between Fitch and Goodman at Ingraham's Ranch, where Fitch was wounded in the knee. After Daggett joined the *Enterprise* staff, Goodman delighted in writing editorials on significant subjects, leaving to Daggett the drudgery of day-to-day journalism. Mark Twain in his *Autobiography*, in a gesture of ostentatious self-abrogation, wrote that Goodman was the only one of the coterie "who had done anything to shed credit upon the paper."[32]

Considerable rivalry developed between Goodman and Daggett over the writing of long commemorative poems whenever there was a national holiday, a special celebration, or the death of a person of note. The two men were the best of friends but distinct rivals in verse-making. About once a week a poem written by Daggett or Goodman would appear in the *Enterprise*, with resulting censure and applause. Steve Gillis, the head of the pressroom, was devoted to Daggett's productions, while Dennis McCarthy was enthusiastic about Goodman's work. At Joe Mallon's saloon Gillis would proclaim, "This is the real stuff. This has the true ring. Hear this, everybody," as he recited Daggett's lines. Then McCarthy would extol the virtues of Goodman's verses: "Talk about poetry! This is the only true music ever written on the ledge [Comstock Lode]. Here's a line, gentlemen, that strikes the heart like a soft beam of moonlight falling from a cloud. I tell you it's the divine fire from Olympus. Where is the man that says that Daggett can write poetry? That man can't write mottoes for a first-class candy factory." In this poetic race Goodman for a time had the lead, as he won a poet-of-the-day contest and received so many requests for verses that he nearly exhausted himself in trying to satisfy the demand. Then Daggett forged ahead, producing a stupendous ode, which he delivered to the Negro community on the anniversary of the Emancipation Proclamation.[33]

On one later occasion the Comstock versifiers had a timed contest. They could spend twenty minutes writing a poem on an announced subject. Goodman won easily: he had half a column of lines when Daggett had barely started. By general consent Goodman was designated "Boss Poet of the Comstock." When Goodman's poem was published anonymously, a reviewer called it "a weak imitation of Wordsworth diluted through a brain enfeebled with the fumes of contraband opium and moonshine whiskey." Daggett made the most of the review, and Goodman accused him of writing it. The feud had reached a stalemate.

As wealthy mining barons sought support for their political ambitions in Nevada, the *Territorial Enterprise* was much coveted. In 1874 Goodman sold his interests for a fabulous price to William Sharon, with Daggett as the "editorial brains." Going to San Francisco, Goodman secured a seat on the Stock Exchange. But, according to his own story, this resulted in his becoming "dead broke."

After failing in an effort to develop a vineyard in the San Joaquin Valley, in 1884 Goodman started a literary weekly, the *San Franciscan*, then sold it to devote himself to the study of Central American archaeology.[34]

Another of Daggett's most intimate journalistic brethren on the Comstock was Charles Carroll Goodwin, born near Rochester, New York, on April 4, 1832.[35] Bernard De Voto has remarked: "Literature has heard nothing of this frontier editor; the West, which is undiscovered by literature, will not forget a career of brilliant and daring controversy."[36] Goodwin's versatility served him as a schoolteacher, merchant, miner, lawyer, jurist, politician, and orator. Going to California at the age of twenty, he started a lumber business, which fire destroyed. Next he turned miner and then studied law. He joined the trek to the Comstock in the early 1860's, where he became a central figure in the coterie that managed and edited the *Territorial Enterprise*. Many revealing stories of the period have come to us through his reminiscences.[37] While Daggett was often brusque and belligerent, Goodwin was consistently gentle and courteous. During the period following the terrible Virginia City fire of 1875, while Daggett was managing editor, Goodwin was the chief, and almost only, editorial writer, although Daggett received credit for many a good article from Goodwin's pen. In November 1875 Daggett left the paper, devoting himself to his business interests in the area. Goodwin then served as editor for two years, from November 1875 to December 1877. Then Daggett resumed the editorship for about a year, until late in 1878 when Goodwin took over once more. By 1880 the Comstock was definitely on the decline. Soon Goodwin went to Salt Lake City where for twenty-one years he was proprietor and editor of the Salt Lake *Tribune*.[38]

Over the years Goodwin wrote much for the *Enterprise* and the Salt Lake *Tribune* and was the author of a number of books, including a book of poems issued in the pre-Comstock period and another, published in 1913, in which he favorably appraises his old Virginia City friends, including Daggett, *As I Remember Them*. Active in cultural and political matters, he was one of seventy-four charter members of the Utah State Historical Society organized in December 1897. At the Utah Constitutional Convention of 1895, when Utah prepared for admission to the Union, he was a leader in the debates, taking an active part in the discussion of the permanent site for the state university.[39]

He was the last of the brilliant galaxy of Comstock editors of the Civil War Period. Bernard De Voto, who worked for a time during his late teens on a Salt Lake newspaper, long afterward remembered how "late afternoons in the office were sometimes made memorable by a white-haired gentleman who smoked stogies and reanimated the West for our young glamor." This white-haired gentleman died at Salt Lake City on August 25, 1917, at the age of eight-five.[40]

Another one of Daggett's intimate associates on the *Enterprise* was Denis Driscoll, affectionately known as "Jerry." Born in Cork County, Ireland, in 1823, as a child he had migrated with his parents to New York City. Learning the printer's trade, for a time he served as compositor for the New York *Tribune*, and in 1861 he became a partner in publishing the *Enterprise*. Severing the partnership in October 1863, he entered business, founding what developed into one of the leading brokerage houses of Virginia City, D. Driscoll and Company. When he died in 1876, he left a considerable fortune.

Dennis E. McCarthy, proprietor of the *Enterprise* from 1861 to 1865, was another of the old inner circle. Later he became proprietor of the Virginia City *Evening Chronicle*, which brought him prosperity. The decline of the Comstock, however, created a financial crisis in Virginia City journalism, necessitating the consolidation of the *Chronicle* and the *Enterprise* in 1881. Although a close friend declared that McCarthy was "one of the truest and best men I have ever met," like many other Comstockers he was an excessive drinker. He died of dropsy in 1885. With genuine grief, Daggett commented: "He was a good-hearted, wrong-headed man, and I shall miss him when I go to Virginia [City]."[41]

The master printer on the *Enterprise* and a loyal member of the informal fraternity that brought out the paper was Steve Gillis. A "bantam fighter from Mississippi," he was "the liveliest soul in the composing room." When Sam Clemens left for San Francisco, Gillis departed, too. Both worked on the *Morning Call* in 1864 and for a while roomed together. After a time both left, and Gillis returned to the *Enterprise*. In 1881 Goodman reported: "Steve Gillis, I fear, is sort of going to the dogs. . . . Two years ago he could have cleared up $60,000 or $80,000, out of Sierra Nevada; but he neglected the opportunity and is penniless now. Moreover, I hear he has taken to drink and has had the delirium tremens once or twice." Yet he outlived all the rest, dying in 1918.[42]

The many interests and enthusiasms of this vigorous and colorful staff were reflected in the various campaigns taken up by the *Enterprise* throughout its existence. For example, after Mark Twain's scathing article on George Turner, Chief Justice of the Nevada Supreme Court, won him a post on the *Enterprise*, the paper issued a relentless barrage against Turner and other judges who supplemented their meager salaries of fifteen hundred dollars a year by selling verdicts on valuable mining claims to the highest bidder. In 1863, in one mining case before the court, Turner demanded and received sixty thousand dollars for himself and ten thousand for his broker. The territorial court became so notorious that William Stewart of the Territorial Council joined in supporting the popular mass meetings in opposition. Eventually, Turner and the other judges of the court, James W. North and C. B. Locke, were forced to resign in 1864.[43]

The repressive measures for Reconstruction taken in 1867 by General Philip Sheridan, military governor for the Fifth Military District, Louisiana and Texas, evoked much bitterness. Dennis McCarthy, formerly of the *Enterprise* and now editor of the Democratic Virginia City *Chronicle*, was furious and in an impassioned editorial demanded "a new rebellion" if that kind of repression were to be visited upon the South. Daggett came into the *Enterprise* office that night after having imbibed "a large and assorted cargo of gin." After an hour of work his editorial colleague, Charles C. Goodwin, proposed that they go out for some hot oysters, for it was a bitter cold night. Daggett refused to leave his writing. He replied savagely, "No sir. That other rebellion cost 4,000 millions of dollars and 400,000 lives," indicating that he intended to squelch an incipient revival of rebellion. Goodwin protested that if the editorial should be published, the

Chronicle editor would get his gun and Daggett would soon be "full of buckshot." Daggett smilingly replied, "I will get up early in the morning and tell him it was you" who wrote it.

The article said that during the war both Sheridan and the *Chronicle* editor were in the service, the former raiding the Shenandoah Valley, the latter leading a raid on government funds, the former succeeding in cleaning out the Valley, the latter in cleaning out government money. Goodwin saw no more of Daggett until the next evening when McCarthy and he were seen walking arm in arm along the street. They had been dining together, and drink had made each a little "mellow." As Goodwin remarked, Daggett was surely "filled with contradiction."

Sometimes Daggett would control his volatile temper, to the surprise of his friends. Once, when Daggett aroused the ire of a fellow editor outside of the state, the editor responded savagely. Asked if he intended to retaliate, Daggett responded, "Answer that? Would you hunt snipe with a howitzer?"[44]

He could be inconsistent. On one occasion he went out on the Divide four miles north of Virginia City to attend a prize fight and even acted as one of the judges. He returned to write a scathing editorial, denouncing prize fighting and its degrading influences and condemning county officials for permitting it. This led Goodwin to comment to Daggett that he reminded him "a little of Saul before he became Paul" and that he "must have seen a great light" as he was coming from the divide. Daggett's response was, "You lack experience. When you have become wiser—I should hate to wait for the time—you will learn that there are times in men's lives when it is a duty to assume a virtue, though they have it not."[45]

Another incident occurred late in the evening of July 6, 1876, when the night wire to the *Enterprise* brought news of General George A. Custer's last stand and the subsequent massacre. Goodwin was obviously shocked when Daggett burst forth with the comment, "Big fellows. Roman noses, fighters those Sioux! I'm proud of them." Daggett had spent some time on his way west among Indian tribes, and he did not hide his enthusiasm for the red man. Yet, a dozen years later, when it was proposed that a statue of Custer be erected in Washington, D.C., it was to Congressman Daggett that Mrs. Custer wrote, protesting against another statue of the general by James Wilson A. McDonald, who had created the memorial to him at West Point. Although critics praised McDonald's work for its accurate portrayal of the fallen general, Mrs. Custer insisted that the statue could not be worse. To many, the face was that of a man of sixty in very unmilitary dress and armed like a desperado. No statue to Custer was erected in the national capital.[46]

Once Daggett composed a biting editorial on the private life of General Thomas Williams, a wealthy Comstock lawyer, to depress his aspirations to become United States Senator. The General appeared with a revolver, and with almost uncontrollable rage demanded to know the authority for the "outrageous statement." "Oh," replied Daggett, "I had the story from Peters," mentioning a lawyer of no distinguished mental capacities. Thereupon, Williams departed to hunt up Peters, who soon appeared at the *Enterprise* office pale and shaken and inquired why Daggett had told such an obvious lie. Daggett soothingly replied that the General had threatened to shoot him, and that Peters was the first son of a b——h that came to his mind.[47]

The *Enterprise* was not above resorting to sensational journalistic tactics when its anger was aroused. When Mr. and Mrs. Frank Leslie, publishers of *Frank Leslie's Illustrated Weekly Newspaper*, a widely read sensational periodical, came to the Comstock in 1877 with a staff of artists and reporters, they were received with courtesy and interest. Yet, in a book issued in the same year, Mrs. Leslie referred to Virginia City as a dreary, desolate, wicked, and Godforsaken community. This was too much for Daggett and Goodwin, who were then conducting the *Enterprise*, and they plotted revenge. As a result, on July 14, 1878, the *Enterprise* devoted the entire front page to a thorough, documented, and unsparing exposure of the alleged background, personal life, sex habits, and shoddy character of Leslie and his wife. They had hired a private detective to gather evidence in New York City. The story of the Leslies was controversial, and the Virginia City newsmen had made the most of an effort to portray it as sordid indeed.[48]

Daggett's aggressive individualism often expressed itself within the intimate *Enterprise* circle. On one occasion a dispute arose over the spelling of a word, and Daggett, proud of his knowledge of the lexicon, reached for a dictionary to confirm his point, grandly asserting, "I'd rather be right than be President." To this Goodwin replied, "That's the way we all feel about you, Rollin." Thereafter, for some time, Daggett was in a savage mood.[49]

When his articles annoyed his readers, instead of withdrawing, Daggett pressed on with even greater belligerence. At one time he became concerned about the methods of a dairy farmer in the region, and when the latter objected, Daggett retorted with more vigor than accuracy, "As I walked along the high board fence of your corral, I heard your cows gnawing bones, and when I turned the corner, they looked up at me and growled like dogs."[50]

In 1880 a reader became irate because of what he deemed the editor's lack of support for U. S. Grant's hoped-for third term. Actually, Daggett was favorable to Grant as long as his nomination seemed a possibility. The irate reader called on the editor, and Daggett abruptly asked, "Well, what in ——— do you want?" The visitor replied that he objected to the way in which Daggett conducted his paper. The latter promptly arose, put on his hat, and, seizing a large heavy cane, caught the visitor by the arm, saying, "Come along with me. You're under arrest, and are going to jail." When the caller tried to escape, Daggett struck his calves with a cane. At the jail the officer in charge asked the nature of the offense, to which Daggett replied, "Insanity. He came in to tell me how to run the paper. Keep a sharp eye on him." Naturally, the man screamed with indignation, causing the jailer to think that he really was out of his mind. The jailer kept him in a cell until morning, when a policeman who recognized him as a normal, respectable citizen released him.[51]

Daggett loved the pleasures of the bottle and the table and seemed to have limitless capacity. One morning, having already eaten, he had breakfast with the silver baron, William Sharon, who remarked, "Heavens, I would give half my fortune for your appetite." "Yes," replied Daggett, "and the other half for my character and lofty bearing." Actually, as Goodwin observed, Daggett's physique and his character "from a Christian standpoint" seemed unworthy of emulation.[52]

Yet, despite his prejudices and eccentricities, Daggett maintained high ideals, and always fought injustice and corruption on any level. His influence on the *Enterprise* has been expressed by Ivan Benson: "His satire was an effective weapon when the *Enterprise* engaged in many noteworthy controversies with individual groups, or rival newspapers. Samuel Clemens learned from Daggett many valuable lessons in the art of fighting, with the printed word, corruption in high places."[53]

As the years went by, the informality of life and labor on the *Enterprise* continued to allow time for indulgence in poetic fancy, as well as editorial duties. Sometimes the poetic muse was called upon under somewhat strange circumstances. Daggett's old friend, Sam Davis of the Carson City *Appeal*, later recalled finding Daggett on a Saturday in July of 1876 using poetry as a means of reviving hope in a rather melancholy Comstock prize fighter who sat across from him in a Virginia City saloon. Daggett had scribbled on a piece of paper six stanzas of a poem which he entitled "A Song of Hope." The first and last stanzas were:

There's nothing so bad as it seems, my friend,
There's nothing so bad as it seems.
   The ills of today
   Will soon pass away,
To meet you again but in dreams, my friend,
To meet you again but in dreams.

There's nothing so bad as 'tis said, my friend,
There's nothing so bad as is said,
   Though heartache and strife
   May last all your life,
Beyond there is hope for the dead, my friend,
Beyond there is hope for the dead.

The pugilist responded to the lines by saying: "It's bang up: You've fought my feeling clear to the ropes. . . . Those words make me weak about the chest."[54]

Daggett's Memorial Day poems of 1876, 1877, and 1879 were high points in the celebration of the occasions and received wide acclaim. On May 30, 1876, his long poem, "Old Unger," dealing with a legendary figure of the Elbe River Valley, was delivered before a highly appreciative audience. Its opening lines were:

With leaf and blossom, Spring has come again,
And tardy Summer, garlanded with flowers,
Trips down the hillside like a wayward child,
Her garments fringed with frost; but in her smile
The valleys turn to green, and tender flowers
Woke from their slumber by the song of birds,
Reach up to kiss the dimpled mouth of May.
With feet unsandaled and with solemn step,
Treading the path that marks the centuries,
We come to lay on valor's silent bed
The fragrant offerings of our hearts and hands;
As we strew with flowers the humble graves
Of men who drew the sword and stepped between
Their country and its foes, the story may
Be told of brave old Unger. He was Chief
Of thousands. Ere the daring Genoese
Of Western seas had seen the sun go down,
His people feed their flocks beside the Elbe,
And spread their nets where with its sluggish flood
The silver waters of the Eger blend.[55]

The *Enterprise* waxed ecstatic:

> It is the finest production which the centennial year has thus far
> brought forth, and ranks with the most splendid efforts of the
> world's great masters. Such delicate taste, such magnificent
> imagery, is only at rare intervals expressed in language, every
> word of which is full of awakened or slumbering power. . . . While
> as sweet as Whittier, it is as strong as was old Homer when he
> set to the music of his verse the bounding life of his own brave
> race, in language which modern scholars strive in vain to imitate.[56]

A year later, as another editor published it, he commented: "It is
worth a place in such a collection as *Bryant's Library of Poetry and
Song*, and ranks foremost among the anniversary poems of the country.
Who would not read it in preference to Bayard Taylor's 'Centennial'?"

Among many other narrative and commemorative poems are the
descriptive, "The Carson Spur: The Grandest Panorama in the Sierra
Mountains," in which prose and poetry are combined, and "Asrik-
Oben," a Memorial Day poem delivered in 1877, which the *Enterprise*
declared had "the same power, the same majesty of language, the
same undertone of delicacy and magnificent imagery" as his previous
effort. It added, "In some countries they would hang a man of Daggett's abilities if he did not oftener make them manifest." The *Gold
Hill News* emphatically declared, "It is the finest poem ever produced
in the state of Nevada."[57]

An orator as well as a journalist and poet, Daggett was often
called upon to speak on special occasions. On the Fourth of July
in 1878 the celebration at Virginia City started at dawn with the
raising of Old Glory on a tall flagpole on the peak of Mt. Davidson,
two thousand feet above the city. Then followed the customary parade
with bands and patriotic organizations in line. Later, at the formal
exercises in Piper's Opera House, Daggett extolled the growth of the
United States, "in every attribute of strength and grandeur unparalleled in the world's history and the annals of national growth." He
praised the government of the United States and "the measureless
products of its field and factories; of its mines of gold and silver."
Even the people of rather free-living Virginia City burst into enthusiastic applause as his eloquence mounted, while he exclaimed: "We
are proud of its school-houses . . . and of the church-spires pointing
upward from every hamlet, and speaking of a faith in Him upon whose
promise our fathers leaned when the days were darkest, and 'whose
judgments are true and righteous altogether.' "

Expressing faith in American representative government when founded upon popular intelligence with the aid of education, "the crowning glory of man," he admitted that "poverty and crime and discontent nurse schemes of disorder in the narrow ways and crowded tenements of the great cities, and fill the air with threatened violence." But to him "their turbulence is no menace to the general peace, and finds no echo on the mountain side, or in the valleys where the daisies bloom." He believed that the cities constituted "the safety-valves of the Republic—the ulcers to which are drawn the baneful humors of the social system—the volcanoes where are concentrated and find vent the smouldering fires of political disorder. It is better that such should be the case rather than that the virus . . . should diffuse its poison throughout the whole land, and sow the seeds of disorder and decay, among the healthy fibres of the body politic." He further was of the opinion: "This spirit of unrest and defiance of the restraints of law will increase in the great cities as their people swell in numbers. This must be expected. But the disease will be local, and never beyond the reach of that surgery through which an evil threatening to the general peace will find speedy eradication."

The Hamiltonian and Jeffersonian approaches to politics continued to divide the people. Daggett asserted: "Carried to their ultimate, both theories would lead to danger—one, perhaps, ending in despotism, and the other assuredly in anarchy. . . . Since there is peril in the extremes of both theories, the correct solution of the great problems consists in discovering the safe and rational mean between them."[58]

Daggett was proud of his effort. Although the White House received the *Territorial Enterprise*, Daggett himself wrote to President Hayes, enclosing a portion of his oration, which he said was "old line Whiggery," embracing a "somewhat novel theory of republican government."[59] But, if Daggett's "Whiggery" distrusted the virtue and restraint of the masses in the large cities, he was not far from Jeffersonian concerns over the uncertain dependability of the landless populace in urban areas. And, local enthusiast that he was, he spent no time on the lapses from sobriety, integrity, and disciplined living that prompted many Americans to look upon small Virginia City as an embodiment of much that was a threat to morality and civilized living and to consider rural Nevada as almost a pocket-borough of the silver barons.

Frontier life was rough and hard, but it was lived with a vigor and courage that always commanded Daggett's affection and respect.

In one of his best-known poems, "My New Year's Guests," written in 1881, he addressed a picture of five hundred California pioneers, concluding with the words:

Bar closely the curtained windows; shut the light from every pane,
While, free from the world's intrusion and curious eyes profane,
I take from its leathern casket, a dinted old cup of tin,
More precious to me than silver, and blessing the draught within,
I drink alone in silence to the "Builders of the West"—
"Long life to the hearts still beating, and peace to the hearts at rest."

V

Daggett's Virginia City

VIRGINIA CITY, SITUATED ON A HANGING SHELF ALONG THE MOUNTAINSIDE, with Mount Davidson rising fifteen hundred feet above it, by 1869 boasted fifteen thousand inhabitants. The mountains crowding about the town limited space for homes and businesses. Some spacious, ornamental residences, such as that of James Fair, a wealthy silver baron, were erected on the upper levels of the mountainside. Yet most homes were simple wooden shacks built close together near the mills and dumps. Few substantial residential structures had been built in the city because of fear that mining prosperity would not last. Instead, men lived in depressing rookeries, causing the comment in 1875 that these places, as well as Virginia's lack of respectable places of public amusement, were a disgrace to the community. Monthly rent for a room was not much below the actual cost of constructing one, yet landlords had no trouble renting. Each evening a thousand bachelors living in such quarters took their meals in restaurants on C Street in the business district.[1]

Daggett was spared the loneliness and austerity of this manner of living. In 1868 he was married to Maggie Curry, a native of Philadelphia, the ceremony taking place in Virginia City. He was then thirty-seven and his bride only seventeen.[2] The couple lived in the spacious home which Daggett built at 45 South B Street, above the business district and a stone's throw from the present Storey County courthouse.[3] On November 29, 1870, a daughter, Grace, was born to them. A year and a half later, a second daughter, Katie, was added to the family. On April 19, 1873, a son, Rollin, was born, but he died five months later. Mrs. Daggett was a charming hostess and took understandable pride in the prominence of her husband and the loveliness of her daughters.[4] As a father, Daggett was as uninhibited as he was as a journalist. At home he would lie on the floor like a hippopotamus, his little girls jumping on him, beating him with tidies

and pillows, and screaming with delight. Daggett "would be vehemently, with strange imprecations and unheard-of anathemas, declaring that in just half a minute he would jump upon them and smash
them into a million pieces."[5]

The raison d'être of Virginia City was, of course, mining. This
meant a remarkable degree of democracy, for a humble miner with
only a pick and shovel might soon become a man of great wealth.
Mine owner and laborer, moreover, freely mingled in the outwardly
egalitarian Comstock atmosphere, for all male citizens, with a few
exceptions, wore the rough garb of the workingman and in general
patronized the same bars, restaurants, and brokerage houses. Mining
claims, often in bitter dispute, provided highly remunerative work
for the legal profession. Speculative ventures and plans for new plants
were constantly being projected. The original Comstock interests had
been taken over by the Ophir Mining Company, a California corporation.[6]

The Comstock bonanza created flush times. In 1874, when Mark
Strouse, proprietor of Central Market, and Lily Edgington, daughter
of a mining superintendent, were married at St. Paul's Episcopal
Church, their presents were declared more numerous and costly than
those ever before received by a local bride. Silver gifts, diamonds, and
other valuables were given in profusion. The store of M. M. Frederick, the most prominent jeweler, alone delivered "a full wagon load."
This establishment, widely patronized by affluent Comstockers, on
occasion would display a ring containing a thirteen-and-a-half-carat
diamond and other stones almost as large.[7]

Wealthy Comstockers could patronize V. Milatovich's gourmet
shop. Available there were the best of California hams, bacon,
mackerel, truffles, French and Italian wines, roasted chestnuts, cheeses,
Dutch sardines, whiskies, and brandies. The proprietor, it was reported, "eats his own grub and drinks his own liquors, and, as a living
proof of their excellence, has a fit of gout regularly every two weeks."[8]

Much of Virginia City life was far less glamorous. The *Enterprise*
frequently reported that ten to forty immigrants from Europe and
the Atlantic states were arriving daily, but often there was not much
work available for them. Many were candidates for disillusionment,
as all had large canvas sacks, which, the townspeople believed, they
hoped to fill with the dollars they would earn. In 1875 the *Enterprise*
remarked: "Some of them are quite impatient to get out into the hills
a mile or two in order to begin breaking masses of solid silver out of
a ledge of quartz, which is unknown to all of our people, but which

they are perfectly familiar with, having seen it some hundreds of times—in dreams."⁹

Many able men thronged to Virginia City, where the fortunate ones amassed wealth and power. In the hierarchy of leadership at Virginia City, six men stood out: William M. Stewart, John P. Jones, John W. Mackay, William Sharon, James G. Flood, and William S. O'Brien, although Flood and O'Brien operated chiefly from San Francisco.

Stewart, like Daggett, was born in New York State and grew up in Ohio. In Trumbull County on the Western Reserve of Ohio, he had a rugged childhood, helped to make brick and assisted in driving cattle over the mountains to Philadephia. He went to Yale, where he was a classmate of Daniel C. Gilman, the first president of Johns Hopkins University, but he did not graduate, for he joined in the California gold rush, going in 1850 via Panama. He prospected in Nevada county but left mining for a law practice there in 1852. Later, he moved to San Francisco, where he was a law partner of Henry S. Foote, former governor of Mississippi. The trek to Nevada took him to Genoa in that territory in 1860, where he set up an office in a log cabin. At that time Nevada was part of Utah, and non-Mormons were very bitter against Mormon leaders. With the help of California friends, Stewart was active in securing the organization of Nevada Territory and became the most prominent member of the Territorial Council. He of course knew Daggett and Samuel Clemens intimately.

Clemens in 1867 became his private secretary, writing *Innocents Abroad* in his room in Washington, D.C. Stewart took a large part in the constitutional convention of 1862. He was active in calling mass meetings to defeat the proposed constitution because it provided for a general property tax. This would have taxed every aspect of mining property so that the miner who had worked without profit would be unable to pay the tax. The constitution was defeated amidst great bitterness. To many, Stewart was the "political Moloch" of Nevada. A second constitution authorized the taxing of the proceeds rather than the property of the mines. Stewart campaigned vigorously and successfully for its adoption and became one of the original senators from the state. Mrs. Stewart at this time was so ardent in her Southern sympathies that her husband sent her to San Francisco with forty thousand dollars to spend while the senatorial campaign was in progress.

Stewart became very wealthy as an able, tireless, and trusted attorney for the large mining interests. In Washington he built a beautiful home, "Stewart Castle," where he entertained extensively. He was a commanding person, six feet two and weighing two hundred pounds, with light-red hair, clear blue eyes, and a ruddy complexion. Indeed, he was so austerely grand in bearing that he was said to "move like a cathedral." But when during one campaign a speaker asserted that he towered "among men like the Colossus of Rhodes," an opponent, quoting the remark, added, "and he has as much brass in his composition."[10]

He aided in the election of the other Nevada Senator, James Nye. Most miners in Nevada had been essentially trespassers on the public domain, so the two men, who were earnestly devoted to the Union, ventured their help in passing war and reconstruction measures and at the same time obtained from Congress confirmation of title to the mines. From 1865 until his retirement from the Senate in 1875, he vigorously supported the Reconstruction program, although he had voted against the second Freedman's Bureau Bill and was more moderate toward the South than many of his contemporaries. He really wrote the Fifteenth Amendment and was the one who directed the struggle for its passage. Nevada became the first state to ratify it. Stewart, unlike some Radicals, aided the Democrats in securing the restoration of Southern states to the Union.

He had been associated with legal cases involving titles worth millions of dollars and much corruption of judges. His fees had averaged $125,000 a year. After ten years in the Senate he found it desirable to resume his lucrative law practice, but once again served in the Senate from 1887 to 1905, dying four years later.

Another mine baron and politician was John Percival Jones. Two years older than Daggett, he was born in England in 1829 of Welsh ancestry. Like Daggett and Stewart, he had spent his boyhood in Ohio, where he attended the public schools of Cleveland. An early Argonaut to California via Cape Horn, he became a farmer, miner, sheriff, and state legislator. Going to Nevada in 1867, he became superintendent and then part-owner of the lucrative Crown Point mine. In the bitterness of the struggle for power on the Comstock, for a time Jones and William Sharon were bitter rivals, and in the spring of 1872 this led to a personal altercation between the two in San Francisco. The *Enterprise* at that time was hostile to Sharon and reported that Virginia City sentiment was almost universally favorable to Jones, for Sharon had no "established reputation for anything—except his own interests." Jones's wealth gave him leisure and the means to embark upon a political career. He served in the United States Senate from 1873 to 1903, a powerful representative of Nevada's interest in silver coinage.[11]

Youngest, ablest, and in many respects the most admirable of the tycoons of the Comstock was John W. Mackay, born in Ireland in the year of Daggett's birth, 1831. His family had come to the United States in 1840. In 1851 he started for California via New Orleans and the Isthmus of Panama. For seven years he worked in California mines, and, when still a relatively poor man, he went to Virginia City, where he gained expert knowledge concerning the timbering of mines. Later, joining forces with James C. Flood and William S. O'Brien, saloon keepers of San Francisco, and subsequently with James G. Fair, he became immensely wealthy. He possessed natural dignity, gracious affability, eagerness to develop his educational opportunities, and generosity to people of all stations in life. He was temperate in eating and drinking and loved music and the drama. His wife preferred to live in Europe and educate their two sons there. While he lived in rather lonely fashion on the Comstock, he maintained a lavish home for her in France and occasionally took trips to Europe to visit his family. He was generous to the Catholic Church with which he was affiliated, and his helpfulness to Daggett caused the latter to refer to him as the "most generous of men." He outlived all of his old mining associates, dying a few months after Daggett, in July 1902.[12]

William Sharon, another of the key figures on the Comstock, had been born in northern Ohio, in Jefferson county, in 1821, had attended college and for a time studied law in the office of Edwin Stanton. He settled in St. Louis, Missouri. Later he practiced law and engaged in business in Greene County, Illinois. Moving to California in 1849, he was a businessman in Sacramento until relocating in San Francisco in 1850. In 1864 William C. Ralston, a daring financial leader who had organized the Bank of California in San Francisco, selected the debonair but crafty Sharon to manage a branch of the bank at Virginia City. There, in banking and especially in mining, Sharon accumulated a fortune. Daggett actively aided him in securing the seat in the United States Senate which he held from 1875 to 1881. In 1875, following the tragic death of Ralston in San Francisco Bay, Sharon had succeeded to the control of the new Palace Hotel in San Francisco, unexcelled in the fabulous luxury of its appointments.[13]

Another "Silver King" was James Graham Fair, who was born in Belfast, Ireland, of Scotch-Irish descent in 1831, the same year Daggett and Mackay came into the world. The family moved to the United States, where Fair acquired his basic education in Illinois. At the age of eighteen he sought his fortune in the California mines. By 1861 he had moved on to Nevada, where he became fabulously wealthy as a mine-owner and banker and served as United States Senator (from

1881 to 1887). In 1872 he built a handsome new residence on South B Street in Virginia City, a square two-story building with imposing white pillars supporting an ornate balcony.[14]

Probably the least admired of the Comstock giants, Fair was a heavy-set person with dark skin and eyes and handsome features. "A master mechanic" and an amazingly shrewd financier, he had titanic confidence in his own ability. He was incorrigibly selfish and egocentric; few people had a good word for him. He loved show but feigned disdain for popular opinion. While Mackay personally drove a shabby buggy, Fair maintained a shining carriage with a beautifully matched team of horses and a coachman. Fair was an intense individual and at times had to take a vacation for reasons of health. In July 1878 he was recuperating at Santa Cruz, California, but in a short time his compusive energy took him back to the Comstock ledge. Divorced in 1883, in later years he was plagued by those claiming compensation for his alleged sexual involvements. He died in San Francisco in 1894, a very lonely man.[15]

The last of the mining leaders of the Comstock were James Clair Flood and William S. O'Brien. Flood was born in New York City on October 25, 1826, of poor Irish immigrant parents. He attended the public schools in New York, served as an apprentice to a carriage maker, and as a "forty-niner" went to California via Cape Horn. After carpentering and mining on the Pacific Coast, he moved east and for a time farmed in southern Illinois. Having married a Mary Leary from Ireland, he again went to California. Eventually a friend, William S. O'Brien, and he became partners in a San Francisco saloon, which must have been well known to Daggett in his San Francisco years. Nearby, in 1862, a new Mining Exchange was established which broadened the interests of the two men. Flood's associate, O'Brien, had been born in Dublin in 1849. Eventually the partners extended their interests to include brokerage and banking activities, and the two men became powers on the Comstock.[16]

The area, of course, had its "ups and downs," as new strikes of silver were made and others proved unrewarding. The years from 1860 to 1863 saw steady movement into the area and rapid development of its resources. A peak in production was reached in July 1863. Then came a decline and before long a revival. A big disappointment came in 1865 when all of the early bonanzas at about the same time were exhausted at the five-hundred-foot level. Over a period of six years the mines had produced ore worth over fifty millions of dollars, but uneconomical managing, faulty technological methods, and expensive litigation between rival mining claimants had brought economic crisis. The rich veins near the surface were approaching exhaustion, and explorations at lower levels had proved fruitless.[17]

But those dedicated to Comstock, and their own, prosperity spared no energy or ingenuity in seeking new veins. John Mackay worked hard to develop the Kentuck mine. Fair, with a reputation as an efficient superintendent of the Ophir mine, in 1866/67 was employed by the Hale and Norcross Company to place that mine on a profitable basis. Success came in a remarkable way, but the business connection terminated in the fall of 1867. Then, as we have seen, the daring William C. Ralston had sent William Sharon to manage the Virginia City branch of the Bank of California. Through shrewd methods the bank soon took over some of the most valuable mining properties. New ores were found, and a boom developed in 1867. Now their control extended over contributory sources of profit: timber, water, fuel, machinery, and ore processing. The huge freight wagons drawn by many teams of horses were replaced by cars on the Virginia and Truckee Railroad, completed in 1872.[18] Sharon and his associates seemed to be practically masters of the Comstock, and they sought control of other properties, including Hale and Norcross, an active mine, which was secured after a bitter struggle, but which soon seemed to have been worked out.

Now two new leaders, Mackay and Fair, confident of the future possibilities of Hale and Norcross, joined with James C. Flood and William S. O'Brien, the San Francisco brokers, and by ingenious endeavors secured control of the property. Rich ore was found, and great wealth came to them between 1869 and 1871. The four manipulators expanded their operations and, by careful planning, within three years had come into the richest treasures of the area, the Big Bonanza. Accordingly, they were acclaimed the undisputed masters of the Comstock. With their profits the group purchased two mills over the Divide at Gold Hill to work the Hale and Norcross ore, previously reduced at a plant owned by Sharon. They also purchased Sharon's interest in the Virginia and Gold Hill Water Company which was the source of water for the mills and towns. Mackay and Fair had minor setbacks as each embarked separately. But major success awaited them. In 1867 the Consolidated Virginia Mining Company was organized to develop much of the Comstock area but did not prove profitable. In 1872 the Mackay-Fair group acquired control of this and of the California mine. These proved immensely profitable, and for five years huge returns were obtained. At first Mackay and Fair were honored for ushering in widespread prosperity, but as economic decline set in, they were widely and bitterly criticized by the public.

This was especially the case because of their control of auxiliary businesses, furnishing timber and water. In 1875 they even established their own Bank of Nevada. Yet competent historians believe that the Mackay-Fair-Flood-O'Brien group played a fairer game than any other mining group on the Comstock.

The rich resources of the Big Bonanza brought prosperity until 1877, but uncertainty was often the atmosphere of the community. In January 1875, as stocks were in a precarious situation, the *Enterprise* reported that Mackay was walking "the hurricane deck of the Comstock as calmly as when stocks were booming their highest." A few days later, it asserted that the decline in the market value of Comstock stocks was "fearful," carrying with it "the hopes and fortunes of thousands in Nevada and California." All seemed to agree that the panic was "unparalleled and without a cause." It appeared to be a "question of endurance," as stock quotations "stabbed as deeply as though they had been daggers" reached a disastrous low. One factor was the precarious financial situation of William C. Ralston of the Bank of California, whose investments had been extended to include a carriage works, a watch factory, a luxurious theatre, rolling mills, and other California enterprises. In August, following a run on the Bank, Ralston resigned. His body was later found in the San Francisco Bay. The *Enterprise* deemed it suicide. Sharon worked strenuously to reopen the Virginia City Branch on October 3, when the band played, and at the request of Ralston's brother, A. J. Ralston, Daggett used his oratory in seeking to inspire confidence.[19]

Details of the mines, stamping mills, and other aspects of the mining industry in Virginia City are fascinating material but need not be repeated here. One sorry aspect of Comstock life was that of frequent mining accidents. Sometimes as many as forty men would die in a single unfortunate occurrence, as in April 1869, when the *Enterprise* front-page columns were bordered in black because of fatalities due to a fire in the Yellow Jacket mine. But there was never an extended period during which in some mine there was not a serious injury or fatal accident.[20]

Perhaps it was because of the hazardous nature of their work that the miners developed a strong union. The Miners' Union maintained attractive halls for social and business purposes. It was generally successful in maintaining four dollars a day as standard pay for underground work. During various periods, as in the crisis of 1875, rumors were abroad that wages would be reduced. The *Enterprise* denounced these, insisting that the very "cordial" feelings between employers and employees on the Comstock were due to the fact that nowhere else was "so large a body of laborers so well paid" and nowhere else did laborers give their "employers so great a reward."[21]

To reduce hazards and increase productivity, ingenious men were constantly working to improve technical aspects of Comstock mining. One of these was Adolph H. J. Sutro, born of German-Jewish parents in Aix-la-Chapelle in 1830. He had come to the United States with members of his family in 1850. Breaking loose from his kinfolk, he went to California in 1851 and later located on the Comstock. This dramatic, dynamic man sought to drain water from the mines and facilitate the problem of removing ore from the deepest levels by his Sutro Tunnel, begun in 1869 and completed in 1878.[22] But by then the last great finds had been exhausted, insofar as they could be worked by existing methods. Speculators eagerly awaited suggestions from Mackay and others that new fields would be opened up. In the mid-1880's new uses for ores brought a temporary revival, but the heyday of the Comstock was over.

Daggett always appeared more interested in the joys of living than the accumulation of money, but he was close enough to the mining situation in Virginia City to make some highly profitable investments. In 1873 a Virginia City journalist referred to him as "already rolling in filthy lucre," with "untold shares in the Belcher" and whole sections of coal and borax lands. For a period he was superintendent of the El Dorado Canyon coal mine, spending a week there in 1876 inspecting the pumps, engines, and other machinery. Stock in the Belcher Mine for a time had been highly profitable. Between September 1870 and April 1872, it rose from $1.50 to $1,525.00 a share. The El Dorado mine, seventeen miles from Virginia City, was one in which extensive deposits of inexpensive coal were found. In 1876 Daggett and a group of associates became involved in a suit against the California Mining Company. The *Enterprise* commented that a large sum was involved and that the matter would interest the courts for some time to come, but the final disposition of the case is not known.[23]

The city was subject to marked fluctuations in prosperity, so there were frequent labor troubles. From time to time the *Enterprise* would record: "The times are hard, and there is much suffering in the city," with much unemployment. In 1878 unemployment in the country had led to the "fearful tramp evil," which in Virginia City was a "veritable plague," as the transients committed many "outrages."[24]

Every afternoon and evening on pleasant days, leisurely throngs promenaded on the shady side of C Street, so that pedestrians in a hurry often had to detour into the street. Mostly men congregated here between four and eight in the evening. Having been "cooped up" all day indoors, they found diversion in swapping experiences. Taking advantage of the crowds, the vendor of cheap jewelry, the razor-grinder, the book agent, and others hawked their wares. Inevitably there was the "Last Chance" medicine man. Perched on a box, his bottles illuminated by the flare of a naphtha lamp, he played the banjo, delivered his sales talk, and distorted his face to the amusement of passers-by. Other hawkers sought customers to use machines for testing the strength of the lungs, or an electrical apparatus to "purify the blood," strengthen the nervous system, and remove "all stains from the teeth." Some of the street salesmen rounded up passengers for a splendid "Concord coach," going to Reno to connect with the transcontinental trains. Other attractions were a spotted boy from the wilds of Africa, a German ballad singer, a Fairy Queen dwarf, and a collection of snakes.[25]

Many amusements and recreational activities in Virginia City were typical of those in almost any American community. Baseball games between the "Socials" of Virginia City and the Silver Star Club of Carson City and racing on the new race course (built in 1871) north of the city were aspects of this. In January 1871 a new roller-skating rink opened and was always so well patronized that a second one was soon made available. In some winter seasons sleighing was highly popular, as the snows were so deep that even heavy ore wagons, hacks, and stages operated on runners. In the springtime an organ grinder, with the inevitable monkey to pick up the pennies offered by the children, was likely to appear, eagerly followed by a throng of boys and girls, although the monkey might be "old, blear-eyed, and emaciated." In the summer came performances such as the Overland Circus with Arab tumblers and trick ponies or the Atlantic and Pacific Circus, which was termed "a moral institution," since the owner did not let his employees use obscene language.[26]

Some diversions were genteel. Daniel Lyons, for example, operated a Dancing Academy for instruction in social dancing. Yet crudity and sometimes even cruelty marked other pastimes. Fights between cocks, dogs and badgers, and bears and bulls were not uncommon.

Prize fights between human participants were not unknown either. In 1875, when about fifteen hundred people attended a prize fight a few miles north of Virginia City, some citizens were surprised at Daggett's inconsistent moralistic reaction. His editorial, reminiscent of the sermons he probably heard in his boyhood, rang with fervent indignation:

Every man who witnessed the brutal exhibition without protest violated the law no less than the principals within the ring, and we regret that a few score of the most prominent were not arrested and made an example of. Without the countenance of such men of respectability, such exhibitions would rarely occur. . . . Had our reporters been arrested it would have received our earnest approval.[27]

"Sinners" in many frontier towns experienced all or a combination of outlets: liquor, gambling, and commercialized sex. Bars and taverns were often the only outlets for masculine sociability. In February 1868 a new saloon, "The Comstock Cave," opened in the Wells Fargo building. Beautifully decorated with mountain and lake scenes, it had an archway of rocks over the bar and glittering lamps in abundance. Pretty waitresses served the "astonishing New Orleans cocktails," mixed by an expert, Eugene Beckman. The new Cave was connected by folding doors with the "Express Saloon," but the two were operated separately. A more "homey" atmosphere was to be found in Mrs. York's North Star Saloon, where a free lunch came with beer and daily papers and pictorial publications were available.[28] The Washoe Club, with its lounge, bar, and card room, was very exclusive. Aside from inferior paintings and statuary, the place compared favorably with luxurious clubs in Boston and New York. An admirable chef added further acclaim to the club's offerings. Daggett proudly wrote letters to prominent personages on the stationary of this club.[29]

Many men on the Comstock consumed as much as a quart of whiskey a day. In 1872 the federal Internal Revenue tax collections indicated that sixteen thousand barrels of beer had been provided there in a year. Some people objected to the indiscriminate sale of liquor to the Piute Indians of the vicinity, many of whom were observed daily in a drunken condition.[30]

Comstock sex life was rather uninhibited. Many of the miners were well-paid unmarried men who frequented houses of prostitution in the Chinese quarter below the railroad depot. On D Street there were two blocks of houses of ill fame, where madames such as Julie Bulette and Mrs. Warren conducted establishments well known in the community. Julie Bulette was a beauty of French extraction, not unknown for generous acts of charity. She often sat in a box at the opera house and maintained a lacquered brougham, the panel of which was decorated with a heraldic emblem resembling "four aces crowned by a lion counchant."[31]

Even those who resisted the allure of the plush houses of vice often sought feminine companionship in hurdy-gurdy houses, where girls would dance with male patrons for a drink or two bits. In 1873 local police said that Virginia City's vice district was ten times as bad as the notorious "Barbary Coast" area of San Francisco in its palmiest days. On one street men and women, victims of liquor and other excesses, lived together in "dens of infamy and degradation," out-rivaling the notorious Five Points District of lower Manhattan in "squalidness and crime."[32] In 1874 the situation became so bad that the city aldermen decided not to issue licenses to six or eight of the vile dens where a "perfect Hell on earth" prevailed, as men, debased and drunken, lay as if dead from 11 at night to morning in the back-yards of the houses.[33] Later, efforts were made to restrict houses of ill fame to the vicinity of D and E streets, as Piper sought to get the women away from the vicinity of his newly opened Opera House, but the Virginia *Chronicle* reported that most citizens seemed to think that if "reasonable limits were assigned for the inevitable nuisance," it mattered little where the houses were.[34]

There were frequent cases of indecent exposure. The *Enterprise* referred to one offender as "a brute wearing the shape of a man."[35] Also not unknown were "Peeping Toms." One of the latter was warned in the press that two or three shotguns were "loaded for his benefit," so that the coroner might have a job almost any evening.[36] Incidents of the raping of young women and even children and elderly ladies were frequent.[37]

In view of the prevalence of speculation in mining stocks, ordi-nary gambling seemed to many less extensive than might have been expected. But in 1870 a Nevada City School Lottery aroused the urge to gamble among residents of Virginia City. Tickets sold "like hot cakes," and it was reported that people were "ready to take chances in any kind of lottery or raffle—let a three-wheeled wagon or a sick cow be put up."[38] Early the next year, Virginia City residents eagerly awaited reports as to the winners. Soon, the *Enterprise* indicated, it was practically necessary to have a lottery journal to keep up with all the lottery winnings in California, Nevada, Montana, and Havana. Prospectuses were regularly posted in the windows of jewelry stores, restaurants, and saloons.[39]

Disappointment, disillusionment, and despair followed many who traveled the road of illicit sex, gambling, and drink. Suicides of both men and women were frequent. Some took laudanum, while others threw themselves before locomotives.[40]

Virginia City was a cosmopolitan city, with residents from many parts of the world. Experienced Cornish and Welsh miners who had fled economic depression in the homeland were there, and the Irish immigration to the United States brought many newcomers to the Comstock. A much larger percentage of immigrants were found in the mines than in the population as a whole, but in 1870 they outnumbered the native Americans in Virginia City. In 1880, out of a population in the county of 16,115, the immigrant population numbered as many as 6,925. Of these, 2,495 were from Ireland and 1,477 from England and Wales.[41]

Three of the most influential and wealthy of the silver barons, John W. Mackay, James G. Fair, and William S. O'Brien, were Irish-born. Each year the Irish of the community celebrated St. Patrick's Day by attending Mass at St. Mary's Church and parading through the streets as the band played Irish airs. An evening ball climaxed the celebration. On Washington's Birthday in 1867, Irishmen from many communities planned a Grand Ball of the Fenian Brotherhood in aid of the Irish revolutionary cause. In 1871 Thomas C. Luby, once editor of the Dublin *Nation,* and General Thomas F. Bourke of Irish rebel renown arrived to give lectures in the area and were given an enthusiastic welcome.[42]

Germans for years supported at least one *Turnverein* with singing and dancing to guitar music. In 1872 the *Turnverein* of Virginia City and nearby communities had a two-day May Festival at Hildebrand's Pleasure Garden, where beer abounded. During the Franco-Prussian War, Germans of the city raised funds for the German Sanitary Fund and were able to send to Berlin a well-molded brick of gold and silver bullion worth $3,123.76. After the fall of Paris to the German army, a great German Jollification was held in the city.[43]

In September 1872 the Swiss of the city observed the anniversary of their country's independence with a celebration that included a twenty-two gun salute. Although there were relatively few Italians on the Comstock in October 1870, they arranged a dinner in honor of the unification of Italy.[44]

The completion of the Central Pacific Railroad meant that Chinese laborers had to find new employment. When some came to Virginia City and other communities some local residents formed Anti-Coolie Associations. To some extent complaint was made that the Virginia City Chinese operated opium dens, frequented by white patrons. In March 1869 the *Enterprise* denounced anti-Chinese organizations, labeling them a type of "Ku-Klux-ism" which was "a burning disgrace."[45] The mining and banking tycoon, William Sharon, tried to pacify anti-Chinese laborers by agreeing in October 1869 not to use the Chinese in mills, mines, or in railroad work north of a specific point in the Virginia City area. When he allegedly broke this promise, thirty or forty Chinese who were working as railroad trackmen were driven away by local people.[46]

The Chinese often had troubles among themselves. In June 1872 a fierce fight developed in Virginia City's Chinatown between two rival factions. Two Chinese were mortally wounded, and fifteen were taken to the city jail. During the same month a disastrous fire, perhaps started by members of one of the factions, destroyed eighty buildings and left over five hundred of the "Celestials" homeless.[47]

The Chinese community had a firm regulation of its own that at least eight doors must be found between washhouses. Some Chinese occasionally found a good location for a laundry, but perhaps it was only seven doors from the next one. Finding a vacant lot between the two locations, they would lease it, erect a little shanty on it, and provide the shanty with one door but no other aspect of a dwelling.[48]

Mexicans, who helped to perform some of the menial tasks of the community, had their own anniversary, that of Mexican Independence, to celebrate. This they did with a cannon and fireworks, band music, and a ball in the evening. Negroes in the town were numerous enough to be served by two colored Methodist churches and one of Baptist affiliation.[49]

Beyond the suburban homes were the "huts and tents of the children of the desert," the Piute Indians. At one time they lived on garbage and discarded victuals, but by 1872 they bought their bread in town at Fitzmyer's and other bakeries. Camping on the Divide, they did not generally get drunk or steal, but they found it difficult to find useful permanent employment.

Sometimes violent threats to the peace of the community prompted action by Vigilance committees.[50] In 1864 and 1865, and for three or four years afterward, mining excitement and strikes, along with the influx of many strangers, had made it possible for outlaws, including the "Garnet Gang" and the "Mortimer Gang," to operate in such a way that people were murdered, disappearing unnoticed. In March 1871 numerous cuttings and shooting scrapes, murders, and incendiary acts prompted the formation of a vigilance committee which took one William Willis out of jail. Placing a rope around his neck, the vigilantes made him acknowledge his own incendiarism and implicate others. Later in the same month one Arthur P. Heffernan, charged with murder, was taken from the local jail and hanged by members of the committee. The *Enterprise* commented that there was "never a lack of force or manhood in a civilized community to protect itself against ruffianism," even though for the time being the law had to be taken into the hands of a few.[51] In July 1871 the viligance committee hanged one George Kirk (who had been warned to stay out of town because of his criminal record), taking him from a house of ill fame kept by "Dutch Mary" on North C Street. Such activity caused Judge Rising to charge the Grand Jury to inquire into and secure the punishment of the vigilantes, whom he termed "murderers," "felons," and "assassins." But Judge Rising became so unfitted for judicial duties because of his drinking that friends had to take him to California. Later, the Grand Jury recommended better law enforcement and a change in the police force.[52]

Virginia City's police force was not the only thing in need of improvement. In the areas of aesthetics and safety, the city needed attention, too. At the edge of the city were cattle yards, the effluvia arising from which were "simply horrible." On summer days in the city itself flies became almost "intolerable." Many people refrained from touching food for fear that some of the flies were "nicely stewed" with the edibles being served. On a winter day, moreover, the streets were often "horribly filthy," snow interfered with the cleaning of the streets, and old gunny sacks, old boots, paper, and other trash accumulated in heaps on the snow banks.[53]

Most of the structures in Virginia City were so flimsy that small fires were frequent and extensive fires not uncommon. On October 26, 1875, a fire broke out and spread wildly while most of the city was yet asleep. For months there had been a serious drought, and now wooden buildings quickly became veritable torches, which a fierce gale from the west carried to the quick destruction of more substantial structures. An area half a mile square in the heart of the city was reduced to debris, hundreds of people were left homeless, and the many mining works were a "pitiful sight." In all, ten million dollars' worth of property was irrevocably lost. Some houses had to be blown up to save mining properties. To perform the job, the wealthy John W. Mackay, "haggard with fatigue, begrimed with dust, powdersmoke, and the smoke of the fire," but "with his old miner instinct and miner's knowledge," set off the charge.[54] School houses became centers of relief, and aid poured in from other communities. Losses included fifty thousand dollars to the Enterprise Publishing Company (with fifteen thousand dollars insurance) and fifteen thousand dollars to Daggett (with four thousand dollars insurance.) The *Enterprise* had to use temporary headquarters and secure new sets of type and steam presses from San Francisco. For weeks, from October 28 to November 16, the paper was issued as a single sheet.[55]

The blame for the fire was placed in part on the failure to provide the business district with fire hydrants, as had been projected four years before. Another factor was that a brothel (permitted to remain outside of the segregated district) was the "hell-hole" in which the "fire of hell" had been kindled. Neighbors testified that the fire originated in "Crazy Kate" Shea's place, when a drunken brawl at six o'clock in the morning resulted in the breaking of a coal-oil lamp.[56]

At a citizens' meeting at the Presbyterian Church (out of the fire area) early in November, Daggett was one of a committee of ten empowered, if it proved desirable, to petition the Governor to call a special session of the legislature to enable the county and city to raise funds by issuing bonds. Building anew was at once undertaken and by February 1, 1876, the *Enterprise* was being printed in a new building on the old site.[57]

Another threat to the tranquility of the community was burglary, thieves entering and ransacking houses almost every night. Once again the *Enterprise* deplored the use of vigilante committees but admitted that they were sometimes the only means for correcting "evils beyond the reach of law."[58]

The gregarious Daggett loved the boisterous excitement of Virginia City. As a member of the *Enterprise* staff, he not only kept abreast of the news but had regular opportunity to avail himself of a free pass to rich theatrical fare. The miners were well paid, and many had no families so could patronize the theatre frequently, enjoying performances by leading companies, which played Virginia City en route to and from the Pacific Coast.

Maguire's Opera House opened on July 2, 1863, and there was no finer theatre even in San Francisco. With a seating capacity of sixteen hundred, its ample foyer provided access to billiard parlors, a cigar stand, green-covered gambling tables, and a bar made from mahogany inlaid with ivory. One drawback was that with the basement housing a livery stable, the atmosphere was definitely affected by undesirable odors.[59] Julia Dean Hayne and her company, the opening attraction, remained for a month. Other leading celebrities later played there regularly. In early 1864 Adah Isaacs Menken, a sensation of the time, arrived from San Francisco. Her opening play, *The French Spy*, did not stimulate great enthusiasm, so she sought attention by playing the title role in *Mazeppa*, a drama based on Byron's poem of that name. In the high moments of the play she was supposedly disrobed, although she actually wore tights, as, strapped to the back of a horse, she was carried up a ramp that represented a mountain slope. The front row was of course reserved for Goodman, Mark Twain, Dan De Quille, Daggett, and the rest. Loud in their praise of the star's performance, they aroused jealousy in other members of the cast. The result was a feud between the management of the theatre and the *Enterprise* journalists. Free passes for the newspapermen were no longer available, and the reporters now ignored the offerings at Maguire's so that effective publicity was no longer forthcoming.[60]

Afterward, John Piper opened his renowned Opera House, which became a landmark in the community and a center of theatrical fare. In later years productions were also presented at numerous other places, National Union Hall, Cooper Hall, the National Theatre, and the Alhambra Theatre, so that dramatic fare was varied. In January 1867 Mrs. Sue Robinson Gentzler and her sister Miss Joey Robinson appeared in the musical drama, *Ben Bolt,* and the "side-splitting farce," *Betsey Baker.* In July 1867 appeared Blaisdell's Bell Ringers, with little Miss Clara, a favorite in Virginia City, as elsewhere, who performed as a comic singer, clog dancer, and cornet soloist. The bell ringers rendered many numbers, including "The Anvil Chorus" and "Home Sweet Home."[61]

Sometimes informality reigned at Piper's, as you could "lean back in your cushioned seat and take your ease, your lager, and your cigar," while waitresses brought refreshments, and favorites like Fanny Hanks and Little Nell appeared on stage. Little wonder that a few weeks later it was reported that the theatre was nightly filled with those "who prefer a hearty laugh to a fit of the blues," and who "find more pleasure in mingling with their fellow men than in sitting moping at home." At that time the jolly comedy, *The Marble Statues,* was presented, the schoolroom scene prompting much merriment as the venerable teacher "handled his paddle in the most artistic manner."[62]

Later, minstrels, including the famous Triers and Burbank (Tambourine and Bones), gave a hilarious performance. Rain, snow, and sleet descended in mid-June 1868 when the famous Lawrence Barrett appeared in *Richard III.* Subsequently, with the distinguished John McCullough, he appeared in *Othello, Romeo and Juliet, Richelieu,* and other classical productions.[63] When Mr. and Mrs. Tom Thumb appeared in the summer of 1869, the *Enterprise* reported that Tom was "a regular little brick. He has a good voice, and sings well. His crow act is novel and well done. He is not much bigger than a corn-fed crow."[64] In January 1870 the Gregory Troupe presented gymnastic feats, including "The Three Flying Men in the Air" and Gertrude Gregory's leap from the gallery to the stage. On other occasions, trained dogs gave an exhibition. When Hermann, "the renowned Prestidigitateur," appeared in April 1870, he was hailed as superior to all previous performers, and as one "certainly entitled to be styled the king of magicians."[65] In June Lawrence Barrett returned in Bulwer's comedy, *Money*, and in Sheridan's *The Rivals*, and early in July John McCullough played Othello with Barrett as Iago. Perhaps such excellent fare was too classical to receive enthusiastic support from many miners who later filled omnibuses each night to see Lydia Thompson's Troupe of "Blondes" present *Sinbad the Sailor*.[66] Occasionally local talent provided the attractions, as when the opera house was filled from "pit to dome" for a grand concert given by the Virginia Choral Society in April 1871.

Despite the great popularity of some, theatre activities, then as today, were a precarious economic venture. In February 1871 the mine magnate, William Sharon, Daggett, and others, sponsored a "benefit" for Sue Robinson, a favorite, who had been appearing at Piper's Opera House. Piper himself had never consented to be the recipient of a benefit but did so in June 1871, because the expense of buying costly scenery and machinery and of paying for top talent had led to a series of unprofitable seasons, and he was considerably discouraged.[67]

In October 1871 the National Guard Hall was packed for two performances by the Fiji Island Cannibals. Favorites of the time, *East Lynne* and *Rip Van Winkle*, attracted crowds to Piper's in November 1873. Another play with equal drawing power was *Ten Nights in a Bar Room*, presented in December 1873. In August 1875 Lawrence Barrett again appeared at the Opera House as Alfred Evelyn in the comedy, *Money*, and as Raphael in *Marble Heart*.[68] In 1877 Maude Adams, the daughter of an old-time favorite, Annie Adams, began what was to be a notable career.

Piper's Opera House was ravaged by the great fire of 1875, but the plays had to go on. In October 1877 the famous Helen Mojesta opened a series of engagements at the National Union Hall. Facilities were poor, and the small attendance at Cooper Hall for the Opera, *Maritana*, was attributed to the fact that people know the hall to be "an excellent place to freeze in" and so denied themselves "the pleasure of listening to a performance alike meritorious and pleasing."[69] But early in 1878 Piper reopened his Opera House, a real asset to the city. In December the famous Hutchinson Family Singers gave a concert there, and on Sunday they presented one or two numbers at the close of the morning service at the Presbyterian Church.[70]

Daggett and Goodman not only occupied preferred seats at Piper's, but they wrote several plays that were performed there, including *The Psychoscope: A Sensational Drama in Five Acts*.[71] The chief characters included Percy Gresham, an inventor; Amos Royalton, a broker; Lucy, Royalton's daughter; Robert Fairbanks, a clerk in the

Royalton brokerage house; and Philo Bundy, a farmer. Among the other personalities were Molly McPherson, madam of a house of ill fame; Minnie Lattimer, a pretty street walker; and Dora and Alice, inmates of Molly McPherson's establishment.

In the first act Royalton's safe is robbed, he is murdered, and Gresham is arrested. In the second act Lucy Royalton, who has been deeply in love with Gresham, now, out of respect for her mother's wishes, considers marriage to Fairbanks. During the conversation there is much discussion of a sensational play, *Social Kaleidoscope*. In other scenes, a rustic, Philo Bundy, having heard of Gresham, is looking for the inventor and encounters Minnie Lattimer, who takes him to Molly McPherson's place, one richly furnished with nude art and other trappings. Philo receives much attention and wine and after going to sleep is robbed of his watch and money. Eventually he is dumped into the street. In the third act he meets Constance Proctor, Lucy Royalton's maid, who, hearing his inquiry for Gresham, tells him that the inventor is serving a life sentence in Sing Sing, where he has continued his inventive efforts but seems to be losing his mind. Another scene is in Sing Sing, from which Gresham makes his escape. The fourth scene is in the Royalton mansion, where a tableau is furnishing entertainment when someone outside is noted using a magic lantern. This is the Psychoscope, Gresham's new invention, which he is invited inside to demonstrate, where he employs it to reproduce Royalton's murder, revealing Fairbanks as the murderer.

In the final act, when Lucy and Fairbanks are about to be married, the minister asks the traditional query, as to whether there is any objection to the marriage, and various persons, including Molly McPherson, Fairbanks' long-time lover, interrupt the ceremony. A police captain takes Fairbanks away, and Lucy, tearing off her bridal veil, rushes wildly down the aisle to fall insensibly into the arms of Gresham. The finale comes as the minister calls for attention:

A moment, friends! Man prospers, but God disposes. Still may His will be done, under whose providence good and evil are mingled throughout creation. It is not for us to read the hearts of men—to judge between the wicked and the just; but, in His gracious name, to extend over all alike our benediction.

John McCullough, a noted actor of the time, played the lead at Piper's, giving four performances in August 1872. On the first night the theatre was filled, but the *Enterprise* reported: "Never, we venture to say, did an audience enter into the portals of the Opera House with a more favorable predisposition, or leave it with a keener sense of disappointment." The paper complained: "It was written in English, but spoken in God knows what dialect; it was designed to have had some tolerable situations and effects, but by some strange fatality they all became intolerable." The second evening a large and fashionable audience was again in attendance with such an improvement from the previous evening as to make "it scarcely recognizable" as the same play. It was said to have been received with unusual enthusiasm, although some, possessing "a mawkish sense of stage propriety," looked with distaste upon the scene from the house of ill fame. Further improvement in presentation apparently marked subsequent performances.[72]

Numerous lecturers came to Virginia City. Noteworthy was the visit of Charles Farrar Browne (Artemus Ward) during December 1863. The boys of the *Enterprise* had a hilarious time, dining and wining with him and taking him on excursions to places of interest such as Chinatown.[73] Mark Twain apparently learned much from him and, as we have seen, Twain himself later returned to Virginia City as a popular lecturer.

In 1869 E. Z. C. Judson, "Ned Buntline," the first of the dime novelists, who wrote popular paperbacks such as *The Gals of New York* (1848), drew a good crowd to his lecture on "Practical Temperance," lightening his moral approach with an occasional good story. John G. Saxe, widely known for his volumes of verse and at the time termed "the humorist par excellence of America," later lectured on "Yankee Land," "The Proud Miss McBride and the Press," and "Poetry and Poets."[74]

In June 1873 Benjamin F. Underwood, an aggressive free thinker, spoke on "The Influences of Christianity on Civilization." Five years later John Tyerman, a popular Australian speaker, lectured at Piper's Opera House on "Is There a Devil? or The Scarecrow of Christendom Unmasked" and before the Liberal Religious Society on "The World's Sixteenth Crucified Saviors—Which is the Right One?"[75]

Henry Ward Beecher, whose alleged moral lapses did not particularly offend the Comstock, appeared in August 1878 to lecture in Virginia City. Advance publicity billed him as the "Greatest Preacher and Orator." Seats were $1.00 and $1.50, with the best seats $2.50 for both nights. As Beecher strolled around town, some residents of course recognized him. His first evening lecture on "Wastes and Burdens" was well attended. Daggett wrote that he was "less of an orator and definitely more of an actor" than many expected. Beecher presented "no magnificent word-painting," as Robert Ingersoll did, but "in simple language some of the world's wrongs were laid bare and the heroic treatment necessary for a cure prescribed." His last lecture was on "The Rule of the Common People," a new one requiring the use of notes. Daggett defended, against the criticism of some, Beecher's denunciation of parts of the press. Daggett indicated that he believed that Beecher had in mind only such sheets as *Chimney Corner, Illustrated Police News,* and *Day's Doings,* which Daggett deemed to have "done more to incite vicious minds to evil practices and to addle not overstrong brains than any other influence in the world."[76]

Various women came as lecturers, too. In 1869 Anna E. Dickinson, woman's rights lecturer, discoursed on "Nothing Unreasonable." Observers found her elocution faulty but admired her as a "hard hitter."[77] In the summer of 1870 Mrs. Laura De Force Gordon, a well-known lecturer, and Mrs. Emily P. A. Stevens, the editor of a woman's rights paper, visited Virginia City. Mrs. Gordon gave an able and eloquent talk on "Woman's Enfranchisement." The general view was that Virginia City was a "man's town," and there seemed little interest in woman suffrage, but its advocates persisted. In August 1871 Elizabeth Cady Stanton delivered several lectures, one on "The New Republic," where women would have equal voting rights, and another "for women only." Later in the same year, Susan B. Anthony spoke on "The Power of the Ballot."[78] Mrs. Sara Jane Clarke Lippincott, "Grace Greenwood," one of the most popular women writers of the day, came to lecture on "The Heroic in Common Life" and to take notes on the Comstock area for the *New York Times.*[79] Other controversial female speakers came to the Comstock. Tennessee Claflin, the advocate of "free love," arrived with her mother in May 1874 as advance agent for her sister, Victoria Woodhull, who was to speak on "Tried as by Fire: or the True and False Socially." Edith O'Gorman, "The Escaped Nun," had lectured at the Opera House two years earlier.[80]

In 1873 Mrs. Maggie Van Cott, often designated the first woman preacher to be licensed by the Methodist Episcopal Church, conducted a revival in the Virginia City Methodist Church. Nightly many came to the mourners' bench. Mrs Van Cott moved among the people in the congregation, urging repentance. One Sunday night she approached a serious Cornish miner and, placing her hand on his head, said, "My friend, are you a laborer in the vineyard of the Lord?" The poor miner scratched his head and replied, "No, mum, I be workin' in 'ee Savage lower level [mine]."[81]

By this time the "liberal" minister, Rev. T. H. McGrath, lecturing on "religious Revivals," questioned the permanent effects of such meetings. But in autumn 1874 McGrath's philosophical and scientific topics gave way to political indictments, as he denounced the Republican party. In discussing "The Moral Aspect of Political Affairs in Storey County," he saw the only remedy for widespread corruption in the destruction of the Republican party and presented evidence of the delivery of votes for a price. The *Enterprise* denied the existence of such contracts, although the sophisticated knew that the buying of votes in Nevada was developing into a public scandal.[82]

There was always an audience for religious speakers such as Mrs. Van Cott or Mr. McGrath, and such offerings were by no means limited. Occasionally a distinguished Methodist such as Bishop Matthew Simpson, "Apostle of Modern Methodism," preached in the city, and in February 1875 Mrs. T. B. H. Stenhouse, author of *Tell It All*, supposedly a revelation of Mormon practices, appeared.[83] A few months later the noted Paulist priest, Father Walter Elliott, lectured on "Certainty in Religion."[84]

Despite its crudeness and widespread debauchery, Virginia City fostered organized religion. Such diverse groups as Episcopalians, Roman Catholics, Jews, Methodists, and Baptists existed side by side on the Comstock. Beginning in January 1867, the Protestant churches held evening prayer meetings five nights a week for six weeks.[85] For the more rationally oriented believer, Mr. McGrath broke with traditional Methodism, forming the First Liberal Religious Society of Virginia City.[86] The Presbyterian pastor, Rev. W. W. Macomber, took it upon himself to improve the morality of local "sinners." On one occasion he criticized some women who, he claimed, put on a private exhibition of living art nudity for a dozen men at a hundred dollars a head.[87] Jewish people sometimes invited a rabbi from Carson City to preside over the circumcision ceremony. After one circumcision, the *Enterprise* on October 13, 1869, observed: "All were merry, though the little fellow who had just been made a Jew squalled most lustily."

Social life for many Virginia City families centered in church activities. Money-raising church fairs were commonly held in late autumn, and local Episcopalians were not averse to church-sponsored social dancing after these.[88] Midnight Mass on Christmas Eve drew large crowds to St. Mary's Roman Catholic Church, whose "excellent choir" was assisted by Rippingham's Brass Band.[89] In 1874 the *Enterprise* observed that churches were making progress in the community and that Sunday was being observed more and more. Comstockers were "fast becoming decently, not bigotedly, religious."[90]

Actors, lecturers, and preachers were not the only celebrities to appear on the Comstock. Others came to see the fabulous mines or for political reasons. In October 1875 there was a large reception for Lieutenant General Philip T. Sheridan, who was visiting Virginia

City's mines. Two months later Baron Rothschild, the youngest member of the banking family, arrived with a party in special cars. Among other visitors was Thomas A. Edison, who spent a day on the Comstock in the summer of 1878, interested in the possibility of developing a machine which, on the surface, could determine whether ore or rock were to be found below.[91] Typical of political visitors was Vice President Schuyler Colfax who came in August 1869, accompanied by his wife and a large party, including the noted Samuel Bowles of the Springfield *Republican.* Daggett was on the reception committee that drove to Reno to escort the group to Virginia City.

Daggett enjoyed meeting such visitors. For many in the city, contacts were made through fraternal orders, including the Masons, Odd Fellows, Knights of Pythias, Red Men, and the National Union.[92] Even members of a temperance order, the Good Templars, had summer picnics and seemed to enjoy themselves, though the *Enterprise* referred to them as "the cold water folks."[93] In October 1870 a state officer, Dr. Carrie F. Young, gave two lectures in the community on "Physiological Temperance." The Templars were not in keeping with Daggett's own enthusiasms, but he was active in Free Masonry. In December 1874, when a Past Master of one of the Masonic Lodges was presented with an "elegant set of silverware," Daggett was the natural choice to make the presentation. Daggett himself had been presented with an inscribed watch on one occasion by Virginia City associates, and he carried a Masonic insignia on the chain.[94] Later, in his Hawaiian career, he was to participate actively in Masonic activities.

Daggett's activities were indeed varied. In 1867 he had added to his responsibilities by becoming clerk of the United States Circuit and District Courts for Nevada. Many of the cases in the courts involved matters of bankruptcy. With the large number of foreign-born persons in the area, naturalization procedures were an important part of his work, too. In October 1868, for example, thirty-six persons in Virginia City became United States citizens. Daggett of course became involved in various controversies because of his federal position. In early 1869 one Lewis Dunn was indicted by a federal grand jury on the charge of violating the Burlingame Treaty with China by expelling a number of Chinese from Unionville, Nevada. Dunn then brought action for damages against the federal judge, the marshall, and Daggett, then clerk. In December, on the wise advice of his counsel, the plaintiff dropped the case.[95]

Daggett owed his federal appointment to a young friend, Judge Alexander W. Baldwin, a remarkable person. Born in Gainesville,

Georgia, in 1841, Baldwin was extremely precocious and was said to have entered the University of Virginia at fourteen and to have become a practicing lawyer as a mere youth. He had become District Attorney in California (where his father was a judge) at nineteen and United States District Court judge in Nevada at twenty-two. During his brief career as a lawyer, he had acquired half a million dollars, a luxurious home, horses, and servants. In the immensely rewarding legal battles over mining claims, he had on occasion confronted William M. Stewart on the opposite side of a case. When Baldwin once interrupted him, the formidable Stewart glared at him and roared, "You little shrimp, if you interrupt me again, I'll eat you." To this Baldwin calmly replied, "If you do, Mr. Stewart, you'll have more brains in your belly than you've ever had in your head." His "rapid and dazzling" advancement terminated at the age of twenty-eight when he was killed in an accident on the Alameda and San Leandro Railroad.[96]

Daggett, though clerk of the federal court, had long continued to serve on the *Enterprise,* and events brought him into close association with William Sharon, one of the wealthy "Silver Kings" of the Comstock.[97] Sharon, as we have seen, was a "chilly, little man, shrewd and closefisted in business contacts." Some of the problems of a mining capitalist are illustrated by the crisis he faced in 1869, when workmen at Yellow Jacket mine were so bitter because of the fear that we would introduce Chinese into the mines and mills that he was threatened with assassination. He addressed the miners between shifts, promising not to use Chinese in the mines, but, as he deemed necessary, on railroad construction to Carson City. When he departed the men gave him three cheers.

In 1872, when Sharon sought the United States senatorship from Nevada, Goodman of the *Enterprise,* who despised him, editorialized:

> You are probably aware that you have returned to a community where you are feared, hated and despised. Your career in Nevada for the past five years has been one of merciless rapacity. You fastened yourself upon the vitals of a State like a hyena, and woe to him who disputed with you a single coveted morsel of your prey. . . . You cast honor, honesty and the commonest civilities aside. You broke faith with men whenever you could subserve your purpose by doing so.

Many Nevadans hated the Bank of California and its manager, who, they believed, had swindled many citizens, and Goodman sought to present a bill of particulars, denouncing Sharon as one who exerted the vast power of his individual wealth and his influence over the Bank of California and its allied monopolies, to lock up money and create a financial stringency; and when his preparations were all completed, he unloaded his stocks on a moneyless market, and chuckled like a fiend as he watched the crash which he knew carried ruin and beggary to thousands of people throughout Nevada.[98]

Sharon, seeking the Republican nomination to the Senate, was opposed by the wealthy John P. Jones, who had been defeated in 1870 for sheriff of Maraposa County, California, and sought political vindication. Nevada was a Republican stronghold where nomination practically insured election, and the nomination went to Jones. He need not have spent a dollar on the campaign for election, but he gave money away lavishly, perhaps to the extent of half a million dollars. When asked his reason for such action, he laughingly indicated that he was having a good time and was setting the pace for the next senatorial struggle. Indeed, this did serve to establish a pattern for Nevada senatorial contests; extravagant use of money came to rule the day. Jones won, and proved in the Senate to be a real leader, as well as an able logician and thinker.[99]

Sharon retired to his San Francisco office but determined to have a seat in the Senate. Realistically, he decided that Goodman had to be replaced, and he is said to have arranged for half a million dollars to be paid the proprietor for the *Enterprise*. This resulted in a new corporation, the Enterprise Publishing Company, organized in February 1874. Daggett was sought as the "brains" for the new venture. Daggett has been called a "pagan opportunist," and certainly he now sold his services to the California manipulator. Yet it must be remembered that Daggett was a conservative Republican by conviction and that generally in Nevada ethical considerations did not then transcend political loyalty. Probably the basic arrangements were made when Daggett journeyed to San Francisco late in January 1874. Goodman and his wife left almost at once for San Francisco and then for a long European tour. The way for Sharon was eased tremendously by the decision of Senator William M. Stewart not to run for reelection. Stewart wanted to recoup his fortunes through a lucrative law practice in Virginia City.[100]

The *Enterprise* now abruptly changed its tone from November 1873, when it had denounced the apparent attempt of Sharon to buy the senatorship. It, however, endeavored to deny the frequent assertion that it was Sharon's organ.[101] Yet, during the campaign, it paid

deference to its financial patron by printing a poem, very probably
written by Daggett, as a tribute to Sharon. The two opening and the
two last stanzas are:

> Who was it worked the Comstock lead,
> When knowing ones had all agreed
> 'Twas worse than useless to proceed?
> > Why, Sharon.

> Who struck old Comstock to the core,
> And found what none had found before,
> The treasure which she now outpours?
> > Why, Sharon.

> .   .   .   .   .

> Who is today the people's man,
> And will do everything he can
> To help them in their every plan?
> > Why, Sharon.

> And, who, if to the Senate sent,
> Nevada's sons to represent
> Will never cause them to repent?
> > Why, Sharon.[102]

The *Enterprise* declared editorially that the existing prosperity
of western Nevada owed more to Sharon "than to any other ten men,
and could his work here be stricken out, with it would go at once
two-thirds of our people, improvements and wealth." Ironically enough,
there was a measure of truth in this highly exaggerated praise.
Sharon was indeed a shrewd manipulator. By clever financing he had
built the Virginia and Truckee Railroad, connecting the Comstock
with the outside world, and still owned half of it, without investing
a cent of his own money. He had, moreover, managed Comstock stocks
to his own advantage. Yet Dan De Quille, the former *Enterprise* reporter and a historian of the region, tells us that Sharon had the au-
dacity to build the railroad and the nerve to advance the money for
the development of mines and the construction of mills, when other
capital was unavailable, so the area owed much to him.[103]

Democratic speakers were bitter against Daggett, one declaring
that he was the greatest "economist of truth he had ever seen," and
"if truth were a medicine, Daggett would be the chief of homeopathic
doctors." Adolph Sutro tried to lead the Independents to defeat the
Republicans and was bitterly attacked by the *Enterprise*.[104] The truth

was that Sharon spent money so lavishly that the attention of San Francisco and other papers was attracted to the situation. It was widely claimed that Sharon distributed $800,000. Another account credited him with so manipulating stock in the Ophir Mining Company by circulating "confidential tips," which the buying public followed with disastrous results to their investments, that he more than got back his collossal expenditures.[105]

The situation was so "rotten" that Rev. T. H. McGrath, the liberal clergyman of Virginia City, attacked the Republican party in a Sunday evening lecture to his congregation. A week later he gave a lecture at the Opera House entitled "The Moral Aspects of Political Affairs in Storey County." McGrath denounced the contracts for votes to be delivered that men whom he knew had seen, and he declared that he would join a Vigilance Committee to drive from the community men who would sell votes. Charges were also made of the wholesale "colonization" of voters, with many who were unregistered casting ballots. But Nevada normally was Republican, and Sharon's tens of thousands of dollars insured a wide margin in the control of the legislature. Soon a caucus of Republican legislators present at Carson City on January 6 unanimously endorsed Sharon for senator. On January 12 he was formally elected, with the joint vote: Sharon, 49; H. D. Mitchell, Democrat, 21; and Thomas P. Hawley, Independent, 4. The *Enterprise* rather brazenly asserted that Sharon had secured the votes of those men "whom money could neither coerce nor corrupt."[106] Democrats and others, however, were bitter at the frauds which accompanied the election and deemed the complimentary vote for Mitchell "a signal rebuke to the arrogant pretensions of non-resident capitalists."[107]

Daggett's pleasant home life received a jolt late in 1875, when his wife was found to have tuberculosis and he was warned that she could not live more than a couple of years. On July 30, 1876, outwardly in her usual health, she left for a visit with relatives in Philadelphia and a chance to see the Centennial Exposition.[108]

In 1876 Daggett resigned as clerk of the court, a step which was constitutionally necessary as he sought a place on the Republican ticket as an elector for Hayes and Wheeler. The Carson *Appeal* endorsed his candidacy, as did the *Enterprise,* asserting that he had "done more and better work for the Republican party in the state than any other man, and for less reward." In the November elections in Nevada, the Republican ticket won, Daggett receiving 10,360 votes to 9,291 for the comparable elector pledged to Tilden. The three

Nevada electors, meeting at the state capital on December 6 chose Daggett as messenger to take the vote to Washington. He set out less than a week later.[109]

He stopped at the home town of his youth, Defiance, Ohio, where he spent part of the Christmas season with three sisters and other relatives. He also visited the shop of the Defiance *Democrat,* on which he had worked as a printing devil more than a quarter of a century earlier.[110] Going on to the capital, he found himself in the midst of the disputed Hayes-Tilden election. On January 9 a friend in Virginia City received a note from Daggett in Washington, saying that the President *pro tempore* of the Senate, Thomas W. Ferry, would not assume the responsibility for determining which votes should be counted as valid, that the questions would be left to the two houses, and that the Republicans were confident that Hayes would win.[111] Ultimately a special Electoral Commission decided the dispute in favor of Hayes. Daggett went to Philadelphia to see his wife, who died on March 21. By April 18 he was back in his beloved Virginia City.[112]

VI

Lone Congressman
from Nevada

AFTER THE INAUGURATION OF HAYES, WHEN DAGGETT RETURNED TO
Nevada, he was no longer clerk of the United States Court and did
not direct the affairs of the *Enterprise*. Naturally, considerable interest
developed as to how he would find an outlet for his energies. It was
rumored that he would be the new Superintendent of the Mint at
Carson City. Residents of that city greeted this prospect with great
enthusiasm. The Carson *Tribune* reported that great reform was
needed in the conduct of the affairs of the Mint and that to the people
of Nevada, Daggett was a "prince in his own right." Visiting San
Francisco, he saw old friends on the *Golden Era*. That journal commented that he looked as young "as when he was one of the Goliaths
of the California press." The *Era* regretted that he had for the time
being "thrown aside the pen," for his talent was "remarkable," few
writers being his equal in exciting "the sympathetic in human nature."[1]
But he did not stay away from journalism. On December 1, 1877, he
resumed the editorship of the *Enterprise*. Other papers wondered
whether he was merely entering into a business investment or whether
he had a "black horse in training for the senatorial race," as had been
the case three years before.[2] They considered other "political contin-
gencies," which were not without significance, for Daggett soon
entered the race for Congress from Nevada. On the Democratic ticket
in opposition was W. E. F. Deal, a native of Maryland who had been
a resident of Nevada since boyhood. He had run unsuccessfully for
the state assembly in 1866, for the state senate in 1868, and later for
District Judge. The *Enterprise* said that he was "a prominent lawyer,
an educated gentleman, and a thoroughly honest man" but a radical
Democrat.[3]

As a Republican Daggett belonged to the dominant party in

Nevada. As the name suggests, Virginia City early contained a large element with vigorous Southern sympathies. But, during the territorial period, a strong government was necessary to cope with frontier law-lessness, and the state was conceived, born, and nurtured under Republican auspices. The need for another Republican state to insure Lincoln's reelection in 1864 and to ratify the Thirteenth Amendment seemed apparent to some, although other motives for statehood related to ending the corruption of the territorial judiciary and securing federal legislation to stabilize the all-important mining land titles. Powerful mining and railroad interests aided the Republican party. Except when factionalism or lethargy resulted in disunity or over-confidence in the party or when workingmen temporarily arose against the "vested interests," Republicans won at the polls. Thus, until 1881 only Republicans were elected to the United States Senate from Nevada. But after 1873, Nevada Republicans were "Silver" Re-publicans, and they had vigorous denunciation for the views of a Stalwart Republican like Roscoe Conkling of New York, when he showed no enthusiasm for silver legislation.[4]

When the Republican State Convention nominated Daggett by acclamation, Republican papers of course applauded. The Belmont, Nevada, *Courier* termed him "one of the ablest writers and speakers on the Pacific Coast," one who had, as an editor, "labored unceasingly for the best interests of the party." Deal challenged Daggett to stump the state. Daggett at first did not accept and told his men on the *Enter-prise* that it would take him two or three weeks to arrange to pay his assessment for even a superficial canvass of the state.[5]

Democrats charged Daggett with being the "Bonanza candidate," and one paper in eastern Nevada stated that the agent of the Nevada Bank in Virginia City had boasted that Daggett could have fifteen thousand to twenty thousand dollars for his campaign. The editor's associates on the *Enterprise* emphatically denied this, indicating that in Congress Daggett could "not be of use to that firm." A complicated local issue involving the taxation of bullion aroused much animosity. Democrats charged that Daggett was an enemy of the working man and that Republicans belonged to a party favorable not only to mining, but also to railroad, interests. The *Enterprise* insisted that Daggett had been a working man and that subsidies to the railroads had dur-ing the previous years brought a thousand settlers into northern Dakota. The mining interests in Nevada, moreover, were paying working men four dollars a day, in contrast with the situation in the South and in urban centers where Democrats were in control. A circu-lar signed E. Blennerhassett, chairman of the Democratic State Central

Committee, charged Daggett "with almost every crime" imaginable, but the *Enterprise* discounted the chairman's authority by branding him an ex-Confederate from South Carolina.[6]

Daggett campaigned in various communities, including Austin on October 15, Belmont on October 17, and Tybo on the following night. In all, he made about twenty-five speeches. A Democratic campaigner later paid tribute to Daggett's effectiveness in the canvass. At one town in eastern Nevada, Deal, the Democratic candidate, stopped at a saloon kept by an Irish Democrat. After being introduced, he treated the crowd to drinks, thanked them for their friendship, and bidding them "Good night," retired to his room. The next day Daggett and other Republican campaigners appeared in the community and visited the same saloon. Daggett threw down four or five dollars and said, "Come on, boys, and have a drink." The boys responded eagerly to the invitation, and in a minute Daggett was shaking hands with each and all. Then his happy nature asserted itself, as he said, "How do ye do, Mike? Well, God bless you, old fellow. Haven't seen you for fifteen years," "Pat, what the devil are you doing here?" and "Corny, you old rambler, where have you been?" These friendly greetings were answered by such expressions as, "Well, he's the same ould Daggett still," and "He's a fine fellow." The men shared jokes and anecdotes of early days when they were together in California or Nevada. When Daggett left, the proprietor said, "Be jabers, I'll vote for Daggett." Many of the others present echoed him.[7]

The mining leaders were generally Republican in politics, and their money may have assisted the party. The state was sparsely settled, with a population in 1880 of only 62,266. Daggett carried eight of the fourteen counties, with 51.82 per cent of the popular vote. He polled 9,727 votes to 9,047 for Deal.[8] He ran slightly ahead of the Republican candidate for governor, John Henry Kinkead of Unionville, a native of Pennsylvania who spent his youth at Zanesville and Lancaster, Ohio, and later had a varied career in St. Louis, Salt Lake City, California, Nevada, and Alaska, finally settling in Nevada. The elections were close enough that two Democrats, Jewett W. Adams, a native of Vermont, and candidate for reelection as lieutenant governor, and D. R. Sessions, candidate for Superintendent of Public Instruction, were chosen. Sessions was elected chiefly because his opponent, John D. Hammond, was a minister, and there was strong popular sentiment against even the suspicion of sectarianism in education. Hammond was Grand Secretary of the Masonic lodge in Nevada and was well known to Daggett in his fraternal associations.[9]

Daggett was a Radical Republican on the Southern question, and the Eureka *Sentinel* probably expressed the fear of many that he would "prove so infernally radical" when he got into "his official harness" that well-wishers might regret a kindly mention of him. But the hope was expressed that he would learn when he reached the East that the "war was over."[10] In this respect Daggett and Hayes had little in common. When Daggett carried the electoral vote of Nevada to Washington in 1876 and remained there until after the inauguration, he did not call on Hayes, because the death of Mrs. Daggett hastened his departure, and, at any rate, he had no special business with the President. In October 1877 he wrote Hayes, assuring him that "the Republicans of Nevada are almost unanimously friendly to your purposes and policies, in which, it may be superfluous to add, I most earnestly acquiesce." He reminded Hayes that he had published "one of the first Republican journals on the Pacific coast, and for ten or twelve years conducted the leading Republican journal in this state."[11] Certainly, Daggett understandably was minimizing the political differences between them.

After the delivery of his Fourth of July oration of 1878 at Virginia City, he sent a copy of it to Hayes, saying that a part of it embraced "a somewhat novel theory of republican government." To Daggett, it was "old line Whiggery," and he asked Hayes, if he thought this reasoning right, to drop him a line on the subject.[12]

On Memorial Day 1879 Daggett, as a Congressman, was not in Virginia City, as in the past, to present an original poem commemorating the occasion. But his poetic ability had become known in Washington, and he was asked to recite an original Decoration Day poem at Arlington Heights Cemetery. Entitled "The Watch on the Heights," the long poem contained these stanzas:

> Now prudish May, flushed with the kiss of Spring,
> And warm embraces of the ardent winds,
> Has draped with robes of flowers her shrinking form,
> Rudely dismantled by the unchaste hand
> Of churlish Winter and her crimsoned face
> Is hiding on the leafy breast of June.
> Again with measured step to martial strain,
> To which the loyal heart keeps noiseless time,
> We come to lay on valor's dreamless urn
> The sweets of spring and garlands of our love.
>
> .   .   .   .   .
>
> As in the dawn when banished Chaos fled,
> The plastic earth, by fiery tempest torn,

Rose into hills and bastioned mountain peaks,
Which now as everlasting monuments,
In fury vitrified and indurate
Around us mark Creation's dreadful throes,
So o'er the homes where peace and blessing slept
The tempest of rebellion and the flood
Of red-eyed carnage rolled from sea to sea;
As by the calm that fell on Galilee,
The crimson-crested waves, transfixed and mute,
Billowed a war-rent continent with graves.

        .   .   .   .

The years with changeless step will come and go,
Like tardy conscripts to the silent hosts
That wait upon the ages, and the buds
Of spring will with the seasons blush and die
While lilacs blossom where the warrior trod;
But time that heals the angry wounds of war
Will gild the glories of the nation's slain.
Sleep on in peace! Though vicious breezes sweep
Around its walls, the Temple will not fall,
For hands that palsied when they smote the arch,
Assault in vain its gates and battlements.
Eternal are its splendors and its years,
And while it lifts its shining front to Heaven
While freedom lives to glorify the earth;
While valor wears the laurels that it wins,
And floats that Banner, emblem of them all,
So long will loyal hearts come with the Spring
To scatter roses where we strew them now
And lay their pledges on these humble shrines,
To guard with jealous eye and sleepless ward
The priceless heritage their fathers won,
And worthy sons gave life and love to save.[13]

The narrative part of the poem dealt with the story of a Saxon king, whose subjects, headed by his brother, rebelled but were conquered. The spirit of treason persisted, and the rebels made a second unsuccessful attempt to overthrow the government. Here was an obvious analogy to the American Union and the unreconstructed spirit of much of the South.

President and Mrs. Hayes and others of the family were present, and wreaths were placed on the graves of the unknown dead. At the close of the reading, Daggett gave the manuscript to Mrs. Hayes, who accepted it with a smile. The Washington *Post* declared that it was one of the finest poems which had "ever been written for an occasion of this kind."[14] In San Francisco, the *Golden Era* asserted that the poem was "pronounced by the combined literati of the country to be the most pathetic and thrilling poem yet inspired by a theme upon which all the greatest of our American poets have written. As a specimen of elegaic verse Mr. Daggett's production is surely worthy of a proud place among the classics."[15]

The *Enterprise* evaluated the poem at length, saying it

> is better and worse than his poem three years ago. . . . The other poem was complete. This takes higher flights than that but is not so even. It is purely a Daggett poem, by which we mean that it is not like the writings of anyone else. The old power and melody are conspicuous, and one thinks while reading it of that famous trip-hammer in the English language which is so nicely poised that the hand which controls the lever can make it break an egg-shell without crushing the edge, or can just as easily cause it to forge with thousand-ton blows the shaft of a steamship, filling the adjacent air with fiery splinters while it wields its blows. If any are troubled by the radicalism of the poem they need but turn to yesterday's dispatches which gave an account of the decoration ceremonies at Winchester, Virginia. These men declare that they are thoroughly reconciled to the results of the war . . . ; and yet they carried the Confederate flag when they went to decorate the graves of their dead. . . . The lesson Mr. Daggett draws in his poem is the right one, that this nation plays with fire when its sentinels are chosen at random.[16]

On one occasion Hayes and Daggett were on the same train. Probably the former was going to his home in Fremont and Daggett to visit his sisters in Defiance. They reached a junction point where there was a lunch stop. Hayes, in leaving the train, took Daggett's satchel by mistake. When Daggett returned, another passenger said, "Do you know the man you were sitting with?"

"Yes," replied Daggett.

"Well, I don't think you do. He's a d——n thief," was the reply.

"Maybe he is," said Daggett, "but what makes you think so?"

"He took your satchel, and left his'n" came the reply.

Daggett saw that this was the case but did not feel disturbed.

Just before the train left, Hayes came back, saying, "I have taken your satchel for mine. I don't know how I did it."

"I don't know either," replied Daggett, "for mine is a bigger one and much heavier." Here he opened his own satchel and revealed a couple of dirty shirts, a deck of cards, and, on top of all, three bottles of whiskey.

At the sight of these, Hayes exclaimed, "Good heavens! suppose I had taken your satchel to my house."[17]

As Daggett went to Washington after the death of his wife, he was one of the numerous congressmen not accompanied to the capital city by wife, daughter, or other female relatives. At first he took up residence at the historic National Hotel on Pennsylvania Avenue, within walking distance of the capitol. Henry Clay had died there in June 1852, and the hotel still shared with the Arlington, Metropolitan, Willard's, Wormley's, the Riggs House, and the Ebbitt House, popularity among congressional members. At the beginning of the second session, of Congress, he had located in what were probably less expensive quarters at 707 Fourteenth Street, N.W. By the next May he had moved a few doors away to 717 Fourteenth Street, and Congressman Thomas Turner of Mount Sterling, Kentucky, had moved into Daggett's former domicile. Daggett remained in the same quarters (where no other members of Congress resided) during the rest of his congressional career.[18] Prior to Daggett's assuming his congressional duties, in the tense struggle between Congress and President Hayes, the Forty-fifth Congress had adjourned without providing for the usual appropriations for the year ending June 30, 1880, so Hayes had called the new Congress in Special Session to meet on Tuesday, March 18, 1879. Daggett was present for the first roll call on the opening day. In the vote for Speaker, Samuel J. Randall (Democrat), of Pennsylvania, was elected by 143 votes to 125 for James A. Garfield (Republican) of Ohio, with 13 votes for Hendrick B. Wright (Democrat) of Pennsylvania and one for William D. "Pig Iron" Kelley (Republican) of the same state.[19] With the organization of committees Daggett became a member of the Joint Committee on the Census and the standing committee on Militia.[20]

Daggett's seat in the House Chamber (number 127 west) was in the last row, but in the fan-shaped arrangement, it was not far from the front and close to the western door of the hall. Next to him— across a narrow aisle—sat Nelson W. Aldrich of Rhode Island, for whom fame awaited. Nearby, in the same rear row, sat Amaziah B. James of Ogdensburg, New York, representing the district in which Daggett was born. Directly in front of Daggett was Thomas J. Henderson of Princeton, Illinois, next to whom sat Jeremiah W. Dwight of Dryden, New York, and next to him, Evarts W. Farr of Littleton, New

Hampshire. After the Special Session, John Hammond of Crown Point, New York, moved to sit immediately to the right of Daggett. In some respects the two men had much in common, for both had been born in the northernmost portion of New York state, and both had been gold seekers in California.

With Daggett in Congress were several men from his boyhood state. Among those on the Democratic side across the chamber was William D. Hill of Defiance, whose home was on the same street as the residences of Daggett's three sisters in the home town of his boyhood. Hill could give him intimate details of the community and friends of his youthful years. Among others from the home state of Daggett's boyhood were the able Benjamin Butterworth and Thomas L. Young of Cincinnati; Frank L. Hurd of Toledo; J. Warren Kiefer of Springfield, destined to be a Speaker of the House; John A. McMahon of Dayton, a nephew of the arch-Copperhead, Clement L. Vallandigham; Thomas Ewing, Jr., of Lancaster, son of the renowned Whig Senator and cabinet officer of former years; Adoniram J. Warner of Marietta, long a leader of the silver movement; and James A. Garfield of Mentor and William McKinley of Canton, destined to be presidents of the United States. One of Daggett's closest friends was Young, slightly younger than Daggett and a native of Ireland. He had served as a musician in the United States army from 1848 to 1858 and later had seen service for the Union. A lawyer by profession, he was close to President Hayes, for, as lieutenant governor of Ohio, he had succeeded Hayes as governor when the latter resigned to become president.[21] The two men had much in common. Young was dignified and courteous, qualities Daggett, too, could exhibit although he was often "rambunctious" to the point of crudity. Young was "genial, sympathetic as a woman, and generous to a fault, with a fascination about him which made him friends wherever he went," and Daggett had often been similarly described, although he had moods of belligerent brusqueness. Of Young it was said, "There was always a serious undercurrent of thought and a tinge of sadness about him, even when he seemed most joyous and happy."[22] Such traits were not uncharacteristic of Daggett's personality, as some of his poems clearly show, but this tendency toward melancholy was not so generally evident in his make-up.

Daggett's impish individualism and uninhibited jocularity, which had found full rein during his Comstock years, were in evidence during his congressional term. He soon gained the reputation of being the most original member of the House ever sent from the West, and when he was in a storytelling mood the cloak room was always crowded.[23]

His conviviality at times interfered with his regular attendance at House proceedings.[24] Wholesale abstention from voting, which was to call forth such drastic procedures a decade later from Speaker Thomas R. Reed, prompted action at this time. Amidst parliamentary maneuvering on May 23, 1879, Daggett was among those not voting. The Sergeant-at-arms was ordered to arrest and bring to the bar of the House all those not excused. Subsequently, when Daggett was asked for an explanation, he asserted that for three of four weeks he had suffered from "a very severe and dangerous malady of the throat" and that he had left the chamber at half-past five for an appointment with his physician at six. William P. Frye of Maine then excited laughter by expressing the wish "that the same disease prevailed generally in the House." Thereupon, Charles O'Neill of Pennsylvania moved that Daggett "be excused and discharged without costs," and the motion was agreed to.[25]

As similar excuses were offered by others, William Aldrich of Illinois explained that he had been in the House for nearly six hours that day, and since the proceedings seemed not very important during the last half-hour of his attendance, he had gone to dinner and returned. He commented: "I stopped to talk with no stranger of either sex." Hiram Barber of Illinois then moved that Aldrich be discharged from custody without costs. This was agreed to but only after Daggett had facetiously interjected: "I move that the gentleman be taken down into the basement of the Capitol and shot."[26]

The rank and file of Nevada citizens, whether Republicans or Democrats, agreed on certain matters which they considered important for their interests, especially exclusion of Chinese laborers, removal of discriminatory railroad rates, remonetization of silver, and adequate taxation of mining corporations. The Republican state convention, meeting at Eureka on September 18, 1878, declared in favor of federal legislation to "absolutely stop the further immigration of Asiatics to our country." The Democratic state convention at Carson City on September 23 had denounced "the Chinese element as an incubus that will paralyze honest labor in any civilized country on earth" and had demanded "such a radical change in the treaty with the Chinese Empire as will forever stop the immigration of the Chinese to the United States."[27]

During the interim between the election of Daggett to the House in November 1878 and his taking his seat in March 1879, the short session of the Forty-fifth Congress had endeavored to deal with the problem by passing a bill prohibiting a vessel's master from bringing to the United States more than fifteen passengers from China on any one voyage. President Hayes vetoed the proposal as contrary to United States treaty obligations. The result was the Angell Treaty with China of 1880, followed by the Chinese Exclusion Act of 1882.[28] In the meantime, Nevada voters had gone on record as to Chinese immigration by rejecting a state constitutional amendment in 1880, which would have permitted such immigration, by a vote of 183 to 17,259.[29]

Another matter central to the interests of Nevada people was the removal of allegedly discriminatory railroad rates. Railroad magnates utilized the most unscrupulous methods to advance their interests. Long- and short-haul discriminations, which had a particularly adverse effect on Nevada communities, were widespread. A careful research student tells us that, in relation to Nevada, "Central and Southern Pacific Railroad men bent national, state and territorial governments to their will while they established their regional transportation monopoly and avoided effective regulation of all railroads." According to this same authority, when leaders in Congress sought to secure railroad regulation by congressional action, even such an enlightened individual as Charles Francis Adams, Jr., testified before a committee of Congress in a way that substantially invoked the Social Darwinist theory that competition "led inexorably to combination with the resulting elimination of the weak."[30]

At the time Daggett became a member of the House of Representatives, the issue of railroad regulation was arousing spirited discussion. Most of the early bills and resolutions to regulate interstate commerce had endeavored to prohibit extortionate rates, and little was said about discrimination. Thus, the chief provision of the McCrary Bill of 1874, introduced by Congressman George Washington McCrary of Iowa, prohibited unreasonable and extortionate rates. Almost as an afterthought one section forbade unjust discrimination. The bill passed the House but was defeated in the Senate.[31]

Yet people in and out of Congress were concerned over what they deemed flagrant discriminations. For many years residents of the Rocky Mountain states, including Nevada, had to pay 25 to 100 per cent higher railroad rates for goods from the East than did inhabitants of the Pacific Coast area, although the goods in transit passed their very doors and often were hauled a distance greater by 25 per cent. Rates charged to Nevada were equally high from every point east of Denver. Thus, the rate to Reno was the same from New York City,

Chicago, St. Paul, Omaha, or even Denver.[32] Three bills had been introduced in the House to require uniform rates and to forbid discrimination between persons and places. Similar measures were proposed in 1873 and 1874, while as many as four bills introduced in 1875 were definitely directed against discrimination.

Congressman John H. Reagan of Texas, who had once been Confederate Postmaster-General, a man of "great personal charm and long devotion to the public good," was for ten years chairman of the House Committee on Commerce and then, after his election to the Senate in 1887, a member of the similar Senate Committee.[33] Much of his time was long occupied with the introduction and advocacy of bills to regulate interstate commerce and to prohibit unjust discriminations by common carriers. The bill he proposed in 1877 was later modified to make it less technical and verbose, the Reagan Bill of 1878 resulting. In the revised proposal, the acceptance of greater compensation for a shorter haul than for a longer haul in one continuous journey was declared unlawful. A minimum penalty of a thousand dollars, half of which was to be paid to the informer, was prescribed. The rigid long- and short-haul provision did much to defeat the bill. It was held that consideration was not given to the legitimate difference between retail and wholesale prices (the latter being properly lower than the former) and that railroads would be forced to abandon service to points where water competition was encountered. The bill passed the House of Representatives on December 11, 1878, but never came to a vote in the Senate, where it was referred to the Committee on Commerce. There it was dropped. Reagan, with undying persistence, introduced similar bills in 1879 and 1880 but failed in each case to secure enactment. In connection with the bill of 1880, Daggett made his most important congressional speech—on February 25, 1881.[34] He had been prompted to do so by a Joint Resolution of the Nevada legislature on February 10, protesting against the discriminatory rates of the Central Pacific Railroad and citing numerous examples of such practices.[35] Daggett proceeded to discuss the history of the Reagan Bill, and with his old-time journalistic flourish launched into florid oratory:

> With their millions wrung from the many they have purchased and enslaved abilities ennobled in better fields of effort. They have subsidized the press. They have fouled the fountains of justice. They have stifled the expression of public sentiment. They have corrupted the ballot, and sought to undermine the morality of every department of State and National Government; and their

accredited agents have abused the privileges of this floor by obtruding their presence among the members during legislative hours.

Nor this alone. Many tongued rumor, the unblest evangel of calumny, has more than hinted that to the glitter of gold have been added the enchantments of beauty to warp the judgments of men, and that the corporate Aladdins of the land, whose influence it is impossible not to feel, even in the inner chambers of the temple, have called to their councils both the sightless son of Ceres and the star-eyed cyprian whose home is on the heights.

I must not, dare not, will not give credence to reports so humiliating to the membership of this House; and, to borrow a figure for the occasion, even were it possible for me to believe them, over my shoulders I would hang the mantle of doubt, and, like the blessed of Noah's sons, walk backward with it to cover the infamy before the world beheld it or our own eyes were blasted by the unwelcome vision.

Like myself, Governor [Leland] Stanford, the president of the company, was a republican when the title carried with it persecution and reproach; when the public addresses of the Bakers and Traceys of California were answered, as they only could be answered, by tumult and violence; when the dissenting Brodericks of orthodox democracy were healed of their apostasy by half-ounce bullets and modest monuments in Lone Mountain. I assisted, and most cheerfully, in his election as governor of California, and well and faithfully did he perform the duties of his high office.

It is therefore with regret that I am compelled to assail the later acts of his life, and make such showings as must bring in serious question his corporate integrity.

Launching then into a discussion of the effects of railroad policy on his home state, Daggett declared:

Their object seems to be to crush, not to develop, the industries of Nevada, and to this end the competition of special rates from California is employed when there is danger of an industry growing into importancce.

He elaborated, again with old-time rhetorical fervor:

And who are the men who have been made the victims of these special corporate cruelties? Are they outcasts, felons, fugitives from prisons, who recognizing no law themselves, should be judged and treated without the pale of law? No, sir! They are part of that grand army of men who years ago became the State-makers of this Republic; who, with ax and rifle on their shoulders, plunged boldly into the wilderness, uncovering its riches, and blazing the way for timid feet to follow. Strong arms and fearless hearts were their heritage, and their lives have been full of hardships and dangers. Many of them have gone by the wayside, with no hand to help, no human voice to cheer, and their humble graves are found in the sands of the desert and under the pines.

These sir, are the men who, venturing beyond the reach of railroad competition, have been singled out as especial victims of unusual railroad greed.

Daggett then proceeded to discuss the progress of the corrective measures proposed by Reagan. Dealing with the Reagan Bill passed by the House in 1878, he declared that it did not completely correct railroad discrimination but did fix a limit based on a principle which, Daggett believed, received the endorsement of a majority of the constituents of four-fifths of the Congressmen. Commenting on the fact that the bill had died in the Senate, he declared cynically:

The manner of its death was never reported by the Committee having it in charge. One Washington correspondent said it died of neglect, another that it was disemboweled and then strangled, and a third that the chairman sat down upon it, I presume by mistake. But, whatever may have been the cause of its death, let him be punished according to his deserving who harbors a suspicion that the funeral expenses were paid by the railroad companies.

Then, with mock seriousness, he remarked, "I am not permitted to believe it." Continuing, he pointed out the progress of the same proposals in the extra session of the existing (Forty-sixth) Congress. He asserted that the Commerce Committee, after due consideration, had authorized the chairman to report it back to the House, but that such action had precipitated drastic measures in corporate circles:

Such action thus early in the session did not accord with the plans of the railroad managers. Should it go to the Senate within two or three months of the opening of the session, it would be difficult to hold it in committee there until the close. Hence, they asked that the report might be withheld long enough for them to be heard before the committee. They intimated that they had some new and overwhelming testimony against the bill, and their request was granted.

Their ablest attorneys were hastily summoned to the capital; their lobby force was increased and redrilled in desperate and shameless tactics; they interrupted communication between the committee and the House; their subsidized journals threw open their throttle-valves, and the assault began. We know the result, if we do not the details of the struggle. The committee yielded to new convictions, and in the end agreed to a new bill instead of the one which they had a few weeks before authorized their chairman to report.

Daggett then indicated that when the committee had finally reported, "in graceless compliance with a popular demand which could not well be disregarded," it was to hand in silence to this House three distinct bills. The first, Daggett asserted, was "the commissioner bill, agreed to by a majority of the committee after the re-hearing, and which, it seems to me, should be satisfactory to the railroad companies." The second was the Reagan Bill, "modestly appearing as an amendment"—a bill that had "already received the endorsement of the people." The third was a substitute bill introduced by Congressman Robert M. McLane of Maryland. According to Daggett, it was one "which says nothing, means nothing, and provides for nothing. It is a ghastly mockery of railroad legislation—something which resembles an uncharged shell from a railroad battery, splattering, fizzing, but harmless, and therefore entitled to no further attention."

Daggett denounced the first bill, the Henderson Bill, named for Congressman Thomas J. Henderson of Illinois:

> The commissioner bill . . . is a dangerous measure, for it wears upon its face the smile of honesty. It is adroitly and carefully drawn; so carefully that its enforcement as a law would not seriously interfere with existing discriminatory railroad practices. Its aim seems to be to supply the people with litigation rather than legislation, and perpetuate evils which it is the duty of Congress to correct.
>
> In a speech before the committee one of the attorneys of the railroads remarked that there was a knife in the fourth section of the Reagan bill, and the trouble seemed to be that his client could not get hold of the handle. . . . But if there is a knife in the fourth section of the Reagan bill, there is a whole cutlery establishment in this commissioner bill, with every edge turned toward the people. Read thoughtlessly it sounds well. It abounds

in sections of tender solicitude for the people and clauses of stern restraint of railroad rapacity. Both are mere mouthings.[36]

This speech, "Railroad Wrongs in Nevada," was widely circulated and received much acclaim. The *New York Times* later devoted two wide columns to the speech, declaring that it furnished "a remarkable illustration of the extortion and rapacity of which railroad managers are capable when unchecked by either competition or legal restrictions." Republican journals in Nevada were highly enthusiastic; the Gold Hill *News* asserted that it was the most able and thorough effort yet presented on the subject. Regret was expressed, however, that Daggett had waited almost to the end of the session to express himself. It was in a way his swan song, for he had only about a week's service before the end of his congressional term. He had been emphatic and effective, but he hardly did on the issue what he had promised during the campaign of 1878, when he said in many a mining camp: "When I am elected, I will introduce a bill to stop this railroad stealing. Of course the bill will be referred to a committee and some rebel brigadier will put it in his pocket. I will steal his bowie-knife, cut off his pocket, get my bill, introduce it again and keep doing it until I carry my point."[37]

There were, of course, practical difficulties. The continuance of the long- and short-haul discrimination seemed to many illogical and unfair, but powerful pressure worked for its retention. Eastern manufacturers wished a favored position for transporting their products speedily to markets on the Pacific Coast, and West Coast businessmen sought favorable rates for their wares to areas east of the Rockies. The so-called Granger states, morever, did not want rates for farm products from Iowa or Nebraska to New York City markets proportionate to those paid by farmers from Ohio or western New York. On the other hand, New York City shipping interests had an obvious interest in opposing disproportionately cheaper rates by rail to the Pacific coast so as to give the railroads commerce which otherwise might go by vessel around Cape Horn or by way of the Isthmus of Panama. At times, therefore, spokesmen for the Rocky Mountain states like Daggett found their interests against long- and short-haul discrimination joining hands with representatives of the New York Board of Trade.[38]

Agitation for effective control of interstate commerce began to get results, as Grangers and Farmers' Alliance men pressed their case, and dedicated individuals like Congressman Reagan worked with unrelenting zeal. Daggett's rhetorical efforts were a minor contribution to the shaping of events. Even railroad presidents came to see that if regulatory laws could not be avoided, it would be desirable to have railroad commissioners to stand between the railroads and the public.[39] The Henderson Bill, written by Charles Francis Adams, Jr., had provided for a National Board of Railroad Commissioners and had frankly recognized the existence of pools, rebates, and drawbacks. One authority tells us that it was "antithetical to Reagan's measure in every sense," hence Daggett's vitriolic denunciation is understandable.[40]

After the noted Wabash Decision by the United States Supreme Court in 1886, federal regulation of American railroads seemed imperative, and a compromise between those favoring and those opposing a commission found expression in the Interstate Commerce Act of 1887. Reagan and Shelby M. Cullom of Illinois both could claim credit for the fruition of years of conscientious service.[41]

Another matter of concern to Nevadans was the free coinage of silver. Such a proposal, sponsored by Congressman Richard Bland of Missouri in 1877 had been altered in the Senate to become the Bland-Allison Bill, directing the Secretary of the Treasury to buy not less than two million dollars' worth and not more than four million dollars' worth of silver each month and cause the same to be coined into dollars. President Hayes had vetoed the bill, but it passed over his veto in 1878.[42] When Senator Jones returned to Nevada, he spoke at a meeting in July. When Daggett was called upon, he paid tribute to the "days of toil and sleepless nights" Jones had given "to the repeal of the iniquitous silver demonetizing law of 1873," and he spoke of the gratitude people of the state owed him as a result.[43]

At the state convention in September, Nevada Republicans hailed "with joy the remonetization of silver as a step toward our emancipation from the grasp of the corrupt money rings of Europe and America," and asked Congress "to complete the measure of our redemption by according to silver unrestrained coinage." In the same year the Nevada Democratic Convention had advocated "the removal of all restrictions on the coinage of silver as a money metal the same as gold—the same as it was before its fraudulent demonetization by a Republican Congress in 1873."[44] Thus, silver agitation continued. In the special session in which Daggett took his congressional seat, a Democrat, A. J. Warner of Ohio, pressed more for the enactment of a free coinage measure, and it passed the House by a vote of 114 to 97, six Republicans favoring the bill and eight Democrats opposing. Daggett was one of the silver Republicans. Indeed, he had secured the inclusion in the bill of the Carson City branch mint (as well as Denver) as a place for receiving the bullion. In the Senate the bill was reported adversely by Senator Bayard of Delaware at the next session, and the measure died.[45] Silver advocates persisted in their endeavors but with no important results until the Sherman Silver Purchase Act of 1890.

Considerable difference of opinion arose as to what constituted adequate taxation of mining properties. The Republicans felt that the mining corporations were paying their fair share of the taxes, while the Democrats believed that the mining corporations were being sufficiently encouraged and demanded that the mining interests should "contribute for the support of government, the same as other property."[46] This, however, was basically a state matter and one with which Daggett was not immediately concerned as a Congressman.

A significant proposal with which Daggett concerned himself was one relating to public lands in Nevada. In 1864, when the state was admitted to the union, the federal government had granted the sixteenth and thirty-sixth sections of the public lands within the state, or one-eighteenth of the area of the state, for school purposes. Comprising 3,900,000, acres these lands of course were scattered in mountain, desert, and arid sagebrush areas. Accordingly, Nevada had been able to sell only about 70,000 acres in fifteen years. Nevada sought, therefore, to exchange the unsold acreage for 2,000,000 acres of non-mineral public lands, to be selected with a view to their salability so as to provide a serviceable school fund.[47]

On March 8, 1879, the legislature of Nevada had sanctioned the acceptance from the United States government of 2,000,000 acres more of land, not yet disposed of by the state, in lieu of the sixteenth and thirty-sixth sections in each township previously granted. Daggett, therefore, introduced a bill to secure congressional sanction of the arrangement. After the Committee on Public Lands reported favorably on it, it was placed on the calendar.[48] In the House Daggett declared that since the bill involved "neither expenditure of money by the Government nor any loss of lands," it seemed unnecessary for him to add anything to the report. Representative William A. J. Sparks of Illinois, who had a sincere and almost pugnacious interest in conserving the public interest in public lands and was to be President Cleveland's Commissioner of the General Land Office, sharply dissented. He contended that the principle in the bill manifested favoritism toward Nevada, for it disagreed with the basis of all other donations or gifts of land by the United States to the various states for school purposes. In previous cases, Sparks said, no state had been allowed to select the *best* lands. Sparks contended that the bill would give Nevada "every acre of public land in the State susceptible of cultivation," since Nevada authorities could select the lands from all nonmineral and nontimber public lands. Daggett denied Sparks's contention but did not really meet his argument. Daggett stated that nearly all the unsold public domain was desert. He explained, "There are not today two million acres of arable land in Nevada; not a million acres that can be cultivated without irrigation by means of artesian wells. It is not the purpose of our State to select the best lands, because there are no such lands unsold." He stated that Nevada wished desert, sage brush, and other lands in quantities large enough to secure development by offering bounties for artesian wells. Thus, lands could be sold to provide money for the irreducible state school fund. He said that in Nevada railroad companies were not taxed on unsold lands or mining companies on anything except improvements, so school taxes had been excessively heavy on the small property owner. The bill passed the House on May 21 by a vote of 138 to 14. It passed the Senate on June 14, and the President made it law two days later.[49]

Daggett of course concerned himself with the usual petitions in the interests of a Congressman's constituents. On April 21, 1879, for example, he introduced bills "for the relief" of John M. Dorsey, William F. Shepard, John S. Luff, and William Haydon.[50] He introduced a pension bill for the widow of an army captain. He brought in petitions for the increase of pensions for maimed soldiers, for pension benefits for soldiers and sailors of the Mexican War, and for the prevention of cattle diseases. He introduced a petition from Mrs. G. A. Custer against the erection of what she deemed an unsuitable statue of her husband. In addition he presented a bill for the erection of a federal building at Carson City. Concerned with reducing the price of public lands within railroad limits, he introduced a bill to that effect, which was supported by citizens of twenty-five Nevada communities, including Reno, Carson City, and Virginia City.[51]

In a broader way, he was especially interested in securing legislation providing for a uniform system of bankruptcy. He also introduced a bill authorizing the postmaster general to adopt a device for canceling stamps. The Reno *Nevada State Journal* expressed the view of many when it asserted in June 1880 that Daggett had been "untiring" in his efforts for his constituents.[52]

At the Republican state convention at Carson City on August 11, 1880, Daggett was renominated by acclamation. At the same time a resolution endorsed his efforts in opposing a change in the mining laws which would have prohibited "the following of fissure veins or deposits" in seeking ore in areas where title to the surface land had not been obtained "beyond vertical lines of surface boundaries." The convention declared that the proposed changes would "work disaster to the labors of the prospector, and seriously retard the development of the mineral riches of the West."[53] The Democrats nominated George W. Cassidy of Eureka, five years younger than Daggett and a native of Kentucky.

In campaigning for reelection Daggett followed a taxing schedule. Along with Judge D. O. Anderson, he addressed a gathering at Winnemucca on October 2. Twenty-one other communities resounded to their oratorical efforts before the end of the month.[54]

Daggett could "wave the bloody shirt" with a flourish. His old friend, Sam Davis, in campaigning for the Democrats in 1878 at Elko drew for the crowd a large picture of Daggett making a speech and used red ink to emphasize Daggett's waving of the Bloody shirt. Now, at Eureka on October 8, 1880, Daggett facetiously indicated that there were probably Democrats present so he would not wave the bloody shirt but would point to what he claimed was Republican-stimulated prosperity throughout the country. Daggett and Anderson visited Carson City on the 26th, Sutro on the next day, and Gold Hill on the 28th. Refuting the claim of Daggett that Republican efforts had produced prosperity, Cassidy at a mass meeting in Virginia City maintained that good times were really due to bountiful harvests and Britain's need for American farm products. Cassidy maintained that Daggett had taken credit for the school land bill but that the idea had been suggested by Governor Bradley and had been worked up by the Democrats, and that all Daggett had to do was "hand it in to Congress." Daggett, he claimed, had talked about what he would accomplish in regard to the reduction of railroad rates but had "not once opened his mouth while in Congress."[55]

Republicans at their subsequent mass meeting in Virginia City on October 29 listened to United States Senator J. P. Jones as he denounced Cassidy's "wild statements" and complimented Daggett, especially on his success, even as a new Congressman, in securing the enactment of the School Land Bill. He termed the bill "the most important Congressional measure ever passed for the benefit of Nevada." Other Republican meetings were held, including the closing one of the campaign at Virginia City on November 1, addressed by Daggett, when Piper's Opera House was packed "from pit to dome." Daggett's old *Enterprise* termed the address "a marvel of research, facts, figures and solemn argument," yet "intensely interesting."[56]

On election day Daggett was defeated by Cassidy, who received

9,815 votes to Daggett's 8,578. The success of the Democrats in
Nevada was general and unprecedented, their candidates for Supreme
Court judge, presidential electors, and nearly all other offices being
elected. Some local Republican newspapers attributed the defeat to
undue confidence, which resulted in apathy, inadequate party organization, and ineffective party management.[57]

The candidacy of William Sharon, the Republican Senator from
Nevada, for reelection was a heavy strain on the ticket. Although
Daggett had aided Sharon in reaching the United States Senate, he
said after the elections of 1880, with his usual exaggeration, that
Sharon had been in the Upper House for six years but had not been
six days in the Senate Chamber.[58] Sharon was a wealthy Comstock
mining capitalist, controlled the famous Palace Hotel in San Francisco, and dominated the Bank of California. Looked upon by many
Nevadans as not in reality a resident of their state, he was sometimes
referred to as the "gentleman from California."

Sharon had tasted the glory of membership in that most exclusive
of political clubs, the United States Senate, and he had not found it an
especially congenial establishment. Thus, he did not have the burning
desire to win at this time, as did his Democratic competitor, James
G. Fair, who apparently was willing to open his money bags to buy the
votes of many poor residents, including many immigrants. The Stockton *Mail* later said that Fair was worth thirty million dollars, so he
was readily able to purchase votes to make himself Senator. One
paper reported that in Washoe (Reno area) and other counties "droves
of men who could not speak English, who had to have an interpreter
when naturalized, who did not know whether Garfield was a candidate
or whether he was running for constable or pound master" were led
up to the polls and voted just as so many sheep, and they did not
vote for Daggett.[59]

When Sharon sought the senatorship in 1874/75, he apparently
bought votes for $2.50. Then the price rose. According to an astute
journalist and political observer of the time, Sam P. Davis, in the
entire history of Nevada politics there had "never been such a
saturnalia of corruption" as in this campaign. Votes were bought
openly on every side, and the price, which at first ranged from $5.00
to $10.00 for a vote, now reached $80.00. Fair's money bags were
opened in every county and precinct on election day.[60]

Daggett later indicated that the fight had been essentially between Sharon and the Bank of California on the one hand, and Fair
and the Bonanza wealth on the other—$20,000,000 versus $100,000,000.
This time Sharon had refused to neutralize the money spent by Fair

by expenditures of his own. Perhaps he realized that he was simply not rich enough to compete successfully. John W. Mackay was Daggett's friend, and it had been expected that he would help finance Daggett in the election. But Fair was Mackay's mining partner, and the latter could not go all out to help the Republicans in an election in which his associate was running as a Democrat. Yet Daggett later said that Mackay had largely helped to finance the Republican campaign in Nevada.[61]

The railroad question may also have helped the Democrats. Sharon had heavy railroad investments, which hardly recommended him as a fighter against what Nevadans believed to be outrageous rate discrimination, and his term in the Senate had tended to confirm this impression. Fair, a rather chilly native of Ireland, was not liked by the populace of Nevada, but many believed that he had a personal interest in the fight against the railroads. Daggett, on his part, may have alienated the votes of some railroad workers. When he went to Congress in 1878, the Union Pacific charged him $16.50 for extra baggage. Vowing revenge, if we may believe a contemporary journalist, he franked seventeen tons of congressional documents, addressed to himself, and when he got home he sent them back again. The men of the road got their revenge in the election of 1880.[62]

But the "saturnalia of corruption" was not over. When the legislature began to assemble, the seemingly victorious Fair was unexpectedly confronted by Adolph Sutro of Sutro Tunnel fame. The *Enterprise* a decade before had termed him "one of the irrepressibles," and so he appeared to be at this time.[63] Sutro, ever a bitter enemy of Fair, had sent a representative into Nevada to announce his own candidacy. Sutro later claimed that Fair had used his money to silence this representative. After the legislature met, Sutro appeared in Carson City and announced that he was a candidate at the hands of the Democratic legislators, most of whom had been elected by the free use of Fair's money. Sutro was in a mood to use money for his ends and, taking rooms at the Ormsby House, began to dispose of $250,000 in cash. Great excitement prevailed, as Sutro was able to break the Democratic party caucus which, it had been supposed, would declare for Fair without question. Fair's adherents, however, proceeded to pad the roll call, announce a full caucus, and proceed with a high hand. Sutro's first victory was thus broken, but he had purchased enough votes of the legislators to elect him. These legislators, however, felt the need for a real excuse to give the voters for their action in deserting Fair, after being pledged to him during the campaign. Sutro's managers conceived the idea of swearing out complaints

against some of the men who had used money corruptly in Washoe
County during the campaign. Arrests were to be made of members
of the legislature on the floor of the House in open session on the
charge of buying votes in the election. The men who had received
Fair's money but who had now been brought up by Sutro planned to
desert Fair as soon as the exposé was made. Fair, however, had a
lieutenant who had taken an active part in the plans of the Sutro men
and knew when the coup was to be made. The previous night, a team
was driven furiously to Reno, and every official before whom complaint could be registered was spirited away. Thus, Sutro's Carson
City attorney was unable to swear out warrants for the arrest of the
men. It was too late to try to get action in other counties, so Fair's
men pressed their advantage, and Fair was elected. The Democrats
on joint ballot controlled fifty-three votes to twenty-one secured by
the Republicans. One state senator was an independent, and in the
balloting one vote was cast for Daggett.[64] Later the Republican governor, John H. Kinkead, was to write President Garfield that "bad
faith" in Republican ranks "coupled with lavish use of money" by
the Democrats had lost the state for their own party.[65]

John Mackay apparently promised Daggett that he would use
his substantial power to get some political preferment for him, and
he invited him to accompany him east on the palatial drawing room
car placed at his disposal by Cyrus W. Field. Boarding the train at
Reno, they reached New York City on November 20 and stopped at
the Gilsey House. Mackay told reporters nothing new about the
Comstock. Daggett seemed eager to talk and indicated to newspapermen that on the trip east Mackay displayed great confidence in the
future of the Lode. In the interview, published in the New York
Graphic on November 23, Daggett said that, although Mackay and
his associates had paid millions in assessments during the previous
three years and had put large sums into improvements without substantial return, Mackay believed that low-grade ore would still be
valuable.[66] Daggett also gave interviews to reporters for the *Herald* and
the *Express*, touching upon Chinese immigration, agriculture in California, and railroad rates on the Union and Central Pacific railroads.
On December 2 Mackay sailed for Paris to visit his wife, whom he
had not seen for three years, and Daggett went to Washington for
the short session of Congress.

Daggett was disturbed by Associated Press dispatches that he had
accompanied Mackay to Europe and by reports that he had come
east on the private car of the president of the Union Pacific. He wrote
from Washington that in imagination he might be "exploring the ruins

of Pompeii, rowing up the Nile" or slaking his "thirst in the broad waters of Tigris," but that physically he was very much in Washington. He insisted that it was also not true that he would receive a diplomatic or other governmental appointment, for at the conclusion of his congressional term he expected to return to Nevada "with no purpose of leaving" what had long been his home state.[67]

During the short session of Congress, Daggett became concerned about the difficulties many Nevadans had under the Desert Land Act. This required that land entered for reclamation by irrigation must be definitely reclaimed by the introduction of water within three years of the date of entry. Daggett hoped that legislation might extend the period by two or three years so that responsible people might avoid forfeiture of their claims.[68]

On occasion Daggett continued to demonstrate his impish individualism. At Pyramid Lake, Nevada, an Indian agency was vacant, and in January 1881 the President nominated a Mr. McMasters of Rochester, New York. Various Nevadans wanted the place, but the Indian Commissioner told Daggett that the position, under an old arrangement, had to go to a Baptist. Previously the agency apparently had been scandalously managed, and Daggett replied, "I presume Mr. McMasters has never seen an Indian outside a sideshow; but if he has capacity enough to steal the whole of the appropriation, and compel the Indians to fish for his benefit and beg their food, he will answer quite as well as the majority of his predecessors."[69]

Daggett later heard from Virginia City that McMasters had declined to serve, so he again sought out the Indian Commissioner, who related that he had received no such refusal. This brought out the irrational in Daggett's make-up, as the Commissioner asked, "What reason is assigned for his non-acceptance of the position?"

"Guess he heard of the fate of his predecessor," replied Daggett.

"What was that?" queried the Commissioner.

Daggett indicated that he had been poisoned: "You see the fellows send out a lot of muffins, who know no more about handling Indians than a hog knows about logic. They soon get to swindling the red brethren, and so the latter send them to the happy hunting grounds with the aid of poison, and by gawd, sir, it's right, too."

"Great heavens," exclaimed the horrified official. "Do you mean to say you approve of such proceedings?"

"Bet your damned life," replied Daggett, "so if you want to vacate some Baptist pulpits send along your ministers and I'll be damned if I don't furnish the poison."

Daggett shouldered his cane and left, and the officials at the Indian Office appeared firmly convinced that the interests of civilization had been advanced by Daggett's defeat for reelection to Congress.[70]

Yet the distinguished historian of Western American history, Hubert H. Bancroft, later asserted that by the election of 1880 Nevada had "lost her able and working congressman, Daggett."[71]

Rollin Mallory Daggett as minister to the Hawaiian Islands
Carter Collection

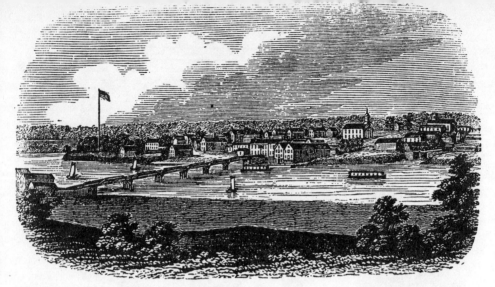

View of Defiance, Ohio, where Daggett spent his boyhood, in 1846
From Henry Howe, Historical Collections of Ohio *(Cincinnati, 1848)*

View of Piqua, Ohio, which Daggett left for California
From Henry Howe, Historical Collections of Ohio *(Cincinnati, 184*

Montgomery Street, San Francisco, in 1856, showing Wells Fargo on corner
and business buildings beyond
From the Hills Collection, The Bancroft Library, University of California

C Street, Virginia City, where the *Enterprise* offices were located
Courtesy The Bancroft Library, University of California

Masthead of the
Territorial Enterprise

WEEKLY TERRITORIAL ENTERPRISE

Published every Saturday by
R. M. DAGGETT.

THE DAILY ENTERPRISE

Is the oldest and best newspaper in Nevada, and the only one having a general circulation throughout the State. Its daily contents embrace the fullest and latest telegraphic dispatches, a careful compilation of general news items, detailed accounts of the most interesting events of the world, editorials on current topics, an elaborate department of local incidents and information, together with varied selections of choice poetry and miscellany—constituting a journal unsurpassed in excellence and attractiveness.

Terms of Subscription:

Delivered by carrier............25 cents a week
By mail, one year, postage paid..........$10 00
By mail, six months, postage paid....... 6 00
By mail, three months, postage paid..... 3 00

THE WEEKLY ENTERPRISE.

The Weekly is issued in quarto form, containing Forty-eight Columns of reading matter, compiled with special attention to the completeness of its general news and the fullness of local intelligence. For readers residing throughout the interior of the State and in the neighboring Territories, who do not enjoy the facilities of a daily mail, the WEEKLY ENTERPRISE will be indispensable, and for those who wish to keep distant friends informed of Washoe affairs it will prove an efficient and economical means.

Terms of Weekly Enterprise:

By mail, one year, postage paid...........$3 00
By mail, six months, postage paid........ 2 00
By mail, three months, postage paid...... 1 00

Saturday.............February 8, 1879

Daggett's daughters Grace (left) and
Katherine (right) with their Grandaunt
Mrs. S. A. Tompkins in Virginia City
   Carter Collection

Daggett's first wife, Maggie Curry,
in Virginia City
   Carter Collection

Daggett of the Virginia City *Territorial Enterprise*
   Carter Collection

View of Virginia City, showing Maguire's Opera House, St. Paul's
Episcopal Church, and some small shops
Courtesy The Bancroft Library, University of California

King Kalakaua of the Hawaiian Islands. The frontispiece of *The Legends and Myths of Hawaii*, on which he and Daggett collaborated

VII

Political Maneuvering
and the
Hawaiian Mission

I<small>N SPITE OF HIS RENUNCIATION OF POLITICAL AMBITION</small>, D<small>AGGETT REMAINED</small> in Washington during the spring of 1881, zealous in his endeavors to advance his own political fortunes. He had been present at what may have been Garfield's last formal address to the public, on the occasion of the unveiling of the statue of Admiral David G. Farragut in Washington. At a memorial service for Garfield in Virginia City in September 1881, Daggett recalled that the President looked somewhat paler than usual but that his eye was bright, and in his five-minute address, "full of thought and pathos, he bathed the monumental marble in a new glory, and gave to its presence an enlarged and lasting significance."[1]

As Daggett maneuvered for political preferment in Washington he had considerable time to visit the Senate gallery, give an interview to the Washington *Post*, and enjoy social occasions. In May he was the speaker of the evening at the annual dinner of St. George's Society of the District of Columbia. Abner's Hall was decorated with United States and British flags, and an orchestra played during dinner and between toasts. Daggett was reported as making "the great speech of the evening, graceful, humorous, suggestive, and eloquent, touching all moods and reaching all hearts. His ingenious fancy and happy diction are aided by a most musical voice, and all who heard him pronounced him a real orator."[2]

Next month Daggett went to New York City, where he was a guest at Delmonico's Restaurant at a dinner of the Stanley Club, an organization formed in 1878 to honor the efforts of Henry M. Stanley, the explorer of the Congo. By this time it seemed that the Hawaiian mission, for which Daggett had been suggested by his friends, was to go to Garfield's intimate associate of former days, Burke Hinsdale, the president of Hiram College. Seeming more urbane than of old, Daggett soon returned to Nevada, where he visited Carson City. A reporter commented:

> Life at Washington has not changed his portly figure, but has given him a look not exactly of the sage brush. His countenance tells of a better quality of wine, a more subdued gaslight and less glaring attacks of sun reflected from alkali. He is reticent upon both his political and literary projects, but talks glowingly of his coal mine.[3]

Daggett continued to have enthusiastic admirers. The Ruby Hill *Mining News* stated that he was one of the few former members of Congress whose recommendations would be accepted by departments in Washington without question, for his name had "never been connected in the slightest degree with any questionable transaction." The Carson City *Index* in June urged him for Superintendent of the United States Mint at Carson City, stating that he was "fearless and unquestionable in his Republicanism."[4]

After the assassin's attack on Garfield in July 1881, Daggett was interviewed by a *New York Times* reporter at Carson City and expressed revulsion at the dastardly deed. After Garfield's death an elaborate memorial service was held in Virginia City. Houses were draped in black and flags were at half-mast. The Governor and his staff, Senator J. G. Fair, and other notables took part in a great procession of over three thousand persons, with a hearse and pallbearers adding a somber note. Even the Piute Indians came to town to witness the occasion. At the formal ceremonies in Piper's Opera House, Daggett gave the funeral oration. He said, in part:

> Of the victim of this human devil I find it difficult to speak calmly. As a friend and counselor I loved him; as a learned and conscientious servant of the people I respected him; for his broad statesmanship, his patriotism, and his fidelity to the right I admired and loved him. In him was combined in manly proportion so much that was great with so much that was good, that I scarcely know where to begin or where to end even the briefest references to his private and public life.[5]

Daggett loved to personalize and even dramatize his own connection with an important person, so he recalled the first time he had met Garfield after his nomination and before his election. It was at the Riggs House in Washington, where the rooms were crowded with visitors. Daggett was soon to leave for the West, and Garfield said to him, "I expect a good account of you in Nevada. All kinds of charges will be made against me during the canvass. My friends will know they are not true, if they affect my integrity, and must refute them."

Daggett also recalled an incident when Garfield was a member of Congress. A young man applied to him for a government clerkship. Garfield ascertained that the man was not prepared for such a place so secured him a laborer's job at the Capitol. The young man rejected the employment, declaring that he was a gentleman and could not degrade himself.

Then Garfield asked, "You were born a gentleman?"

"I was," came the reply.

"And therefore think yourself above earning an honest living," Garfield continued. "Now listen to me, young man. You say that you were born a gentleman, and doubtless believe that you can sustain that character better by begging or stealing than by accepting the only employment you seem to be fitted for. Continue in that belief, and you will bring up either in the penitentiary or the poor house." Daggett asserted that the young man profited by the rebuke, accepted the menial work, and had come to hold a responsible position in the United States Agricultural Bureau.[6]

After Daggett's congressional term was over and he had returned to Virginia City, he appeared to have more time for his literary interests. One of Daggett's colleagues in Congress was Samuel Sullivan Cox, who had been a Representative from the Columbus, Ohio, district during the Civil War and later from New York City. He had gained the sobriquet of "Sunset" because of his glowing description of an Ohio sunset.[7] Early in 1882 Daggett sent Cox a woodcut print of the latter which had appeared in the San Francisco *Post*. Some asserted that the likeness resembled "that of a scarred and leprous desperado." Daggett inquired of Cox as to what had happened to him. Cox replied in part that "there ought to be a law enacted for the special benefit of those recreants of the 'enterprising press' who maliciously appropriate the pictures of Guiteau, quack doctors, and other murderers, and print them on applebutter presses with biographical mention of 'Distinguished Public Men.'" This led Daggett to send Cox an original poem, "Nevada Sunset." In part, it was:

> The day is spent; behold the setting sun,
> With golden pencil tipped with silver light,
> In farewell greeting reach among the stars
> And touch the palette of eternal hues

That glorify the walks of other worlds
And paint the vaults and tapestries of Heaven;
Then with a single stroke of skill divine
So gild the cloudy canvass of the skies
That art stands awed, and seeks, but seeks in vain
To match its splendor.
      Not in Arctic seas;
Nor by the Adriatic or the Alps;
Not where the Himalayan minarets
Rend into shreds the clouds of Kumanon;
Or where the sun, as drops the plummet down,
Dyes red with vapors with its eyes of fire;
Not where, o'er looking bright Sicilian skies,
The Syracusans watch the amber skies
Or where the clouds, on balmy breezes borne,
Their shadows troop across Aegean isles
Are looped such pictures from the evening stars.
      Ye who would view these beauties, come with me
To some brown hill in Autumn, sloping down
From Tahoe eastward, where the rocky waves
Lower and gentler in recession thence,
Die out in ripples on the desert plains
The sere and scentless herbage at our feet,
The gnarl'd nut-pine and fragrant juniper,
Scarce feel the breath, cool from the frost heights,
As if the fragments of a world had dropped.[8]

Cox replied:

I knew that sunsets were not limited to Ohio, and that the farther
west you go, the more set in his ways and beams he becomes.
You have over-matched my pile of glory with your exquisite
versification. . . . Yours takes the palm. If I could make my pet
name negotiable, I would transfer it without recourse to the
ex-member from "Nevada's bannered peaks."[9]

Daggett continued to be in demand as a speech maker, in 1882
presenting a medal to a Mr. Van Duzen for the Virginia City Miners'
Union because of Van Duzen's heroic efforts in saving lives of fellow
miners in the lower levels of the Comstock. The same year Daggett's
most ambitious single literary effort appeared, *Braxton's Bar: A Novel.*[10]
In those days of low costs, it sold for $1.50. Based in large part on his
own experiences in crossing the country, it presents a vivid account

of the hazards of a gold seeker in encounters with Indians, cholera, and thirst. It recreates the anxiety and frustration of the gold hunter in the fields of California. The work demonstrates the vivid imagination and literary abilities of a talented writer and has been judged "the best novel to be produced" by a California Argonaut.[11] His work was basically narrative, packed with exciting melodramatic action, and he was not averse to rather cheap fictional devices. A contemporary journal, *The Friend*, appraised it:

> It is a book about the style of Mark Twain and Bret Harte, in which frontier life is depicted with a bold dash of the pen. From our personal knowledge derived from a visit to the mines of California in 1849 . . . the sketches of this volume are not very much overdrawn.[12]

Hubert H. Bancroft, the historian of the West, believed that Daggett's novel stood out above many tales of pioneer days in California and that it displayed some of Bret Harte's "conspicuous features."[13] The *Argonaut*, a leading San Francisco literary journal, declared: "Although prone to be sensational in parts it is a fair picture of early California life, and many incidents evince the fact that they occurred in the author's experience.[14]

Hawaiians became especially interested in the novel, because at the time of publication it looked as though Daggett might become minister to the Kingdom. In November the Honolulu *Pacific Advertiser* praised this "live book," commenting that the author had lived the life he portrayed and showed "himself not only a brave adventurer, but a generous hearted and philosophical observer." The Honolulu *Gazette* thought that Daggett excelled in "descriptive writing, and when illustrating the scenery of the West, whether beautiful mountain views or dreary stretches of prairie, it is with the finished touch of the poet."[15] Even in this novel Daggett could not abstain from moralizing, a fact noted by the *Enterprise* reviewer.[16]

By the end of 1881 Daggett was being prominently mentioned as Republican candidate for governor in 1882. Some asserted that he would not accept the nomination. The editor of the Eureka *Leader* wrote Daggett regarding the matter. The latter replied that there was "no shadow of truth" in the report first published in the Gold Hill *News* "on the authority of a Democratic county official" that he would not accept the nomination. Daggett said that, "owing to the animosity of the Central Pacific Railroad," he did not wish to jeopardize party success by pushing himself forward but would await the judgment of the convention. The *Leader* commented that Daggett was "not popular in some circles" but that he was a man of "undoubted character," who was "too honest to follow the decrees of the cliques and too independent to cultivate the good will of pothouse politicians." Other Republican papers expressed interest in Daggett's candidacy.[17] The movement was gaining momentum when interested friends pressed upon President Arthur Daggett's selection for minister to Hawaii. Much political maneuvering was involved.

Rutherford B. Hayes had been materially indebted to a number of Ohio politicians and editors for helping to bring him to the White House in March 1877. One of these was James M. Comly, editor of the *Ohio State Journal* in Columbus from 1865 to 1877. Born in New Lexington, Ohio, in 1832 of Quaker ancestry, as a mere lad working on the *State Journal* he had become acquainted with John J. Piatt and William Dean Howells. His service in the Civil War made him a brevet Brigadier-General at its close. Later Grant rewarded his services to the Republican party by making him postmaster at Columbus.[18]

Hayes had twice been governor of Ohio, from 1867 to 1871, and Comly urged him to run again in 1875. Hayes refused at first, but Comly persisted, and eventually Hayes accepted the nomination and won over the incumbent, William Allen, in a hotly contested fight.[19] During the days of intricate maneuvering associated with the disputed presidential vote of 1876, Comly went to Washington on January 2, 1877, and conferred with many Republicans. He worked especially to prevent a rift between the Grant administration and the Hayes men, and upon his return to Columbus he served as a liaison between Republican leaders in Washington and Governor Hayes in Ohio.[20]

His health impaired by the Civil War and worsened during strenuous efforts for Hayes, Comly was critically ill at the time of the latter's inauguration. His sickness eliminated him from consideration for a major appointment. Doctors advised that a stay in Hawaii might prolong his life, so he reluctantly asked Hayes for the post of United States minister there. The appointment was secured, and Comly proceeded to the islands of tranquil leisure, where he sought an outlet for his literary ambitions. He wrote one book, several essays, and some short stories, but few were ever published.[21]

In Hawaii Comly found the diplomatic quarters with no flags or even official envelopes, with books that were "archaeological specimens," and furniture that "would be dear at $10, even with wood at $19 a cord." He felt "four thousand miles farther away than Sheridan was at Cedar Creek." To Comly the Islands semed rather desolate, and the "good climate, beautiful surroundings, nice people" hardly compensated for active life in Ohio. He became so homesick that in 1879 he spent two or three months on leave in the United States. By April 1880 he lamented that the "present seems like living at a poor dying rate." The work seemed such as to make him unfit for future achievement. The duties were "monotonous and detestable," as they included visiting with other diplomats, engaging in speechmaking ceremonies, receiving and entertaining American visitors, and dealing with trivial matters such as identifying criminals, releasing drunken sailors from jail, mailing stamps to stamp collectors, and preparing reports for the Hawaiian Board of the Evangelical Association.[22]

Comly's journalistic flare almost terminated his diplomatic career. Shortly after his arrival in Honolulu, he wrote rather "racy" letters to his old newspaper. In these he described Hawaiian official life as "diplomatic monkeyism" and made sarcastic allusions to the aging white residents from missionary families who controlled the basic economic life of the islands. He soon abandoned this practice.[23]

Grant was Comly's political friend, and his failure to secure the presidential nomination in 1880 was a keen disappointment to the diplomat. With Garfield's nomination and election, Comly knew that his own status was in doubt. Although in a private letter in 1878 Comly pictured his official duties as chiefly "going to take another drink," and although Mrs. Comly longed to return to Ohio, he now sought reappointment.[24] The accession of Garfield prompted Comly to secure the services of Andrew W. Francisco, general manager of his old paper, the *State Journal,* to protect his interests. Comly wrote that he had just suffered a serious hemorrhage, felt "shaky on his pins," and was most anxious about his future. The Hawaiian climate under the circumstances seemed a necessity to him, and he was anxiously "waiting for the verdict" from Washington. Francisco well knew how much Hayes owed Comly, so he wrote to the ex-President, asking what could be done in view of efforts of leaders on the Pacific Coast for Daggett. Hawaii was a "banishment" for Comly but seemed imperative in view of his health.[25]

Although Francisco did not want to make the journey to Washington, he went there in May 1881. He found that Daggett had never left the capital after the adjournment of Congress. The Nevadan and his friends were bringing to bear Pacific Coast influence and were also counting on Blaine's assistance to secure the Hawaiian appointment for Daggett. On March 1, before Garfield's inauguration, Senator John Jones of Nevada, Senator John F. Miller, and Congressmen R. P. Pacheco and Horace F. Page of California had sought an appointment with Garfield.[26] Two weeks later the two Nevada senators, Jones and

James G. Fair, urged Garfield to appoint Daggett to the Hawaiian
position, stressing his thirty years of residence in the West and his
long career as a leading editor who had rendered conspicuous service
to the Republican party.[27] These pressures were part of what Whitelaw
Reid of the New York *Tribune* had in mind when he wrote to Garfield
on March 21: "I hope the mob infesting all the approaches to the
White House is gradually being fought off a little. When I last heard
from any of my friends there you were having a terrible time of
it."[28]

Everyone seemed to be office-seeking. By May Francisco found
that "pressure on the President . . . was terrible." Mrs. Garfield had
become ill with a malarial, possibly a typhoid, condition, and with
mounting patronage troubles the situation set the President "wild."
After three days in Washington Francisco obtained a ten-minute interview with Garfield, while two senators, some congressmen, and others
"looked daggers" at him. Francisco presented letters from former President Hayes and from George Nash, then Attorney General of Ohio
and later governor, to support Comly's case. Garfield commented that
he understood Comly would like to leave Honolulu, and Francisco
replied that Comly had so expressed himself if a better place could
be found for him. Finally Garfield, who on occasion committed himself
too readily, said that he thought it could be arranged, but that, in
any event, provision would be made for Comly.[29]

Francisco had by this time concluded that Daggett had no real
prospect for the Hawaiian post. Some weeks later, however, he learned
that there was much competition for the position. When Governor
Charles Foster (known as "Calico Charlie" because of his dry goods
store career during the war) returned to Columbus from a visit to
Washington, he told Francisco that a few days before Garfield was
shot, they had gone riding together. The President seemed to think
that Comly had been taken care of by four years in Hawaii and ought
to have "saved some money."[30] He indicated that Alfred Lee, who had
served as editor of the *State Journal* after 1873, while Comly was ill,
and had been private secretary to Governor Hayes, was one for whom
Hayes wished provision to be made. Hayes had appointed him Consul
General at Frankfort-on-the-Main, but, with the new Garfield Administration, he was looking for another place.[31] Benjamin Butterworth, the
influential Congressman from Cincinnati, and his friends were seeking
the Hawaiian post for a local citizen named Vogeler. The conflicting
and burdensome pressures greatly irritated Garfield, and, somewhat
troubled by the strain of making a decision, he indicated that Lee
had been appointed by Hayes out of personal considerations, and now

he was entitled to provide similarly for his own friends.[32] Garfield indicated that he felt bound to do something for his old associate, Burke A. Hinsdale, the president of Hiram College in Ohio. The Garfields were indeed intimate friends of Hinsdale and his wife, for both families had earlier been closely associated in the affairs of the college. Financial difficulties had become oppressive at the college, and both of the Garfields felt obligated to help Burke and his wife Mary. The Hinsdales had hoped for an appointment in Europe, but Garfield found none available that provided an adequate salary. The Hawaiian post paid a salary of $7,500, while the next available positions were those of Charge d'Affaires in Denmark or Portugal at $5,000. In June 1881 Garfield wrote Hinsdale that he had directed Secretary of State Blaine to recall Comly so as to provide for his appointment. Garfield offered the attractions of comparatively low living costs and the opportunity for meritorious service. Hinsdale was a Disciples of Christ minister, and Garfield appealed to both his financial and idealistic impulses. The Hawaiian king had just started on a trip around the world, and it was feared that he contemplated either the sale of the islands or a commercial treaty with European powers that would embarrass the United States. "Delicate and important diplomatic work" loomed on the horizon. Hinsdale expressed disappointment that he would miss European travel, but he found consolation in the relatively high salary and the opportunity for rest and work of his own. He prepared to put his affairs into shape, so that he could leave at any time that seemed desirable after two or three weeks.[33] But all of this planning was abruptly altered, when twelve days later the President was shot down by a disappointed office seeker in a Washington railroad station. Hinsdale went to Washington and spent much time at the White House. He even preached a sermon eulogizing the wounded President at Garfield's church, the Vermont Avenue Christian Church.[34] For weeks Garfield's life was in the balance, and with it the future of Hinsdale as a diplomat. Daggett did not know it, but an interesting period in his own career hinged upon the same uncertainty.

With Garfield's death in September, prospects for the Hawaiian post under Arthur, the new President, were clouded in doubt. On May 8, 1882, Comly asked for a two-month leave of absence to visit the United States.[35] John Sherman, the Republican Senator from Ohio, fully realizing the conflicting forces at work in the party in his home state, seems to have delayed a new appointment for more than a year. But on April 1, 1882, Senator Jones and George W. Cassidy of Nevada, Senators Miller and James T. Farley of California, Senator James H. Slater of Oregon, Congressmen Horace F. Page, Campbell C. Berry,

Romualdo Pacheco of California, and Congressman Melvin C. George of Oregon joined in urging Arthur to appoint Daggett to Hawaii. They asserted that he was "a gentleman of distinguished ability who had had a creditable career in Congress" and "that his appointment would meet with universal approval on the Pacific Coast." The President referred the matter to the State Department.[36]

Arthur was a "Stalwart" Republican, and Daggett had close association with that Republican faction. The wealthy and influential Senator Jones of Nevada, as we have seen, was highly favorable to him, as was the immensely rich John Mackay of Virginia City, a powerful member of the Republican National Committee. On May 15, 1882, Comly received a telegram through the Collector of Customs at San Francisco, notifying him that Arthur wished his resignation. Comly complied at once.[37]

On June 12 Arthur presented his nomination of Daggett for confirmation by the Senate, which confirmed it on July 1. Ten days later Frelinghuysen wrote Daggett, enclosing the necessary official papers, including the commission of his office and the letter of credence to the King. Compensation was to be seventy-five hundred dollars a year with four hundred a year for rent and expenses of the legation. Frelinghuysen remarked: "The Department entertains the confidence that your intelligent and zealous attention to the interests of the United States now confided to your care will be conducive to the harmony and friendly relations existing between the two countries."[38] On August 4, having taken the official oath at Virginia City before Notary Public Ricketts, Daggett sent the document to the Secretary of State. It was asserted that this was the first time a minister to a foreign power had taken the oath in Nevada. Naturally, Daggett was now out of the race for governor of Nevada, and his old cronies felt that they would miss the "jolly and ever-cheerful Daggett."[39]

The San Francisco *Tribune*, pointing to the appointment as another one of "them literary fellows," commented:

> If there is a gentleman in the world constituted by nature and education to adjust himself speedily to the manners and customs of the Cannibal Kingdom it is the same Rollin. He has a fair taste for bananas, is an expert swimmer, a hammock in the shade on a hot day is a regular oasis to him, while the grief of his life for years has been that the manners and customs of civilization seem to impose on poor human nature to wear clothes.

The San Francisco *Chronicle* expressed the belief that the change from Comly was desirable, for he had grossly betrayed the interests of the United States, and has played directly into the hands of the sugar monopoly, which is robbing the Treasury of millions annually. He has purposely closed his eyes to the degrading effects of the contract-labor system on the Islands, and has done all in his power to perpetuate a system as brutalizing as African slavery in its worst aspects.[40]

Secretary of State Frelinghuysen, to whom Daggett would be responsible during his Hawaiian years, was the scion of a noted New Jersey ministerial family. He had had a long career in the Senate and had few enemies but almost completely lacked experience in foreign affairs. After the brilliant but somewhat erratic career of the previous Secretary, James G. Blaine, the Washington *Post* expressed the general belief that Frelinghuysen would provide "a commonplace and routine management of the State Department."[41] Daggett sailed from San Francisco August 9 on the *Suez*, arriving at Honolulu a week later. Next day, when Comly and Daggett called informally on the King and Walter M. Gibson, the Minister of Foreign Affairs, they asked what time would be agreeable for the formal presentation of Daggett's credentials.[42] At the government building, Aliilani Hale, five days later, Comly officially presented the one-time Ohio printer's devil to his Majesty. Daggett in turn presented the King with a letter from President Arthur. His own appropriate remarks concluded with a gesture of good will: "Permit me to assure your Majesty that nothing shall be omitted on my part to promote and cement those friendly political, social, and commercial relations which, rising above all other considerations, make nations kindred, and a brotherhood of mankind." The King replied with a similar ritual of good will.[43]

A few days before, upon Daggett's arrival in Honolulu, there was a stirring impromptu reception for him, with a torchlight procession headed by the Royal Hawaiian Band. Coaches were crowded with young American torchbearers, while transparencies read, "Daggett and McKinley mean Representative protection" and "Stand by the Old Flag." In response Daggett said, "The Yankee is an evangelist, and everywhere, be he chasing whales in the Arctic, gathering cocoanuts in the tropics, or opening up new markets in the South and West, he preaches the Gospel of Freedom."[44]

On August 24 an elaborate farewell dinner was given for Comly in the Hawaiian Hotel. The trees in the courtyard were hung with colored lanterns; vines running over the verandas were provided with red and yellow lights; the pavilion for the band was brilliantly illuminated; and the dining hall was beautifully decorated. The Royal

Hawaiian Band played during dinner and afterward. Peter Cushman Jones, a lawyer of the American community, introduced a large array of speakers, including Comly and Daggett. Guests toasted "The President of the United States," "His Majesty the King," and "Our Late Minister Resident." Then Comly proposed a toast to Daggett, commenting: "Mr. Daggett is like the young cub whose troubles are all before him. [Laughter.] When the trouble does begin, the best luck I can wish him, that he may be like the old maid in the play, 'Always ready and never wanted.'" Daggett replied that he did not like to speak of himself and felt like a Nevadan who was charged with murder. After an hour or two of cross-examination the accused turned to the judge and said that he would prefer to drop the whole matter than be kept on the stand talking about himself. Daggett concluded by paying tribute to the Islands and to Comly.[45]

Sanford B. Dole, a prominent lawyer who later played a major role in events leading up to the annexation of Hawaii to the United States, commented:

> Mr. Daggett speaks of these Islands, meeting place of Oriental and Western and Eastern civilizations as sacred ground; it seems to me that it is likely to be a rather hot place and that our community may be in the position of a kernel of corn between two millstones. [Laughter and applause.] But we feel sure that America will not forget the descendants of her citizens, who while they might have honorably stood aloof, willingly marched to her assistance in her great struggle for the supremacy of Representative Government, and will not without protest, see the work of her sons and their descendants in the direction of Representative and Constitutional Government here swept away. [Applause.][46]

At this dinner Peter Cushman Jones contended that American interests were not sufficiently represented in the government, the result being essentially "taxation without representation."

The enthusiasm for the United States associated with the impromptu ovation for Daggett and the farewell dinner for Comly thrilled American residents. Some believed that these occasions had not given opportunity for the rank and file of Americans in Hawaii to show respect for Daggett, so a committee of fifteen planned to arrange a popular formal reception in his honor. Daggett appears to have given tentative approval to the project, but both Dole and Jones were of New England background and, not without reason, they looked upon the "Palace Party" as inefficient and corrupt. Daggett apparently was somewhat disturbed by the aggressive Americanism associated with the Comly reception and with the proposed occasion. He declined the offer, expressing his "profoundest thanks" but pointing out that two public occasions and the length of time since his arrival in the Islands counselled against another reception at that time. This declination definitely disturbed members of the committee. In reporting the matter to Frelinghuysen, Daggett said that at the dinner for Comly some of the speeches attacked the ministry and even the government itself. Such utterances, he believed, were "out of place," and he had declined another reception because of the previous "radical" expressions, which, if repeated, might lead to "intemperance of action."[47]

The outward condition of the legation property was not attractive. Daggett reported that the official records were in good condition but that the library was of little value, the furniture scant and almost worthless, and the flagstaff rotten and unusable. He at once ordered a new flagstaff, planned needed repairs, and proceeded to rent a number of spacious cottages on the grounds of the Hawaiian Hotel, where he had the archives of the legation transferred.[48]

Daggett, unlike Comly, reveled in the hospitality and honor bestowed upon him and wrote a Nevada friend of the warmth of his welcome. Soon the Carson City *Appeal* was predicting that in less than a month he would be riding about the country with the King on the most intimate terms. The paper remarked that Daggett's friends would not be surprised to learn within a year or so that he had married into the royal family.

Daggett, with his irrepressible penchant for writing, was ever quick to grasp the pen and had been in Honolulu scarcely a month when he wrote Secretary Frelinghuysen his observations on the Hawaiian political situation, based upon "conversations with representative men who assist largely in creating opinion and in shaping political events." Daggett remarked that some days before his arrival the legislature had adjourned and that it was apparently completely under native control. This he found not surprising, in view of the fact that natives outnumbered Americans almost ten to one and the ballot was given only to native and naturalized citizens. He declared that two motives seemed at work as the voters chose legislators. One was that a loan might be effected and necessary appropriations made for the coronation of the King in February 1883. The other was the possible repeal of the long-established law forbidding sale of liquor to natives. Daggett, who thoroughly enjoyed liquor, claimed that "the missionary influence" had been responsible for the law, but that commercial and other interests were changing the situation so that the natives deemed the law "a grievous humiliation," since even native-born high officials had been denied privileges accorded to others. After October 1, 1882, liquor was to be sold to natives under certain restraints. Daggett expressed his opinion: "I do not think the privilege will be greatly abused. The natives of these islands are a singularly tractable, lighthearted, noncombative, and law-abiding people, and unlike the North American Indian and other meat-eating natives of colder climates, do not generally crave alcoholic stimulants."[49] Historians of Hawaii hardly agree that Daggett was a reliable prophet in this regard. One of them declares that repeal led to "evil consequences."[50]

Daggett from the time of his arrival cultivated frequent contacts with King Kalakaua. Thus, when the United States Steamship *Alaska* arrived at Honolulu early in September 1882, he took occasion to present the commanding officer, Captain George E. Belknap, and other officers and notables to the monarch.[51]

On August 26 Daggett asked the State Department to grant him a leave of not more than fifteen days to visit the various islands of the Kingdom. The leave was granted, but the expense of the trip was to be his responsibility. In October the new minister took a trip on the steamer *Likelike*[52] to visit the island of Maui with the King's sister Princess Liliuokalani, her husband John O. Dominic, Governor of the island of Oahu, and Captain Belknap of the *Alaska*. Making a pleasant run of nine hours they reached Lahaina, where bouquets and leis were sent out to the Princess and other visitors. Continuing their journey, a few hours later they were ready to land at Maalaea Bay, where horses had been provided for them by their host, Judge Kuihelani. After breakfast they were taken across the narrow isthmus to Wailuku, where they inspected various plantations and spent the night at the Judge's home. Later, a special train took them to Kahului and Spreckelsville (named for the San Francisco sugar refiner), where they inspected the sugar mills and machinery. Then they visited Paia and, returning to Kahului, they visited various persons of prominence. Journeying via Lahaina, they found the Governor's residence profusely decorated with leis, flowers, and lanterns and the shores lined with torchbearers. There Dominic, Belknap, and Daggett made a brief visit to the shore, but the people of Lahaina were disappointed that the Princess did not join them. Daggett found the trip immensely enjoyable and expressed his interest in repeating the excursion at almost any time. The following week he made another visit to the same island and then to the island of Hawaii, where he inspected numerous sugar plantations.[53]

Daggett had a shrewd sense of the importance of state occasions and patriotic celebrations for the popular imagination. On November 28, 1882, in accordance with custom, Hawaiian Independence Day was celebrated by a display of flags, a midday salute, and a military parade. Daggett thought that the native people showed very little enthusiasm, but good relations with the United States were emphasized by the Royal Band and military units paying their respects to the American Legation. Daggett made a congratulatory call on the King.[54]

During the same month Daggett stimulated wide observance of the American Thanksgiving Day. Services were held at the two English-speaking churches, Fort Street Church and St. Andrew's Cathedral. Daggett issued a notice inviting American citizens to attend the Fort Street Church. The King and Queen attended with other dignitaries. This ceremony at Fort Street Church was definitely a step in the enhancement of American influence, for that church was of Congregational affiliation, representing New England missionary traditions, in contrast to the Episcopal church, which had been looked upon as strengthening English influence and continuance of the native monarchy.[55]

At the service Daggett made some introductory remarks and read President Arthur's Thanksgiving Proclamation. Then the choir and congregation sang a Thanksgiving Hymn he had composed for the occasion.[56] After the church service the King visited the American Legation and spoke of the great development of the United States and of Hawaii's friendship for the Republic. A year later Daggett was again to issue an official notice of the Thanksgiving service at Fort Street Church.[57]

During these early months of Daggett's residence in Hawaii, the King was preparing to occupy an elaborate new palace, which cost the taxpayers $343,595. The King was a Mason, and on December 27, 1882, celebrated as St. John's Day by Masonic orders, there was a formal palace opening with Masonic bodies of Honolulu attending en masse in full evening dress and regalia. Speeches were made by various Masonic leaders, with Daggett, himself a Mason, concluding:

> For the benefit of the substantial charities of our Order we pay dues to our lodges; but there are dues to the Grand Lodge above which must be met—not in gold or silver or precious stones, but in cheering the hopeless, in raising the lowly, and in assisting the weak so that when at last we are called to final refreshment in "that house not made with hands," eternal in the heavens, we may not be found delinquent on the ledgers kept by the Record-

ing Angel there; and with these dues paid our paths will be made
luminous through the paths of darkness leading up to everlasting
love and light, where the fundamentals of Free Masonry find
expression in the inscrutable dynamics of the universe and in
the wisdom and mercy of God. [Loud and continuous applause.][58]

The outstanding ceremonial of the period was of course the be-
lated coronation of the King and Queen on February 12, 1883, nine
years after their accession, as a means of strengthening the prestige
and influence of the monarchy. As early as September 15, 1882, Daggett had suggested that at least one American vessel of war be present
at the coronation. He indicated that no political trouble was expected
but that the presence of the vessel would have a wholesome effect on
American interests in the Islands. Shortly thereafter he informed authorities in Washington that this was all the more important because
"not improbably" all of the British Pacific squadron would be in the
Islands at the time of the coronation. Daggett was gratified to learn
in November that the Navy Department planned to provide at least
two American vessels to be at Honolulu at the time of the coronation.
The *Lackawanna* arrived on January 25, and the *Wachusetts* on February 3. Daggett saw that their officers were presented to the King.
By that time the English *Mutine* and the French *Limier* were in the
harbor. Soon Sugi Magoshichiro, Envoy Extraordinary and Minister
Plenipotentiary, arrived from Japan. Daggett was present at a dinner
given by the Hawaiian government in the Japanese envoy's honor on
February 3, and at one given by the Japanese minister six days later.[59]

The coronation took place in a pavilion and amphitheatre in front
of the palace, decorated with the coats-of-arms of the nations of the
earth. Representatives of the principal countries were in attendance.
The ritual combined European precedents with the sacred observances
of the native kingdom. A costly jeweled crown, a scepter, and a sword
of state, all made in Europe, were used. The King placed the royal
crowns (never to be worn again) upon his own head and the
Queen's.[60]

The American vessels, the *Wachusetts* and the *Lackawanna*, gave
the traditional twenty-one-gun salute at sunrise, sunset, and at the
conclusion of the coronation ceremonies. Daggett, along with the
United States Consul and most of the American naval officers, attended the ceremonies in full dress. Rank was bestowed on a number
of princes and princesses, and twenty-three convicts were pardoned.
The observances continued for two more weeks. On February 14

Daggett attended the unveiling of a statue of King Kamehameha I. On later occasions fireworks, the conferring of decorations, a state ball, a native feast, a regatta, and other races were attractions that commanded Daggett's interest. February 22 was not only Washington's birthday, the observance of which Daggett had marked by flag displays and a twenty-one-gun salute by the *Lackawanna,* but Daggett's fifty-second birthday. Calls at the legation were numerous, and in the evening a concert, with the King in attendance, was given in Daggett's honor by the Royal Hawaiian Band at the Hawaiian Hotel.[61]

On March 21 the *Lackawanna* departed for Callao, Peru. Daggett wrote that while he was not disposed to give much heed to "threats of coming political disorders, made and repeated here and elsewhere," the presence of a United States war vessel was "a guaranty of peace and a ceaseless benefit to commercial interests" in the Islands. On April 17 the *Wachusetts* also left for Callao, so only a Russian and a German war vessel remained, and these were soon to leave. Daggett reported that many American merchants and businessmen had requested that the *Wachusetts* remain, as they feared that the Chinese might prove aggressive and lawless and that the Hawaiian government would be unable to cope with the situation. About six weeks later an American vessel, the *Hartford,* came into port and remained until June 18, when the *Essex* arrived.[62]

In 1883 Daggett's interest in emphasizing American ceremonial occasions resulted in the first public observance of Memorial Day in Honolulu. Most business houses were closed, and flags were at half-mast throughout the city. Daggett joined officers from the *Hartford* in a parade in which the Royal Hawaiian band and about a hundred carriages took part. The local G.A.R. post of over thirty members then decorated the graves of three or four Union veterans. Thereafter, Memorial Day was observed in the Hawaiian Islands."[63]

On the Fourth of July that year many business houses for the first time closed in celebration. The Palace was illuminated, many gun salutes were fired, the King and his ministers attended the exercises of the day, and there was a ball in the evening. Daggett was chairman of the day.[64]

The government newspaper, the Honolulu *Pacific Commercial Advertiser,* commented on the occasion:

We attribute this feeling of unanimity amongst the Americans in a great measure to the prudent and patriotic course pursued by Mr. Daggett, the American minister resident, who has, we doubt not, subserved the purpose of his Government in fostering and maintaining a spirit of friendship and hearty accord with the people and Government of these islands, and in keeping alive legitimate American interests.[65]

Soon Daggett was to pay a visit to the mainland. In May he had sought a leave of absence to attend to "urgent business" on the Pacific Coast. He received permission late in July, leaving on the next steamer for the mainland. At that time he at once visited Virginia City, where he had long been a leading citizen. There a petition nine feet long, signed by citizens of the area, asked him to lecture on the Hawaiian Islands. He declined with the statement that United States laws did not permit a minister to lecture on the country to which he was accredited.[66]

He soon had more intimate considerations in mind. He returned to the San Francisco Bay area, where his more than six years as a widower came to an end. On October 1 he married Lizzie Hinds of Seattle, the eldest of three sisters and "an heiress." Her stepfather was Captain Marshall, well known as a shipmaster all over the Puget Sound area. The very quiet ceremony, with a sister of the bride as an attendant, and with the usual reception, was performed in Oakland, California.[67] The young lady, just a little over twenty-one years of age "and quite pretty," may have visited Hawaii on one of the vessels of which her stepfather was shipmaster. Daggett was thirty-one years her senior, but he was known for his extraordinary personal magnetism, and the aura associated with the position of minister-resident probably did not detract from his impression on the young lady. A week after their wedding the couple arrived in Honolulu. The bridegroom took pains to thank the Secretary of State for the leave of absence and stated that he had returned "refreshed, re-invigorated, and re-married." Previous to this time he had resided at the Hawaiian Hotel, but now the bridegroom and his bride established a residence on Alakea Street.[68]

Daggett had first arrived in Hawaii in 1882, when King Kalakaua, who had become the ruler in 1874 was running into serious trouble, and we have already considered the diplomat's early reactions to the situation. The difficulties were deep seated, involving tensions between native and Western interests, between English and American influences, between missionary and avowed secular leaders, and between rival members of the native dynasty. When Kalakaua was chosen King in 1874, the cabinet and American interests favored him, while the British favored Queen Dowager Emma. It was believed that with Emma on the throne there would be no hope for a reciprocity treaty with the United States. The movement for Emma prevailed on the island of Oahu, where Honolulu is located, but had no time to spread to the other islands. It was generally believed that bribery secured Kalakaua's election by the legislature.[69] Although many natives and foreigners alike loved Emma and respected her splendid traits, they had little confidence in her as a political leader.[70] This may be one reason for her defeat.

To protest Kalakaua's victory, a howling mob of Emma's partisans surrounded the courthouse, sacked the buildings, and assaulted the legislators with clubs, although the mobs generally refrained from violence to foreigners out of fear of intervention by the man-of-war in port. H. A. Pierce, then United States Minister, had anticipated the riot and had agreed with Commander Belknap of the U.S.S. *Tuscarora* and the Commander of the *Portsmouth* upon a signal for landing troops. Finally, the Hawaiian Minister of Foreign Affairs appealed to the United States Minister and the British Commissioner to help put down the riot. One hundred and fifty United States marines and seventy British servicemen thereupon quickly dispersed the mob and arrested a number of those involved.[71]

On the next day Kalakaua was sworn in as King under protection of American troops. Ironically, the King, who earlier in his career had led in anti-American agitation, now owed his life and throne to United States intervention. For several years thereafter he depended on the support of the foreign community. In October 1874 Elisha H. Allen and H. A. P. Carter went to Washington to negotiate a treaty of reciprocity. Next month the King embarked on the U.S.S. *Benicia,* placed at his disposal by the United States. He was well received in the United States and returned to Honolulu in February 1875. A treaty had already been concluded, and the Hawaiian legislature ratified it July 18, 1876, after stubborn opposition, especially from English members of the House and partisans of Queen Emma, who denounced it as a step toward annexation. By this time the King, who had long believed that a monarch should rule, not merely reign, became more aggressive. The Reciprocity Treaty brought a boom in sugar. Claus Spreckels, who had been a leading sugar refiner in San Francisco, having acquired land in Hawaii for a sugar plantation sought extensive irrigation privileges on the island of Maui. When the ministers proved unfavorable to this, the King requested their resignations without stating the reason for their dismissal. Constitutionally, he had this right, but such arbitrary action was without precedent in Hawaiian history and was looked upon as a dangerous innovation. Next day a new cabinet formed and granted Spreckels the water priv-

ilege for thirty years at five hundred dollars a year. Spreckels thereafter became a malevolent influence in Hawaiian affairs.[72]

Some endeavored to improve the situation but without success. By
1880 another crisis had developed. Long a power in the government
was Walter Murray Gibson, a former Mormon leader. Born at sea while
his parents were migrating from England, he grew up in New York
and New Jersey. Later he was an adventurer in California, Guatemala,
and the Dutch East Indies, then went to Utah, where he embraced
Mormonism and interested Brigham Young in a grandiose scheme
for disposing of Mormon interests in Utah and establishing the Latter
Day Saints in Hawaii. He went to Hawaii in 1861, acquired large
tracts of land which he held in his own name, and was expelled from
the church in 1864. By 1880 he was a close confidant of the King and
sought to appear as the champion of native Hawaiians.[73] He also
courted missionary favor, as he professed conversion, attended prayer
meetings, and spoke in favor of temperance. At this time the King
was especially influenced by an Italian adventurer, Celso Caesar
Moreno, who sought a subsidy for a steamship line to China. A syco-
phant, Moreno had encouraged the Monarch's desires for a loan of
ten million dollars, largely for military purposes. Moreno, by bribery,
was able to secure the granting of the ship subsidy. He paid the King
and his henchmen to press it through the legislature, but the subsidy
was never to be paid. Then the King dismissed his cabinet once more
and installed Moreno as Prime Minister. The foreign community de-
tested Moreno. Diplomatic representatives of the United States, Great
Britain, and France declared that they would have no further official
intercourse with the government so long as Moreno was premier. A
popular meeting of indignation was held, with the result that the
foreign community united with native support to remove Moreno from
office. Five days later Moreno was out.

Soon the King began a tour around the world.[74] The American
government was much concerned about the effects of this tour upon
American influence. Such was the situation when Daggett entered
upon his duties in Honolulu in the summer of 1882. Now the King
proceeded to pursue a policy that appeared to repudiate every ideal
of statesmanship, and the adventurous and unscrupulous Gibson, who
became head of the cabinet in 1882, aided and abetted him.

During the next half-decade Gibson held each of the cabinet
positions, on occasion several of them simultaneously. Other ministers
were in and out of office, but Gibson stayed on. He was intelligent,
had acquired an extensive practical education, and was extremely
shrewd. Some of his ideas were constructive, but he was selfish, un-

scrupulous, and often ruthless, with the result that Hawaii suffered under Tammany-like political chicanery.[75]

The year 1882 marked a high point in political corruption. Over twenty-four thousand acres of land were transferred to Claus Spreckels to settle a claim he had purchased for ten thousand dollars. As has already been noted, a long-established prohibition against providing intoxicating liquors to the natives was lifted. The appropriation bill amounted to twice the expected revenues and led to such difficulties that the next July Daggett reported to the Department of State that he was taking an early opportunity "to urge upon the Government, in a friendly spirit," some further reductions in expenditures. In order to flatter the King's vanity, sanction was given for the issuance of silver coins bearing his features. Spreckels arranged to have these coined at the San Francisco mint and profited to the extent of $150,000 from the arrangement.[76]

In 1883 the cabinet was again reconstructed and for some time Gibson occupied the most important positions.[77] Then the powerful Spreckels decided to support Gibson and supposedly would add strength to the ministry. One observer commented that this could hardly augur well, for Spreckels always demanded *quid pro quo* for any service rendered. A. Francis Judd, of a missionary family and chancellor of the Kingdom, wrote early in 1883 that Gibson had unjustly dismissed three members of the Board of Education so as to get that bureau in his own hands. Judd hoped for radical reform by stimulating native sentiment for good government, but he lamented, "I am not too sanguine, as I know how fickle they are."[78] In the elections of 1883 only three white men were elected to office, and a reaction against Gibson and Spreckels took place. Paul Neumann, an American citizen, was appointed Attorney General in place of Gibson. Daggett believed that Neumann was a man of unusual abilities and "thoroughly American in sentiment." But Neumann did not please American capitalists, such as S. B. Dole, and after a time he was sharply referring to Dole's "boyishness" and "fractious spirit."[79]

In 1884 reaction against Gibson and his crowd continued, and eight or nine foreign-born legislators who, according to Daggett, were fairly representative of "the commercial interests of the Kingdom were chosen." The American Minister looked upon this as "fortunate" and as serving "to operate as a restraint to extravagance." Gibson, Spreckels, and their friends endeavored to secure a charter for a dubious "state bank" and to set up a lottery. They also offered an opium-licensing bill. Great bitterness developed. Resolutions against the ministry (especially Gibson), signed by 1,590 persons, were presented on June 23. A few days later Gibson was knocked down upon leaving the legislative hall but was not seriously injured.[80]

The Banking Bill was defeated, and a more equitable general banking act was passed. The lottery bill was withdrawn, and the opium bill was defeated. In spite of the heavy government patronage exercised to promote the passage of these bills, resistance was such that responsible citizens could rejoice that much evil had been prevented.

But in 1886, the year after Daggett's departure from Hawaii, legislation giving the government the right to sell the opium monopoly license for thirty thousand dollars was passed. Other scandals of the time involved sale of public offices, defrauding of customs revenues by the abuse of royal privilege, illegal leasing of lands to the King, neglect of public roads, and sale to lepers of exemption from segregation. Daggett had been realistic enough to realize that, while much indignation against fraud and corruption properly existed among both native and foreign-born elements, a constructive charge was difficult, for "capable and conscientious men" were far from "plentiful."[81]

Daggett had early been concerned about aspects of the Hawaiian government's financial situation. In 1883 he had reported to the Secretary of State that the deficit for the previous fiscal year was $201,900, with expenditures of $1,385,531. He also had become concerned, as had Hawaiian businessmen, about the large circulation of Hawaiian silver coins, the minting of which had profited Spreckels.[82] Daggett was especially distressed over the silver inflation which meant that silver coins were at a discount of 5 to 8 per cent. Being accepted for customs duties, these coins in effect lowered the value of the duties collected and thereby decreased the benefits accruing to products from the United States, imported under the Reciprocity Treaty of 1875. An involved exchange of correspondence followed, concerned with the intricacies of foreign exchange, but Gibson finally admitted that there seemed to be "a manifest departure from the intention of the treaty—a departure which the Government" had "no desire to countenance." The fact that gold was at a heavy premium resulted in the failure of the Hawaiian government to enforce the law requiring customs duties to be paid in United States gold. Daggett pressed for action on this matter, and the legislature passed a Gold Standard Act, which required duties to be collected in United States gold beginning on August 1.[83] Naturally, this seemed something of a personal victory for the American Minister.

But economic problems continued, as the "spend-thrift policy of

Kalakaua was glaringly obvious."[84] Daggett reported to Washington in mid-January 1885 that a "general business depression" had developed which was "beginning to test the financial standing, not only of the retail dealers of Honolulu, but of many wholesale houses of reputed strength and responsibility." The large indebtedness of the sugar and other industries, the marked decrease in the price of raw sugar, and the apparent excessive circulation of silver coins contributed to the distress. To alleviate the situation, the Hawaiian government proceeded to retire from circulation over two hundred thousand dollars in Hawaiian silver coins. Other steps were taken, but serious, even alarming, problems persisted as Daggett came to the close of his Hawaiian Mission.[85]

VIII

Reciprocity and
Return to Private Life

MANY OF THE PROBLEMS BETWEEN THE UNITED STATES AND HAWAII during the years of Daggett's ministry were deeply rooted in early developments.[1] One of the important questions of the later years was continued reciprocity of trade with the United States. Congress had rejected proposed reciprocity treaties with Hawaii in 1855 and 1867.[2] But, when King Kalakaua visited Washington in January 1875, Hamilton Fish, Grant's Secretary of State, concluded a highly significant reciprocity treaty with the King's plenipotentiaries, Elisha H. Allen and Henry A. P. Carter. The United States was to abolish duties on a short list of Hawaiian products, including sugar, and Hawaii agreed to place a long list of United States products on the free list.[3] The Hawaiian legislature and the United States Senate ratified the treaty almost at once, but strong protectionist sentiment in the House stalled acceptance of the measure.[4] In 1867, in general, support for reciprocity was looked upon as giving aid to a movement toward annexation, but a group of undetermined strength opposed reciprocity as tending to hinder annexation.[5] Now, in May 1876, the House grudgingly acquiesced, as Hawaii's strategic position for the United States was emphasized.[6] The treaty could be terminated at the end of seven years or at any time thereafter. This immediately stimulated production of rice and sugar and especially redounded to the benefit of Claus Spreckels, who had gone to California in the Gold Rush and later became the largest sugar refiner on the Pacific Coast. Originally opposed to ratification of the Treaty of 1875, as he feared Hawaiian competition, he proceeded to capitalize on the situation. Taking advantage of the new treaty, he entered into arrangements with Hawaiian planters to send their raw sugar to his California refining mills duty free. He also invested heavily in the Hawaiian

146

economy. Going to the Islands in person, he developed important interests in Hawaiian plantations and secured valuable water rights for irrigation from the native government. Since independent sugar producers were virtually forced to sell their sugar to his California refineries, by 1880 Spreckels enjoyed a practical monopoly of the Hawaiian sugar crop.[7]

United States Treasury officials and sugar and rice interests in the United States became alarmed. Hayes's Secretary of the Treasury, John Sherman, was informed in August 1878 that the reciprocity duties were one-sided and that the agreement was costing the United States more in loss of duties than the entire gain in exports to the Islands. In succeeding years Spreckels and other investors expanded into importing and transportation lines and also moved into politics. As American investments grew, sentiment for annexation became vocal, and Great Britain and Germany sought trading privileges to counteract the trend. The American Minister, Comly, was able to secure recognition by the Hawaiian government that American reciprocity privileges were exclusive.[8]

In the United States eastern sugar refiners, anti-Spreckels newspapers in California, and Louisiana mouthpieces of the cane sugar interests there raised a cry against continuing reciprocity. Henry A. Brown of Saxonville, Massachusetts, had opened a nine-year campaign as the leading champion of domestic sugar and rice. Eastern sugar refiners, Chambers of Commerce in Atlantic Coast communities, and representatives of southern rice and sugar bombarded Congress with petitions for the abrogation of the Convention, and bills to that effect were introduced into Congress. Representatives of the other side of the question stressed the importance of American interests in Hawaii in competition with those of Great Britain. As 1882, the year for possible termination of the agreement, approached the old arguments pro and con were clearly emphasized. It soon became evident that the Senate was unwilling to terminate the convention or extend it. Hawaii's basic prosperity, however, was contingent upon continuing trade, and the Kingdom pressed for assurance that the Convention would be officially extended and not depend upon American sufferance.[9]

In his Annual Messages of 1882 and 1883 President Arthur urged extending the arrangements for another seven years. Daggett, commenting on the reference to reciprocity in the Message of 1882, stated that he believed Hawaiian sentiment would favor, and the government there could not successfully oppose, complete reciprocity as a consideration for continuance of the treaty. This, he believed, would make the "Islands a commercial dependency of the United States, and irrevocably assign their future to the control of American sentiment." Daggett of course was actively involved in numerous disputes between Americans and the Hawaiian government as to the proper interpretation of the treaty provisions. Americans in the Islands insisted that the treaty provisions for the free entry of American "manufactures of wood and metal" included pianos and parlor organs. Protracted negotiations led the Hawaiian government to yield to the American contention.[10]

This controversy prompted Daggett to comment to Frelinghuysen that the treaty provisions were not very specific and were subject to varying interpretations. He suggested that a detailed schedule of all articles exempt from duty be drawn up and agreed upon.

He also became intimately concerned with discussions as to whether the treaty was being used as a cover for unlawful procedures, especially as alleged evidence was presented that sugar shipments were being illegally imported into the United States as products of the Hawaiian Islands under cover of the Reciprocity Treaty.

In December 1882 Frelinghuysen asked Daggett to investigate the charge that Chinese sugar was being taken to Hawaii and then sent to the United States as products of the Islands so as to take advantage of the Reciprocity Treaty. Daggett reported in March 1883 that he found "after careful investigation" that only four vessels (two British and two German) had entered the Islands from China and that no sugar was discharged by them. He asserted that secret landing would be difficult, for only at Honolulu could freight be discharged without the aid of lighters. In a few islets freight might be landed, but only in daylight when the channels were calm. Chinese sugar, moreover, differed in texture from the Hawaiian product and would have to be mixed with Hawaiian sugar to avoid detection. Thus, Daggett concluded that Chinese sugar had not been imported into the United States via Hawaii as Hawaiian sugar.[11]

But the Collector of Customs at San Francisco and the United States Consul at Hong Kong continued to express fears on this score. The latter, John S. Mosby, writing in April to Collector C. L. Sullivan at San Francisco, stated that the steamer *Glenelg* had cleared from Hong Kong for Honolulu with eight hundred tons of sugar on board and that other ships were about to leave, all apparently intending to land the sugar in California as a Hawaiian product. Frelinghuysen and the Secretary of the Treasury, Charles J. Folger, concerned themselves with the matter. Accordingly, Daggett investigated the case of the three ships, the *Glenelg*, the *Madras*, and the *Livingstone*, which had arrived from China during the first five months of 1883. He received sworn statements about the *Glenelg* from the consignees of the cargo, from the Hawaiian Collector General, and from a customs guard on duty on the vessel, and comparable testimony about the *Madras*. As a result, he gave an unequivocal answer regarding these vessels: "From none of them have sugars been discharged in any port of these islands either illicitly or by payment of duties." Frelinghuysen, pleased with Daggett's careful inquiry, wrote him, "I desire to compliment you and to thank you for the very full and ample report which you have submitted on the subject.[12]

By this time Folger had appointed a commission (O. L. Spaulding, John E. Searles, Jr., and A. K. Tingle) to inquire into the charges of smuggling. After a thorough investigation of several months in San Francisco, Portland, and the Hawaiian Islands, the commission reported that it could find no substantiating evidence. Allegation of fraud, the committee report indicated, appeared to have no foundation other than the fact that there had been a tremendous increase in the quantity of sugar sent to the United States under the treaty, but this increase could be explained as evidence of the success of reciprocal trade.[13]

Daggett personally favored not only continuing reciprocity but enlarging its scope. Recognizing sugar-raising as the paramount interest of the Islands, he asserted: "The abrogation of our reciprocity treaty would be severely felt in these islands, for under its operation property values have everywhere increased, especially in real estate, and every industry has prospered." Since 75 per cent of Hawaiian imports were from the United States, and 18 per cent of those from the United States had a duty on them, he favored "absolute reciprocity." This, he declared, "would not only relieve our commerce of duties on this 18 per cent of our exports to these islands but would virtually put an end to the direct trade with other foreign countries, and correspondingly increase our own, for the imports from Europe consist mainly of such commodities as are subject to duty under our treaty."[14]

On June 9, 1884, President Arthur sent the Senate a request from the Hawaiian King to extend the reciprocity agreement seven years, and the President asked the advice of the Senate "before directing the negotiations to proceed." Although the Senate voted to postpone action, on December 6, 1884, Secretary of State Frelinghuysen proceeded to arrange an agreement with Hawaii extending the Convention for seven years. Daggett's services in this connection were at an end, for the agreement was not ratified until after the new

Cleveland Administration and a new minister to Hawaii had come upon the scene.[15]

The very success of reciprocity so stimulated the sugar industry that a severe labor problem arose. The native population had declined so that in 1875 the number reached a low point in the nation's history. The decline continued, so that in 1884 Daggett reported to the Secretary of State that over a period of four and a half years, beginning in 1879, Hawaiian deaths numbered 11,254 while births were 9,150. Some of the fatalities were due to the smallpox epidemic of 1881, while 583 occurred at the leper colony of Molokai.[16]

As early as 1850 native labor had not been equal to the demands of the developing sugar industry, and the Royal Hawaiian Agricultural Society was established to cope with the problem. Although whaling was the mainstay of economic life at that time, 180 Chinese coolies were imported in 1852 to work on sugar plantations. After 1870 the whaling industry was rapidly dying, and sugar became increasingly important. American and European labor were not favorable to Hawaiian employment because of low wages, the greater opportunities in the United States and Australia, and the remoteness of the labor field (Europeans faced the heavy expense of the trip around Cape Horn). China, on the other hand, seemed to provide a convenient source of labor, and the Hawaiian Masters and Servants Act of 1850 had legalized contract labor. Anyone over twenty-one could contract to provide his service for not more than five years. Contracts executed in a foreign country for labor to be performed in Hawaii, moreover, were legal.[17]

The Chinese were in many respects desirable workers, but many of them sought the personal independence possible for them as operators of small stores or vegetable farms. Planters were dominantly interested in an adequate labor supply at the lowest cost, while the Hawaiian government was becoming concerned that unmarried Chinese men in numbers presented an abnormal and undesirable social situation. Some opposition arose to the Chinese laborers, especially as they were deemed responsible for introducing the smallpox epidemic of 1881. For a time the Hawaiians had looked to Polynesia, the Azores (Portuguese), and India as sources of supply. But the United States feared that laborers from India would enhance Britain's interest in the Islands. Blaine, as Secretary of State in 1881, declared that immigration of Chinese and Anglo-Indians could not be permitted to the Hawaiian Islands in wholesale numbers, for "the Hawaiian Islands cannot be joined to the Asiatic system. If they drift from their independent station it must be toward assimilation and identification with the American system." Blaine even suggested that labor trained in the rice swamps and cane fields of the South might be used instead. After he retired in December 1881, it soon became apparent that Hawaii had abandoned the idea of introducing laborers from India, and those from the Polynesian Islands had proved unsatisfactory. Consequently Daggett, as United States minister, had to consider chiefly the problem presented by the Chinese. By 1883 a thousand Chinese laborers were in quarantine at Honolulu, and over four thousand more were en route to the Islands. The trend accelerated because of removal of restrictions previously imposed in China and the Chinese Exclusion Act of 1882 in the United States.[18]

As Chinese flocked to urban life in Honolulu, Hawaiians feared that the influx might change their own way of life drastically. In April 1883 Daggett reported that there were about twelve thousand Chinese in Hawaii. Four thousand were on plantations as laborers, while the rest were rice planters, gardeners, shopkeepers, fishermen, tailors, boot- and shoemakers, domestics, and peddlers. Daggett stated that they were "steadily depriving the natives of their means of support and that a continued increase in the numbers of these laborers would hasten the destruction of the native people and eventually render it difficult for the Hawaiian government to protect the large foreign investments that dominated the commercial life of the Islands. Daggett personally had presented the gravity of these dangers to the King and Gibson, the Foreign Minister. As a result, the Hawaiian consul General at Hong Kong was instructed to discourage further Chinese immigration to the Islands. A few days later, on April 9, the Hawaiian cabinet formally passed a resolution, that, due to the "injurious disproportion of the sexes," there being twenty thousand more males than females in the population, steps should be taken to prevent unrestricted migration.[19]

Daggett reported that shipping interests and sugar magnates looked with disfavor upon this curtailment of cheap labor. On July 13 the Hawaiian cabinet rescinded the resolution of April 9 and authorized the arrival, under certain restrictions, of not more than six hundred laborers in any six months. As a result of the change in policy, on July 14 Gibson wrote to T. Bulkley Johnson, the British Consul General at Hong Kong, that Hawaii had "never been prepared to discountenance a limited immigration of Chinese accompanied by a proportion of females." He further explained that employers of Chinese laborers in Hawaii had stated that a large number of Chinese laborers returned to China each year at the expiration of their contracts, so that now the Hawaiian government deemed it prudent to permit further immigration to replace those departing. The duration of this situation would depend on the results of negotiations pending between Hawaii and China and the character of the migration, including the number of women arriving. Gibson authorized Johnson to permit steamships to bring not more than six hundred passengers in any three months from Hong Kong to Hawaii, but only on vessels of established lines, at that time the Pacific Mail Steamship Company and the Oriental and Occidental Steamship Company. Both of these kept their vessels well equipped and clean, with experienced physicians on board. On July 14 Gibson wrote to H. A. P. Carter, Hawaii's minister to the United States, asking him to inform the Chinese minister there of the terms of the partial resumption of Chinese immigration. It represented "no change of policy" on the part of the Hawaiian government, he wrote, but recognition that the previous emergency appeared to have passed.[20]

For several years the Pacific Mail Steamship Company operated four vessels between San Francisco and Australia, which stopped at intermediary points. Their vessels on the China line also made such stops, as did those of the British line, the Occidental and Oriental. In August 1883 Hawaii granted exclusive privileges to those two companies for carrying Chinese emigrants from China to Hawaii.[21]

But Claus Spreckels, the sugar baron, conniving with Hawaiian officials, soon altered the picture. This business magnate, a large owner in the Oceanic Steam Navigation Company, recently established for trade between San Francisco and Hawaii, informed the Pacific Mail Steamship Company that unless his previous demand that the calling of the company's Australia-bound steamers at Honolulu be discontinued, he would see that its privilege of landing Chinese at that port were abrogated. Understandably, the company declined the proposal. Spreckels was as powerful as he had claimed. On October 15 Gibson served notice that Hawaii had entered into an agreement with the Oceanic Steamship Company, giving it the exclusive privilege to transport Chinese immigrants. Since the Oceanic line did not serve the China-Hawaii route directly, it offered the Occidental and Oriental line the use of its exclusive privilege. The representative of the Pacific Mail line claimed that, if carried out, this would violate the treaty of 1849 between the United States and Hawaii. Daggett took up the complaint of the British government. The Hawaiian government replied that immigration from China was restricted as a matter of sanitary control—a domestic consideration—hence there was no contravention of the treaty. This obviously ignored the definite acknowledgment only a few months earlier of the well-equipped and clean condition of the British company's vessels. By March 1884 the Hawaiian Foreign Minister announced that no steamship company any longer held authority to transport Chinese laborers, so there was no discrimination against the Pacific Mail Steamship Company. In April six hundred Chinese arrived, contracted for under a previous order. Thereafter, no more than twenty-five could be brought on a single vessel.[22] Seemingly under pressure from Spreckels, the Pacific Mail Steamship Company now merely delivered mail but declined passenger and freight traffic, to the definite dissatisfaction of the general public.

But concern regarding dependence on Chinese workers continued. Complaints were based upon opium smoking, smallpox scares, social problems due to a disproportionate number of males, concern over assimilability, and fear of numbers. The workers, moreover, were moving off the plantations, and the result was that Gibson and the King maneuvered to substitute workers from Japan. A special envoy was sent to Japan, offering very favorable terms. In April 1884 Count Inouye, the Japanese Foreign Minister, declared that Japan was willing to permit voluntary migration of Japanese laborers to Hawaii but would not enter into a formal convention before a general revision of the previous treaty of 1871 could be agreed upon. Hawaii, nevertheless, had at long last secured permission for the coming of Japanese laborers. Under the treaty of 1871 only 116 Japanese had entered Hawaii between that year and 1884.[23] In June 1884 Hawaii appropriated fifty thousand dollars to promote this new effort, and Robert W. Irwin, Hawaiian representative in Japan, endeavored to recruit the needed workers.

Early in February 1885 the *City of Tokyo* arrived with 943 Japanese laborers, including 267 women and children. Hawaii paid their passage and guaranteed them wages of nine dollars a month for twenty-six working days. Daggett reported that the newcomers seemed "as a whole, to be a hardy and tractable class of laborers," and that the planters engaged them promptly. With the laborers came Mr. Jiro Nakamura, as Consul of the Japanese Empire, to reside in Honolulu and look after the interest of his countrymen. On June 17 a second shipload of almost 1,000 persons arrived. Subsequently negotiations between Hawaii and Japan formalized the understanding in the Hawaiian-Japanese Labor Convention, signed January 28, 1886, which proved mutually advantageous.[24]

Leprosy had long troubled the Islands. Note was made in 1863 of the rapid spread of the disease, and in 1865 a law was passed aimed at isolating confirmed cases and establishing a receiving hospital for treating early cases. But the disease increased and segregation of course led to bitterness and difficulties of enforcement.[25] Early in 1884 a letter signed by a long list of citizens of foreign states in Hawaii was presented to Daggett, as well as to representatives of Great Britain, France, and Portugal, expressing great anxiety and alarm over the rapid spread of leprosy in the Kingdom.[26] Daggett informed the State Department of his own concern over the situation. Upon investigation three positive cases and nineteen suspected cases were found in the public schools, but the Hawaiian government deemed that it was aware of the situation and that no cause existed for alarm. Unfortunately, a corrupt government was tempted to sell exemptions from segregation to property-holding lepers, and the program of isolation and treatment broke down.[27]

But by this time Cleveland's accession to the presidency meant that Daggett would soon depart from his diplomatic mission. The new Secretary of State, Thomas Bayard, wrote on March 25, 1885, asking for Daggett's resignation, and on April 7 the Senate, having confirmed the nomination of a successor, recalled him.[28]

Daggett's successor was George W. Merrill of Nevada, who arrived in Hawaii June 5. A week later Daggett presented him to the King at Iolani Palace. The monarch expressed sorrow at taking leave "of a gentleman with whom I have enjoyed such pleasant relations" and whose representation at the Court had always "been most honorable and courteous" and tending toward mutual understanding. On June 15, 1885, the Honolulu *Bulletin*, reflecting the regret of the community in a parting "Aloha" to him, commented: "While serving his own country's interests with the utmost fidelity, he leaves no breath of resentment behind him, for either arrogance of meddlesomeness. Society in this capital will miss the ex-minister and his amiable partner for a good while to come."

The same day the King drove down to the wharf to bid good-by to his two congenial friends. The band played "The Star Spangled Banner" as Daggett and his wife left on the *Mariposa* for the United States. The Honolulu *Advertiser* declared that Daggett "took care not to mix up in the domestic policies of the Kingdom. His career was therefore a successful one, and he leaves many true and tried friends behind. . . . We are certain that he will ever be found to be a willing and vigorous champion of the Kingdom and people."[29]

He had indeed acquired a lasting affection for Hawaii and its people, and he never tired of composing poems or giving addresses based on Hawaiian themes. He and his wife returned a year and a half later for a pleasant renewal of friendships. When they left on the

S.S. *Australia* on February 16, 1887, they were "literally weighed down with floriculture."[30]

During his ministry Daggett sought the greatest possible personal remuneration. Early in his diplomatic career he had drawn on the State Department for salary based on his time while in Virginia City "waiting for instructions" and while "in transit to the post of duty." He was informed that he had interpreted the regulations in a way far too favorable to his own interests, but, with some adjustments, an accounting favorable to Daggett was eventually made.[31]

Daggett thoroughly enjoyed his assignment and seemed very reluctant to leave. He loved activity, and because of his long journalistic career diplomatic correspondence was to him something of a diversion, rather than a burden. Always excited by the dramatic, he found delight in patriotic and other celebrations. On the last Fourth of July of his mission, in 1884, the celebration on the grounds of the Hawaiian Hotel included "eloquent" remarks by Daggett, who dealt at some length with the traditions and history of Hawaii and the rapid development of the United States.

Daggett was never a conformist. Indeed, as the following incident illustrates, his disregard of social norms marked him as one who sometimes lacked good taste. After Daggett's arrival in the Islands, he paid a courtesy visit to Queen Dowager Emma in her retirement.[32] She showed him all over her regal residence, described her native art treasures, and finally brought him to a full-length portrait of her son, the Prince of Hawaii, who had died many years before.[33] The portrait, which pictured the young prince in all the bespangled regalia of his exalted rank, amused the American minister, who commented:

"Looks like a pert boy! Trot him out!"
"But, your excellency," protested the Queen, "the lad is dead."
"The h—— you say!" responded the surprised minister.[34]

Daggett seemed to delight in his own unconventionality. In Honolulu he received distinguished visitors in his shirt sleeves, with his suspenders hanging about his hips, his trousers rolled up to his knees, and his legs bare. The legation in Honolulu was furnished after his Virginia City ideas. In his reception room was a round table just about the right size for poker, half a dozen chairs, and a long wooden spigot that passed through the wall into the next room, where it connected with a barrel of whiskey. A tin cup suspended by a chain from the spigot was a constant invitation to imbibe. It is said that the British Commissioner, James H. Wodehouse, was always athirst and that the pledges of friendship and fealty between the

representatives of the great English-speaking nations could be heard
for great distances, in direct relation to the activity of the tin cup.

In September 1883 it was reported that Daggett had been introduced to a book canvasser as a "minister." The agent was somewhat
surprised because there was nothing clerical in Daggett's demeanor,
although he always wore a white necktie and stiff collar in public.
Daggett told the canvasser that he was "damned" glad to get the book
and took his new acquaintance to a bar for a drink, where he recounted stories "about the hula-hula dance" in Tahiti, which made
the companion blush. Continuing, Daggett boasted of "laying the
entire cabinet out" in a game of poker, so the canvasser could not
help but wonder what kind of men were carrying the Gospel to the
Islands.[35]

Apparently Daggett's relations with the King were similar. He
is supposed to have initiated the monarch into the refinements of stud
poker. The King was a man of gracious manners and could converse
easily in English or Hawaiian. He was devoted to music and art and
had strived to advance himself as a speaker and writer. Mark Twain
in 1866 found him to be a young man of dignity "who would do no
discredit to the Kingly office."[36] In spite of his studied, crude eccentricities, Daggett was a man of elaborate courtesy on formal occasions. He possessed wide knowledge of history and literature, and was
gifted with amazing facility in verbal expression. To some degree he
was a "pagan opportunist," a role developed by thirty years of experience on the Comstock. He and the King had much rapport, since
the King was heir to pagan aspects of the Hawaiian traditions. The
two men incurred the stern and even irate disapproval of the missionary element, which deemed their conduct "licentious."

Samuel C. Armstrong, born in the Islands of missionary parents,
and whose father had been for sixteen years Minister of Public
Instruction, was now carrying on a venture in idealism as founder
and head of Hampton Normal and Industrial Institute for Negroes in
Virginia.[37] But he retained deep interest in the affairs of Hawaii, and
in April 1883 he wrote to President Arthur concerning his understanding of the situation in the Islands, as communicated to him by
"gentlemen of the highest repute":

> My object is to secure your attention to the fact, that, under
> the present amiable, intelligent, but utterly incompetent King
> Kalakaua, the Hawaiian people are in a state of physical and
> moral decay through their own weaknesses, and through the
> vices and bad examples of foreigners; and that Mr. Daggett, the

present United States Minister Resident, is from his licentiousness and otherwise, an unsuitable representative of the American nation, which, during the past sixty years, has established the institutions of civilization in that country.[38]

At the time of the funeral of Victoria Kamahumalu of the royal family in 1875, certain pagan sexual rituals were revived. Now Armstrong transmitted information to Arthur regarding the continuance of these. One of his correspondents was the Rev. C. M. Hyde, President of the Punahau Theological Institute at Honolulu. Referring to the "hula" dances, which the King "had had prepared for his own delectation," Hyde commented with indignation: "Think of worshipping Kalakaua's private parts, extolling his licentious practices; acting them out to the life, boasting how many pretty women he had been intimate with . . . how much he had paid for the use of a prostitute in Berlin, etc., etc. I wish Kalakaua could be hooted out of decent society."[39]

Armstrong also sent the President an extract from a private letter received from the Honorable A. F. Judd, of a missionary family, who was serving both as Chancellor and Chief Justice in the Islands. This stated:

> One more disagreeable element here is Minister Daggett. He has not returned a call made on him, so far as I know, and has made no friendships except with Rev. Mr. Gibson, Dominis and a few hotel bummers. He is a low, vulgar, blasphemous fellow of brilliant parts, and if it be true that he represents that the clamor here is but that of a few disappointed "outs" he is a liar too. No pure man can but despise him and he has no influence with Americans. I heartily wish we could have a gentleman here like Genl. Comly. Can you not make some representation to the State Department of his complete unfitness?[40]

Later, after Queen Liliuokalani ascended the throne, some missionaries praised her Christian character. But, when it served their purposes, some of the missionary group denounced her as immoral, wicked, and heathen. They complained about her private life, her countenancing of native "hula" dances, and her favorable attitude toward opium and lottery establishments.[41] But evidence shows that, whatever his personal habits, Daggett had a sophisticated appreciation of the conflict of interest between the native Hawaiians, the missionary element, the foreign business community, and the increasing number of Orientals. He was a realist who worked hard at communicating all available facts concerning matters pertinent to the interests of the Islands and the United States. He was in close touch with the King and with foreign emissaries and spared no pains in securing recognition of commemorative days of the Hawaiian and American traditions. A strong idealistic vein in his make-up was evident in his many speeches and messages. To some these noble utterances may have appeared hypocritical, but Daggett believed that any society must defer to the moral and religious ideals that are often unattained amidst the stresses of life, where "the spirit is willing but the flesh is weak."

Daggett was minister during the years when the Islands were moving toward what seemed inevitable annexation to the United States. Decline in the native population, conflict between native and missionary moral attitudes, lack of disinterested leadership, and economic concerns of American and European residents—all these signs pointed to crisis. Although sympathetic toward the native culture, Daggett stimulated enthusiasm for American traditions and institutions, and probably contributed to the eventual outcome. While he was minister, the political situation was troubled, and the way was was being paved for the crystallization of opinion that "stable government," independent of the native "kanakas," or sorcerers, would be most easily attained by annexation to the United States.[42]

During his residence in Hawaii, Daggett developed new literary interests. Amidst his diplomatic duties, he found time to learn of the legends and traditions of the Islands. He became an intimate friend of the King who, in spite of his weaknesses, was like Daggett a man of considerable learning and culture. Thereafter Daggett often used Hawaiian themes as a basis for his poetic efforts.

One of Daggett's old friends of San Francisco days was Charles Warren Stoddard. Stoddard traveled widely and some of his best-known writings were based upon South Sea and Hawaiian topics.[43] From 1881 to 1884, during part of which time Daggett was minister there, he lived in Hawaii. After the manner of the time, Stoddard kept an "album" to which friends contributed. For this in March 1883 Daggett wrote a poem, "Hookupu," which follows:

> As there was gold and purple in his thought,
> He raised a tall *Kahili** at his door,
> And claiming *Hookupu,*** some hundreds brought
> Fair largess to him; but he wanted more

* A Hawaiian royal emblem.
** A gift from the people to royal Hawaiians.

And down on him his tribute galleon bore,
With guns of love and armament of smiles
Demanding "Words! words! e'en a single line!"
Come forth, O heathen muses of these Isles!
While in your name I offer eight or nine.[44]

The people of Hawaii loved Daggett's poetic flights and he delighted to satisfy them. In July 1883 he contributed a long poem, "Kealumoku's Last Vision," to the Honolulu *Hawaiian Gazette*. The opening lines are:

O Westward turn my face, and let my eyes
Enfold the glories of the sunset skies,
And take them thence in death, to light my way
To Rono's halls and Kane's fadeless day.
For me the clouds will paint the West no more
Nor tireless billows fret the coral shore,
Nor leaf nor blossom come, nor twilight's calm,
Nor morning's kiss beneath the sheltering palm;
For music soft as voice of singing streams,
And whispers sweet as children's guileless dreams,
Lift up my soul and plume it for its flight,
To isles of rest beyond the seas of night.[45]

He also contributed a long narrative poem, "Kaina," named for a noted warrior, a lieutenant of Kamehameha I (1758–1824).[46] His best-known Hawaiian poem was "Waikiki," which the public asked to have republished from time to time. Its eight stanzas closed with the lines:

O Waikiki! O scene of peace!
O home of beauty and of dreams!
No haven in the isles of Greece
Can chord the harp to sweeter themes;
For houries haunt the broad lanais,
While scented zephyrs cool the lea
And looking down from sunset skies
The angels smile at Waikiki.[47]

During his Hawaiian years Daggett contributed to the first issue of the *San Franciscan*, which was announced as a possible rival to the well-established *Argonaut*. Associated with its chief editor, Joseph T. Goodman (of *Territorial Enterprise* fame), were the able Arthur McEwan, Thomas E. Flynn, and W. P. Harrison. The journal paid

"generously" for its stories and articles, but old friends contributed
gratis to the first number (February 16, 1884), which presented "an
array of talent never since equalled in any one issue of a journal in
California or on the Pacific Coast."[48]

Goodman believed that the *Argonaut* had "become snobbish and
entirely subservient to the railroad interest," which had aroused
highly intense antimonopoly feeling on the West Coast.[49] He solicited
contributions from his old Western literary friends, Daggett, Tom
Fitch, Charles W. Stoddard, C. C. Goodwin, Dan De Quille, Sam Davis,
and Mark Twain—all of the old literary group except the individ-
ualistic Bret Harte and the Bohemian with a very irritable disposition,
Charles Henry Webb, who had long before cast his lot with the East.[50]
Seeking a contribution from Mark Twain, Goodman wrote: "Now,
just take a day off . . . as you would to go to a logging-bee, if you
lived in the backwoods—and give us a taste of your quality." But Mark
Twain was a busy, popular author and twice gave a negative response,
causing Goodman to experience his first "setback." Undiscouraged,
Goodman insisted that Twain contribute something, if nothing more
than a congratulatory letter "reviving memories of the old days."
Goodman knew that he would have no such difficulty with Daggett,
who, he told Twain, "has become a public character and likes to see
his name in print in any connection that will give it currency. He
even wanted me to print some doggerel concerning him in the
Argonaut, as he said all that sort of thing helped along a man in
public career."[51]

Mark Twain relented and sent in his contribution, "The Carson
Fossil-Footprints," for which Goodman sincerely thanked him by
saying, "God Bless you for the article."[52] Mark Twain's contribution
dealt with a controversy that arose when he was in Carson City in
1864. Stone was being cut for buildings at the state capitol, when the
stone mason discovered strange imprints of prehistoric birds and
animals, some of the impressions resembling the footprints of a huge
primeval man. The scientific facts gathered from this led to a hotly
debated controversy in the scientific world. By 1885 Mark Twain was
to take delight in hitting at scientists, who were so seriously involved
in the arguments, and at the members of the first Territorial Legislature. So he developed a story that the tracks were really made on
a rainy day by members of the early legislature: "The cave bear tracks
were made by Mr. R. M. Daggett. . . . The tracks attributed to the
old Silurian ass were not made by the old Silurian ass. I made them
myself."[53]

Daggett's contribution was on "Strange Hawaiian Traditions," emphasizing the Hawaiian legends relating to the creation. Daggett accepted a view, then current, that Hawaiians descended from tribes of ancient Hebrews. Daggett concluded that the similarity between the Hawaiian and Hebrew accounts of the creation, the Deluge, and other events recorded in Pentateuch could only "be regarded with wonder." Daggett later contributed to other issues of the *San Franciscan* a number of Hawaiian legends in new form, amplifying some of the traditional accounts. He thus endeavored to create interest for a volume he sought to have published relating to the same subject.[54]

Goodman asserted in the first number of the *San Franciscan* that since Mark Twain, Joaquin Miller, Henry George, and Bret Harte had received acclaim elsewhere, "no writer of considerable note had arisen" in California, which had "not been hospitable to her men of genius," and that he hoped to bring about a "literary revival on the Pacific Coast." To this end Daggett wished to contribute.

As Daggett had left the diplomatic service and returned to the mainland he had two basic concerns. One was the choice of a place for retirement. The other, which was to occupy his time while he sought the permanent residence, was the completion of what he had long had in mind, two ambitious literary projects: a history of the Hawaiian Islands and an epic interwoven with mythology, with King Kamehameha for its hero.[55] In his retirement he had time and energy for such undertakings, but he soon found that the publishing and marketing of one volume would present difficulties enough. The practical-minded Daggett knew that his old friend, Samuel Clemens, had his own publishing firm. The two men had been intimate in the early buoyant days at Virginia City. As a Congressman Daggett had offered to help Clemens by introducing an amendment to the copyright law that would help defeat pirating of Clemens' works.[56]

With such relationships in mind, Daggett, who had taken his wife for a visit to the national capital, wrote early in November 1885 from Willard's Hotel in that city, to Clemens. He related how he had spent his spare time as minister to Hawaii in obtaining the chief historic legends of the Kingdom. He then collaborated with the King on a collection of "legends of love, chivalry and barbaric pomp, extending back over seven hundred years, and in a measure, connecting the dynasties of that period." Daggett said that he had prepared the first draft of all but two chapters and that the stories were "novel and dramatic." He indicated that he planned to remain in Washington for at least four or five days and would then visit New York before returning to the West Coast. He invited a reply from Clemens if the latter thought the project "worthwhile."[57]

Old friendship was revived at once. Clemens invited Daggett and his wife to come to Hartford. This was exactly what Daggett had hoped for and perhaps why he had included the suggestive comment that his wife and he would be in neighboring New York City. The Daggetts spent two delightful days with the Clemens family. Mrs. Daggett was "greatly charmed" by the Clemens household, and Mrs. Clemens' mother, Mrs. Langdon, seemed to Daggett a "splendid" person. The ex-diplomat brought with him the Hawaiian material he had already prepared. Now intimacy was resumed, and soon, in correspondence, Clemens was no longer refered to as "Friend Clemens" but as "My Dear Sam." Clemens was very enthusiastic about the projected book. The day after the departure of his guests, he wrote to Charles Webster of his publishing firm, extolling the proposed volume as one that broke fresh ground, "untouched, unworn, and full of romantic interest." He felt that the King's name would boost sales and help the publishing house to keep up its standards as one that brought out books "only for Kings and full Generals." Of course, he said, it was Daggett to whom the King had told the sagas, and it was Daggett who was doing the writing, connecting the stories into a historical chain. Daggett indicated that he would "not have to divide with the King," so he could afford to accept modest terms. Clemens suggested that without the King's name in connection with the volume, Daggett should get 15 per cent of the profits above cost (what Clemens said that he been paid for *Innocents Abroad*); with mention of the King in the Introduction as collaborator, 40 per cent of the profits; with both names on the title page as authors, 60 per cent of the profits.[58]

Daggett and his wife left for California on November 14. He planned to "hurry up the king" in what remained for him to do. The promoter in Daggett's make-up stood forth, as he sought Clemens' aid in enabling him to get an article in *Harper's, Scribner's,* or the *Century,* so as to "excite something of a hunger" in Eastern circles for more Hawaiian legends. Daggett felt confident that he could "work the matter up on the Pacific Coast." Clemens replied a few days later with suggestions, so Daggett wrote the King to speed him up and promised to get busy with his share. Daggett was one who was sensitive to the personal details of friendly relations and took time to compliment Clemens: "Allow me to congratulate you on the attainment of your 50th birthday. Twenty years ago I expected you would have been hanged before you were fifty. Now look at you! Famous, wealthy, and the center of a charming household, and d——d if my wife doesn't even think you are handsome. If good luck continues, you will reach the Buddha in a single translation."⁵⁹

John Mackay, Daggett's wealthy Comstock friend, had apparently helped finance Daggett's earlier literary endeavor, *Braxton's Bar.*⁶⁰ Understandably, Daggett suggested to Clemens that the same generous source might be tapped again. In mid-December he wrote Clemens that he had passed Mackay on the Grima Desert as the latter was on his way to some mines in Arizona and Mexico, and he had been able to have "but a moment's time with him." But Daggett was optimistic, commenting that Mackay "is a hard man to run down, but I shall come across him before long and shall broach the matter to him."⁶¹

Eventually a contract was signed, but the contract provided for no specific date for publication, and the printing of the book was delayed. The volume eventually came out in 1888 as *The Legends and Myths of Hawaii. The Fables and Folk-lore of a Strange People. By His Hawaiian Majesty Kalakaua, Edited and with an Introduction by Hon. R. M. Daggett.*⁶² Five hundred and thirty pages in length, it was extensively illustrated. In his fifty-five-page introduction, Daggett summarized the physical characteristics of the islands, reviewed the aboriginal manners and customs, modes of life, implements and manufactures, discussed the ancient religion with its various divinities, and paid tribute to the work of Christian missionaries.

The main body of the work consisted of twenty-one legends, most of which had a historical base, dealing with every phase of Hawaiian character and achievement. Some of the tales bore a striking resemblance to the myths of ancient Greece and Rome. The first legend, which was characteristic of the others, was about Hina, the Hawaiian Helen, who was seized by Kaupeepie while she was surf bathing and taken to his island fortress. There she spent fourteen years, until her sons by her first husband, having reached manhood, headed an invading army and killed the Hawaiian counterpart of Paris in his stronghold, along with the inner circle of his warriors.⁶³

The Honolulu *Hawaiian Gazette* praised Daggett for his "fairness and intelligence" in producing the book but complained that he had used too much literary license in "reconstructing" the material so as to alter "the mental and moral atmosphere" of the times depicted.⁶⁴ The San Francisco *Bulletin* deemed it "a most important contribution to the recorded folk-lore of the world." The New York *Tribune* published a two-and-a-half-column review, concluding: "But in truth the entire series of stories is of value and interest, and when we consider how steadily and with what fearful rapidity the people of Hawaii are approaching extinction under the influence of Western civilization, it is a matter of thankfulness that so much of their tradition and folk-lore has been thus preserved and given permanent and even admirable literary form."[65]

The work unfortunately was not a financial success and contributed to the serious difficulties of Clemens' publishing firm.[66] For Daggett it was a very pleasant addition to the accomplishments made possible by his diplomatic career, and it helped to satisfy his almost insatiable craving for literary recognition.

IX

Closing Years

With Daggett's return from Hawaii and the publication of his volume on Hawaiian traditions, his active career was essentially over. His youth had been one of amazing vitality and achievement. One who knew him well said that he was a "thorough representative of the idea the French philosopher had in view when he said, 'We can do anything at twenty.' "[1] For almost a quarter of a century the Comstock had been his home, but now its fabulous fortunes were in decline, and journalistic ventures were precarious indeed.

With Daggett's wide experience as a Congressman and diplomat, many believed that he might well be chosen Senator from Nevada in 1886/87.[2] John Mackay had often been urged to run for the Senate but resisted the promptings. Now, as Senator John P. Jones was running for another term in the Senate, Mackay and Jones were at odds over business matters, and Mackay was inclined to throw his support to Daggett, for whom he had high personal regard. But Mackay was sensitive to the demands of decorum, and when it came to his ears that Daggett, as Minister to Hawaii, had received visitors barefooted with his trousers rolled up to his knees, Mackay termed him "a savage" and withdrew his support.[3]

Perhaps in the midst of his Hawaiian service Daggett sensed that he had reached the climax of his career. Because he often expressed his deepest thoughts in verse, he penned a poem, "On the Summit," the first lines being:

Life's hill is climbed. Behind me troop the shades of purple dreams;
The vine wreathed rivers, broad in youth, and shrunk to narrow
    streams;
The stately pines that swept the clouds, the peaks that pierced the
    blue,
Stand stunted in the olden light that mingles with the new.

The shadows of the past grow dim; its voices all are low,
Like moans in caverns where the tides of ocean ebb and flow.[4]

After returning from Hawaii and taking care of official duties in
Washington, Daggett and his wife spent the winter of 1885/86 in San
Diego. Mrs. Daggett had two sisters living there, and the climate was
reminiscent of Hawaii. Daggett wrote in December 1885 that the
weather was "delightful," for one could "write with one's coat off
and a window open." He added that he could readily dispense with
the balance of his clothing "were it not for the looks of things."[5]

Several months later Daggett went to visit his old friends and
old haunts at Virginia City. There, as usual, he responded readily
when his poetic talent was sought. On Memorial Day 1886 he presented original verses entitled "In the Dawn."[6] Later he appeared at
the Virginia City Fourth of July celebration, as poet of the day. For
that occasion, he used a theme derived from his knowledge of Hawaiian folklore, writing a long poem, "The Image of Kanola."[7] Two years
later, in October 1888, when he again visited the old Comstock community, a long-time friend, John F. McDonnell, penned a sentimental
poem, "A Welcome Home," in his honor. But the passing of years
meant the vanishing of familiar faces. In 1885 Daggett had written to
Mark Twain that one of their old cronies, Dennis McCarthy, was dead
of dropsy and that he was "beginning to miss everybody" in Virginia
City that he ever cared about but that a peculiar fascination kept
him from staying away.[8] In the early summer of 1889 another old
Comstock friend, "a strong, brave man," John Van Buren Perry, passed
away, and Daggett penned a poem to him.[9]

When the Daggetts visited Virginia City in the spring of 1886,
they were seeking a suitable home for their retirement. But, with many
friends gone, with the Comstock largely emptied of its treasure, and
with Virginia City emptied of a large part of its inhabitants, Nevada
now had no permanent appeal for Daggett and his wife. Although he
had once thought of retiring to the vicinity of San Bernardino, California, the northern part of the state was nearer to the scenes of much
of his active life and he found a restful haven in the Blue Mountains,
between San Francisco and Sacramento.

Their new home was about seven or eight miles north of Vacaville,
a community named after Manuel Cabenza Vaca. After 1880 the cultivation of tokay grapes, cherries, plums, peaches, almonds, English
Walnuts, and figs in the area had become increasingly important.[10]

Daggett's home, at Holly Mount, a thousand feet above the Vaca
Valley, was thought by some "magnificent," by others "modest." It

was situated in the midst of acres of vines and fruit trees and surrounded on three sides by high rolling hills, slashed with ravines
and covered with a dense thicket of oak and bay. Among the rocks
of the ravines were raccoons, badgers, owls, and even foxes. Quail,
bluejays, and linnets came with the end of the winter rains, remaining
until the holly ripened, and eagles sometimes soared over the green
slopes. Looking eastward from the front verandas of the home one
could see many, many miles of the Sacramento Valley, dotted with
villages, farmhouses, and green fields, and, beyond the river, miles
of the Sierra Nevadas, capped with snow. To the extreme south could
be seen the San Joaquin River and at night the lights of the San
Francisco-Stockton steamers winding in and out of the tortuous
channels.[11]

In their new home Daggett and his wife lived a rather isolated
life, in decided contrast to the diplomatic whirl of their Hawaiian
years. Daggett amused himself with horticulture and continued his
literary career.[12]

Daggett's experience in Hawaii enabled him to translate a sheaf
of Hawaiian songs, including "The Appaponi," "Haaipu," and "Waikiki" for the San Francisco *Chronicle.* His interest in the affairs of the
Pacific persisted. During 1889, when Great Britain, Germany, and
the United States were involved in a dramatic crisis in the struggle
for empire at Apia in the Samoan Islands, Daggett expressed his
feelings in a poem, "Apia." The opening stanzas are:

> The embattled winds, like a God of wrath,
> Smite the isle with savage might;
> And the Palm goes down in the tempest's path,
> And the mango reels in fright.

> Now the thunder ships with their anchors cast,
> Are white with the driving spray
> And are tossed and rent by the battling blast,
> Entombed in the reef-ribbed bay.[13]

But Daggett's versatility led him into other paths. As one who
knew much about coal deposits in Nevada, he wrote a long discussion
of "Fossiliferous Coal,"[14] which appeared in the New York *Tribune*
early in 1890.[15] Two years later he wrote to the Sacramento *Union*
protesting a reference in *Lippincott's Magazine* to Gertrude Atherton
as the granddaughter of the first editor of the *Golden Era.*[16] The same
year he wrote a long narrative poem, "Cabrillo," commemorating the
voyage of discovery along the California coast of the Portuguese ex-

plorer, Juan Cabrillo, three hundred and fifty years earlier. Daggett's charm and reputation as an orator at neighborhood ceremonies brought him much acclaim. Thus, with his other interests, he kept occupied.[17]

Once in a while Daggett would journey to San Francisco to see old friends and visit familiar haunts. In 1890, King Kalakaua, a very sick man, visited California in the hope of improving his health, and Daggett went to the Palace Hotel to see him. When his card was sent up to the King's suite, as it was later reported, the King turned to his Lord Chamberlain, McFarlane, and said, with a gesture of high command, "Let him be admitted and the drawbridge raised. We are at home to none else today." The King never recovered from this illness; he died on January 20, 1891.[18]

Sometimes, with the tenderness of which he was eminently capable, he would write an endearing letter to his aging sister Betsey in Ohio, who in his boyhood had been a mother to him. In 1887, having heard that she was losing "something of the energy and vigor" that had been supremely evident in her personality, he advised: "You have reached what Victor Hugo calls 'the youth of old age,' when one year is worth a dozen of the thoughtless whirl of the earlier life, and are situated just as you should be to justly and rationally enjoy the good things of this world, and you must do it. By a life of industry you have richly earned the repose and comfort of advancing age, and do not allow yourself to be swindled out of it."[19] On another occasion he wrote her: "You are perhaps a little too old to turn a handspring or ride a bicycle in a Bloomer costume, but to one who has reared a family of worthy children, who has added her mite to the wealth and glory of the Republic, and whose life has been blameless, old age should be a season of satisfaction and calm enjoyment. The sunrise of life is brilliant and dazzling, but it is not equal in real beauty to a serene and cloudless sunset. So kick up your mental if not your bodily heels."[20]

With considerable leisure time, a strong penchant for writing, and a long-established literary reputation on the Pacific Coast, Daggett contributed to the well-known periodicals of the West. In the latter half of the nineteenth century, San Francisco was an important literary and publishing center. One of the most interesting periodicals was the *Wasp*, founded in 1879. It lived up to its name, stinging the crudities and hypocrisies of its day. It was distinguished for its colored cartoons, as well as its satirical attacks on "a thousand abuses."[21] The amazingly bitter Ambrose Bierce, who like Daggett had spent his boyhood years in Ohio, was editor for five years after 1879, and he "stung busily here, there and everywhere."[22] "Full-page cartoons shrieked blasphemies at the enemy, and editorials blasted the very foundation of the opponent's platform."²³ After 1885 the *Wasp* did less stinging and more reporting of society, the theatre, art, politics and finance. It was then that Daggett contributed to the journal.

But Daggett's satirical poems were worthy of the most virile of the *Wasp*'s social iconoclasm. One poem he contributed, "My Stately Friend," opened:

> In twilight gloom the mousing owl, with visage staid and wise,
> Sits like a statue, with a scowl cut in its rayless eyes;
> With freezing grandeur, up and down he moves his stately head,
> As if to wither with a frown or strike intrusion dead.
>
> He hoots, and doubts not at the sound all living things rejoice,
> That leaves are shaken by the ground that trembles at his voice;
> In port a king, in aspects grand, of dignity the soul,
> With look sublime he grasps the sand and breakfasts of a mole.
>
> And owls there be in human guise; we meet them every day:
> Their step is slow, their looks are wise, their gaze is far away,
> As if the purple and the green, the lowly and the sweet,
> Were only fit to live unseen and die beneath their feet.

Daggett concluded the poem, tongue still in cheek:

> They are the buds and blooms that spring from hearts of
>   gold and green,
> The perfume that on viewless wing exhales from sweets unseen;
> And souls are leafless, scentless when, dark, solemn, and sedate,
> Their mien implies to other men, 'Behold, how talk the great!'²⁴

During the latter part of the nineteenth century, the "great California magazine of the times was the *Overland Monthly*."²⁵ Daggett, as a leading Western writer, made his contributions. In November 1894 he offered the "Story of O'Doud Diggin's," a tale of an Irish-born miner, Timothy O'Doud, in California during the years 1852-55, who for a time spent his golden treasure in profligate fashion but eventually used his resources to establish a small business in New York City.²⁶ Two months later Daggett's "My French Friend" was published as the second in a series (the first by another author) on "True Tales of the Old West." Ostensibly based upon Daggett's acquaintance with a Parisian-born argonaut, Armand Daudet, it ends with Daggett's meeting his old associate in San Francisco in July 1852, where he was the latter's guest at a luxurious French restaurant. Evidently Daudet had taken this way to spend the last of his earnings, for the next morning he was a suicide, having jumped from the Clay Street wharf.[27] Daggett's next contribution was one of literary criticism, "Motion and Emotion in Fiction: The Real versus the Realist." In it he denounced the pedantry of the previous quarter of a century, which had urged "the acceptance of the self-styled 'realistic' novel as the only scholarly and imperishable form of fiction." He deplored its "redundance of borrowed aphorisms," its efforts "to record the thoughts rather than the actions of humanity," and its rigid avoidance of plot. To Daggett,

> whenever the attempt is made to put the stamp of reality on years of domestic bickerings resulting solely from a disputed interpretation of a Scriptural verse; whenever broad-chested men are made to pass harrowing days and sleepless nights over occurrences to be sensibly whistled to the winds, and robust women are tortured into premature graves by a knowledge that their husbands have read Voltaire or laid a wager on a horse race; whenever, in short, men and women in the ordinary walks of life are deprived of common sense, and made to think and feel with a saintly furor unknown to the bread-winners of the nineteenth century—then is fiction of the worst description being served to the public in the guise of realism.

Daggett then made an appeal for a revival of storytelling, bemoaning the fact that it had become a lost art.[28]

Daggett further displayed his versatility in a poem in recognition of his own sixty-fourth birthday, entitled "To John W. Mackay," a man whose generosity Daggett appreciated. Published in the *Overland Monthly* in September 1895, it included the following lines:

I'm sixty-four today, John—well entered on four score
And you're not far away, John—a few months less or more.

Could Time be coaxed to wait, John, by blarney or with gold,
Who would not baffle fate, John, by never growing old?

Some pressed the grapes of sin, John, while others played the fox;
You wisely gathered in, John, the vintage of the rocks.

But gold was only part, John, of Fortune's gifts devout;
You drew a sunny heart, John, to keep wealth's mildew out.

Our life-paths now diverge, John, but looking up, I hope
That somewhere they will merge, John, beyond the Sunset Slope.[29]

A month after the publication of Daggett's poem to Mackay, Mackay's older son, John W. Mackay, Jr., was killed in an accident near the family chateau in France.[30] With two friends young Mackay had engaged in a steeplechase race in which he was fatally injured. He was buried with "the pomp of a prince."[31] Daggett expressed his sympathy to the Mackays in a sensitive poem, "O Tell Us Why."[32]

A more joyful episode occurred in Daggett's life a couple of months earlier. Late in August his younger daughter, then twenty-two, was married to John P. Roelofsz, a native of Amsterdam, who owned a large fruit ranch near the Daggett home. Several years before, his older daughter Grace had married Ross Campbell of Santa Rosa. Both daughters lived in California after their marriages.[33]

Apparently during these years Daggett lost much weight. In 1890, when he visited San Francisco, a journalist remarked that Daggett had been very fat but now appeared like "a pugilist in training." Daggett replied:

> Everybody seems to be shocked by my leanness, just as you are. Judge Mesick was quite scared this morning. "Daggett," says he, "it isn't natural for you to be with jowls, and a paunch. It ain't exercise that's the matter with you. See a doctor. You're dying."
>
> "Dying," says I, "I'm as strong as an ox. Let me show you. Give me something to raise—an anvil or anything" and I bared my arm. "Just let me raise something for you." "All right," says Mesick, "go out and see if you can raise me $5,000."[34]

About five years later Daggett came down again for a visit with friends and had lunch with a group at the Palace Hotel. Daggett was much concerned at the time with the German-British rivalries in South Africa and commented, "I say that if the few Americans down there have decided that old Kruger is right it must be so. You never see Americans taking sides with the wrong element." He then elaborated by asserting that Americans generally looked carefully into a matter before expressing themselves and in South Africa were too few to try to dominate, hence they were exercising discretion.[35]

From time to time Daggett contributed to San Francisco papers. In October 1897 the San Francisco *Chronicle* published a long interpretative article, "Some of the California Writers of the Early Fifties." In it Daggett made an extensive and penetrating analysis of the literary milieu of the earlier period, with appraisals of George H. Derby, Elbridge Gerry Paige, Alonzo Delano, John R. Ridge, Ferdinand Ewer, and others.[36]

By this time Daggett noticed that even friends who seemed young to him were becoming gray, and he penned a poem, "The Young Gray Head":

> Brow unfurrowed, eyes still burning
> With the fires of long ago,
> Answer me, the heart returning,
> Through what agony and fears
> Through what storm of bitter tears
> Came this blight of frost and snow.
>
> Came it when the sun was shining,
> Came it when the skies were dark,
> With no cloud of silver lining,
> With no hand to ward away,
> With no heart to bend and pray?
> Do not answer, but hark!
> In the breath of April flowers,
> In the silence of the night,
> In the stories of the hours
> It is whispered, fancy-told,
> Angels paint the gray with gold
> In the land of endless light.[37]

The last years of Daggett's life were rather lonely, for his wife had died. (Details of her death are unavailable.)[38] Brooding over the loss and seeking solace in writing, he penned two poems, "Withered Leaves" and "Waiting."[39]

As the months passed, the seclusion of Holly Mount became oppressive and in 1898 Daggett moved to San Francisco to be near his daughter Katherine and her family. His health failing, he wrote to his old friend, Charles C. Goodwin of Salt Lake City, that he "was assured of the future and was ready."[40] By early November 1901, afflicted with a tumor on the bladder he became a patient at Homeopathic Hospital, San Francisco, where he died on November 12, 1901.[41] A Swedenborgian minister officiated at the funeral, after which Daggett was buried in Laurel Hill Cemetery, San Francisco.[42]

Daggett's death signalized the end of an era of adventure, speculation, and expansion. He had lived during the administrations of eighteen presidents, had seen the frontier advance until it disappeared, and had seen fortunes made and lost in silver and gold.

Just as Daggett's life was spent in a world of kaleidoscopic change, his personality was one of amazing variegation. His char-

acter at times seemed to his Comstock friends that of a "pagan opportunist" with somewhat shopworn morals. Yet they testified that when
he would meet an elderly lady on the street, grasp her hand tenderly,
and inquire about her health, his eyes sparkling with warmth, she
would swear that any aspersions against him must be utterly un-
founded. In Hawaii he drank with abandon, taught the King to play
stud poker, and in general conducted his personal life so that missionaries bewailed his "licentiousness." Yet there he composed a Thanksgiving hymn sung with enthusiasm by Hawaiians and Americans alike.

During much of his mature life, organized religion for Daggett
was a matter for detached, if sympathetic, observation. Yet, although
he had departed drastically from the religious orthodoxy of his youth,
his deep religious feeling from time to time found comfort in the
writings of Emmanuel Swedenborg, who had also greatly influenced
such men as the fathers of Henry and William James and of William
Dean Howells.[43] His exposure to moderate Calvinism during his Ohio
boyhood, moreover, had had a very different effect on him than had
more rigid Calvinist doctrines upon his friend, Mark Twain. We are
told that Calvinism's "influence upon Mark Twain was profound and
. . . in some respects permanent."[44] In his old age, Mark Twain's
"incurable Calvinist mind saw all the events of his life . . . as a chain
of causation forged by some power outside his will."[45] Rebelling
against the theology that seemed to dominate him, he "poured vitriol
promiscuously over the whole human scene."[46] On the other hand, in
spite of his worldliness, Daggett's boyhood exposure to Calvinist doctrines, modified by humane insights, provided him with a "buckler
and a shield" that served him throughout life.[47]

During his active career, his life was far removed from the atmosphere of prayer. Yet, that he was deeply imbued with the Biblical
traditions and religious sentiments of the Judaeo-Christian heritage,
if not with every aspect of its self-discipline, is illustrated by an
episode in Washington during his congressional career. At the time
a restless widower, Daggett went for a walk on a Sunday afternoon.
Approaching a Negro Methodist Church, an usher inquired if he were
a Methodist. With more agreeableness than truth, he said yes, and
was ushered to a front seat. Some recognized him as the Congressman
from Nevada, and soon asked him to pray. He had prayed little in
twenty years and was almost paralyzed with nervousness, but he
knelt in the center of the aisle and began:

> Lord of all power and might, who, while ever able to chasten the
> wicked with the rod of thy vengeance, but who also bends the ear

of mercy and lowers the hand of infinite forgiveness to repentant sinners, let this groveling child of iniquity supplicate before thee.

A fervent "Amen" then swept over the congregation. Daggett proceeded:

Heaven laden, and sore of foot, we travel through the vale of life, where the stones are rough, the thorns ever constant, and the temptations many. How often have we reached out to pluck the forbidden fruits and cull inviting flowers, to find that one was rotten and the other exhaling the scents of eternal sin!

At that point, an Amen arose like a wail from five hundred fervent lips. The Congressman then continued, "Place in our hands the staff of Divine grace, fill our hearts with love for Thy Will, and plant in our hearts the hope of a Heavenly hereafter." The Amens from the congregation became veritable shouts. Daggett then added: "Fill the cruse with the oil of gladness and bind up our lacerated feet with the Balm of Gilead." The congregation shouted in unison, "Amen, and the Lord save us."

At this juncture, Daggett seemed to have entered into the spirit of the congregation and really "warmed up" in his petitions, as perspiration streamed down his face and his hands were lifted upward. Daggett "tore whole pages from the Holy Word, as he led his hearers through the Red Sea, assaulted the walls of Jericho, camped on the plains of Moab, and took complete possession of Jerusalem." The congregation had never heard such eloquence. They swayed in their seats and shouted, rose up, yelled, danced, and swung their arms aloft. Silence ensued as Daggett lowered his voice and closed:

Let the mantle of Thy immeasurable forgiveness be the shroud that encircles our soul when the perishable cerements of earth wrap our mortal bodies, and may our eyes view the glories of Thy eternal brightness through the alabaster gates of the New Jerusalem.[48]

Yet, when religious zeal became too intense, as it seemed to him was the case with his sister Esther, who back in Ohio visited the local prison seeking to convert the wayward, he could be delicately ironical. Writing to Betsey, he commented:

Poor Esther! Her life has been one of great care; but she has stood up under it with sublime fortitude and has well earned a crown and a pair of wings on the other side; and she will get them, too, if such things are distributed to the Godly when the Recording Angel makes out his final balance sheet. I do not want any wings myself. I don't think I would look well in them. . . . But Esther wants them, and ought to have the nicest pair in the Kingdom come. . . . Nor should she accept a second-hand pair that someone may have thrown aside for a newer pattern. She is entitled to the best manufactured.[49]

Into his three score years and ten of strenuous living, Daggett poured enthusiasm, energy, bravado, sagacity, and mental vigor. His own life, as well as that of his forebears, illustrates the western movement of population in American history. Rollin Mallory Daggett never lost the impetuous individuality of the true frontiersman.

Notes to Chapters

KEY TO ABBREVIATIONS

BL	Bancroft Library, University of California, Berkeley
DAB	*Dictionary of American Biography*
Era	San Francisco *Golden Era*
FR	*Foreign Relations of the United States*
HL	Huntington Library, San Marino, California
HML	Hayes Memorial Library, Fremont, Ohio
LC	Library of Congress, Washington, D.C.
MTP	Mark Twain Papers, University of California, Berkeley
MVHR	*Mississippi Valley Historical Review* (now *Journal of American History*)
NA	National Archives, Washington, D.C.
OH	*Ohio History* (previously *Ohio Historical Quarterly, OHQ,* and earlier *Ohio Archaeological and Historical Quarterly, OAHQ*)
OHS	Ohio Historical Society (previously Ohio Archaeological and Historical Society)
OPR	Ohio Presbyterian Records, Synod Room, College of Wooster, Wooster, Ohio
OSM	Ohio State Museum
PHR	*Pacific Historical Review*
Scrapbook	Rollin Mallory Daggett Scrapbook, Bancroft Library, University of California, Berkeley
TE	Virginia City *Territorial Enterprise*

INTRODUCTION

1. *TE*, Apr. 19, 1877.
2. Charles C. Goodwin, *As I Remember Them* (Salt Lake City, 1913), 185-91.
3. "Notable Men," No. 1, San Francisco *Call* (Nov. 1878), clipping in Daggett Scrapbook, hereafter cited as Scrapbook.
4. Wells Drury, "Journalism," in Sam P. Davis (ed.), *History of Nevada* (2 vols., Reno and Los Angeles, 1913), I, 459-502.

5. Myron Angel (ed.), *History of Nevada* (Oakland, Cal., 1881), 321-22.

6. Effie M. Mack, *Mark Twain in Nevada* (N.Y., 1947), 215, citing Sam P. Davis, "The Enterprise Poets," *San Francisco Examiner,* Jan. 22, 1893.

7. *Mark Twain's America* (Boston, 1932), 136.

I: EARLY YEARS IN NEW YORK AND OHIO

1. Carter Papers. The genealogical material was collected by the late Miss Flora Carter of Defiance, Ohio, a daughter of Daggett's sister Betsey. A detailed account of the general westward movement from the New England states is found in Lois K. Mathews, *The Expansion of New England* (Boston, 1909). See also Stewart K. Holbrook, *The Yankee Exodus: An Account of the Migration from New England* (New York, 1950).

2. Franklin B. Hough, *A History of St. Lawrence and Franklin Counties, New York* (Albany, 1853), 291.

3. Edwin Phelps, "Memoirs," ed. by F. P. Weisenburger, *Northwest Ohio Quarterly*, XVII (Apr.–July 1945), 72 ff.

4. Lois K. Mathews, *The Expansion of New England,* 147-70.

5. F. P. Weisenburger, *The Passing of the Frontier* (Columbus, Ohio, 1941), 6-7, 48, and by the same author "Northwestern Ohio a Hundred Years ago," *Northwest Ohio Quarterly*, XVI (Jan. 1944), 12-21.

6. Phelps, "Memoirs," 92.

7. Defiance *Crescent-News,* Oct. 9, 1903; Gideon Daggett to Gardner Daggett, Andersontown, Indiana, Aug. 30, 1838, Carter Papers.

8. To Betsey Ann Daggett, Defiance, Ohio, July 27, 1837, Carter Papers.

9. Recollections of the late Elbert E. Carter of Defiance.

10. Phelps, "Memoirs," 85. Recollections of one of the Daggett party regarding the trip are found in the Antwerp *Ohio Bee,* copied in Defiance *Crescent-News,* Oct. 9, 1903. Betsey Daggett Carter often recalled that the party visited Brock's Monument, recollections of Maude M. Carter.

11. J. W. Scott, "Memoirs," in H. S. Knapp, *History of the Maumee Valley* (Toledo, 1872), 542.

12. Giddings to his wife, Apr. 22, 23, 1837, Giddings Papers, OHS.

13. Charles E. Slocum, *History of the Maumee River Basin* (Defiance, Ohio, 1905), 207 note.

14. D. Higgins, "Memoirs," in H. S. Knapp, *History of the Maumee Valley,* 279.

15. Edwin Phelps, "Reminiscences," Defiance *Express,* July 1, 1886.

16. Cincinnati *Gazette,* June 22, 1837.

17. Defiance *Crescent-News,* Oct. 9, 1903.

18. Charles C. Goodwin, *As I Remember Them* (Salt Lake City, Utah, 1913), 185-91.

19. The family plot can still be found in the old cemetery.

20. *History of Defiance County, Ohio* (Chicago, 1883), 105-08.

21. Carter was admitted to the practice of law in the Federal Court in Cincinnati in October 1855 and was elected as a Democrat to the Ohio Senate in 1868. He died on January 29, 1881, Defiance *Democrat,* Jan. 30, 1881.

22. He was also elected in 1857, 1859, and 1860.

23. Defiance *Democrat,* Aug. 15, Sept. 19, Sept. 24, 1844, Mar. 27, July 17, Aug. 14, 28, 1845.

24. Columbus *Ohio Statesman,* Jan. 6, 1846.

25. Oliver N. Johnson, "Ohio in the Mexican War," Master's Thesis, The Ohio State University, 1926.

26. *Ohio State Journal,* May 21, Aug. 8, 1846.

27. *Ohio Executive Documents,* XI, Part I (1846), 108.

28. *Congressional Globe,* 29th Cong., 2d Sess., Appendix 216-17.

29. Defiance *Democrat,* Feb. 18, 1847.

30. *Ibid.,* Feb. 25, May 20, June 17, Dec. 9, 23, 1847.

31. At Third and Clinton Sts. Later, in 1859, the family moved into a new residence at Third and Jefferson that was a showplace of the community.

32. David Hockman, "Reminiscences," *Maumee Valley Pioneer* (Grand Rapids, Ohio, 1890), I, 2-8.

33. Ms. Records, First Presbyterian Church of Defiance, College of Wooster Library.

34. *Ibid.* The exact nature of the offense is not indicated in the records. When a new church edifice was erected in 1909, a window was dedicated in her honor.

35. Sermon of Jan. 17, 1841, OHS.

36. Sermons of June 26, 1842, and March 31, 1844, OHS.

37. Sermon of Jan. 3, 1841, OHS.

38. Sermon of Oct. 23, 1842, OHS.

39. Paul H. Boose, "Moral Policemen on the Ohio Frontier," *OHQ,* LXVII (Jan. 1959), 38-53; "In Cases of Extreme Necessity," *Historical and Philosophical Society of Ohio, Bulletin,* XVI (July 1958), 191-205; "Let the Men and Women Sit Apart," *OHQ,* XV (Jan. 1957), 33-48.

40. Letters of Mrs. Emma Carter Hooker to Mrs. Betsey Carter, Sept. 27, Oct. 20, 1895, Carter Papers.

41. Defiance *Democrat,* Sept. 18, 1845.

42. *Ibid.,* Jan. 1, 1846, Jan. 7, 1847.

43. Daggett to Emma Carter, San Francisco, Feb. 19, 1859, Carter Papers.

44. Defiance *Democrat,* Jan. 7, 1847.

45. *Ibid.,* July 31, 1845, and Jan. 14, 1847. High water similarly affected other portions of the state, especially Dayton.

46. *Ibid.,* July 10, 1845, July 9, 1846.

47. *Ibid.,* Aug. 19, 1847, June 28, 1848, Apr. 28, 1849.

II: OFF FOR CALIFORNIA!

1.   The story of the discovery of gold and the rush to California has often been told. See Rodman W. Paul, *California Gold: The Beginning of Mining in the Far West* (Cambridge, Mass., 1947); John W. Caughey, *Gold is the Cornerstone* (Berkeley, Cal., 1949); and William S. Greever, *The Bonanza West* (Norman, Okla., 1963).

2.   Melvin R. Thomas, "The Impact of the California Gold Rush on Ohio and Ohioans," Master's Thesis, The Ohio State University, 1949.

3.   Defiance *Democrat,* Jan. 3, 14, Feb. 17, 1849.

4.   The party reached San Fernando, fifty miles beyond the Rio Grande, in June. The change from roast beef and wheat bread to corn cakes cooled the ardor of six, who returned to Defiance. Later four others had to be left behind at Chihuahua, Mexico. Those reaching California found that the trip had taken not four months but eight, and gold was not so plentiful "as had been represented." Yet two of the party later wrote from the Stockton area, reporting some success, as one had mined $175 in gold in two weeks. Defiance *Democrat,* May 19, Dec. 22, 1849, Jan. 5, 1850.

5.   *Ibid.,* Jan. 30, 1849, Dec. 21, 1876.

6.   Cincinnati *Gazette,* Jan. 8, Feb. 26, Mar. 26, 1849.

7.   Columbus *Ohio Statesman,* Jan. 3, Mar. 23, Apr. 6, 1849.

8.   John H. Kemble, "The Panama Route to the Pacific Coast," *PHR,* VII (Mar. 1938), 1-13. A variant from the Panama Route was through Nicaragua. For one Ohio group taking it, see Schuyler C. Marshall, "Four Buckeye Argonauts in California," *OHQ,* LXII (Oct. 1953), 368-72.

9.   Robert Thomas, "Buckeye Argonauts," *OHQ,* LIX (July 1950), 260-61.

10.   Robert S. Fletcher, *Eureka: From Cleveland by Ship to California, 1849-1850* (Durham, N.C., 1959).

11.   Among many accounts are: Ralph Bieber, *Southern Trials to California in 1849* (Glendale, Cal., 1937), and Owen C. Coy, *The Great Trek* (Los Angeles, 1931).

12.   Cincinnati *Gazette,* Nov. 29, 1849.

13.   Letter of George E. Smith in *Ohio Statesman,* Oct. 19, 1849.

14.   Cincinnati *Gazette,* Oct. 20, 1849.

15.   Letter of Joseph W. McCorkle, Dec. 20, 1849, in *Ohio Statesman,* Apr. 19, 1850.

16.   Letter of Shannon, Aug. 12, 1849, in *Ohio Statesman,* Nov. 10, 1849.

17.   Piqua *Weekly Register,* Sept. 14, 1850.

18.   Daggett to William Carter, Piqua, Ohio, Jan. 23, 1850, Carter Papers; *Shelby County Yeoman,* in *Ohio Statesman,* Feb. 4, 1850.

19.   During the cholera epidemics of 1832 and 1849, churches commonly held days of fasting and prayer. Charles R. Rosenberg, *The Cholera Years* (Chicago, 1962).

20.   Defiance *Democrat,* Feb. 9, 1850.

21.   *Ohio Statesman,* Apr. 6, 1850.

22.   Obituary in *Defiance Weekly Express,* Nov. 21, 1901. For a dis-

cussion of Independence and similar towns, see Walker D. Wyman, "The Outfitting Posts," *PHR*, XVIII (Feb. 1949), 14-23.

23.   Daggett loved to look upon himself as a very early pioneer, so in the story he set the date as 1846. Actually his mother was dead and he was deeply attached to his sister Betsey, thirteen years his senior, who had nurtured him in youth. To simplify the story he substituted "my widowed mother on the banks of the Ohio" for Betsey, who lived on the banks of the Maumee, a river which would not have been recognized by many of his readers. The story is in the *Era*, October 16, 1853. A friend of pioneer days asserted that he had wandered unharmed among the hostile Sioux, sleeping in their wickiups at night. His odd behavior caused them to deem him a harmless lunatic. Charles C. Goodwin, *As I Remember Them*, 185-86.

24.   *Era*, Oct. 30, Nov. 4, 13, Dec. 4, 1853; Hugh J. Mohan, *Pen Pictures of the State Officers, Legislators, Public Officials and Newspaper Men* (Virginia, Nevada, 1879), 58-59.

25.   *Era*, Apr. 16, 1854.

26.   Myron Angel (ed.), *History of Nevada* (Oakland, Cal., 1881), 321.

27.   To his wife, Mary A. Mitchell, dated Sacramento, California, July 24, 1850, Piqua *Weekly Register*, Sept. 14, 1850.

28.   *Ibid.* The census of 1850, not wholly accurate, counted fifty-five hundred Ohioans in California, or about 6 per cent of the state's population.

29.   *Era*, Sept. 10—Dec. 31, 1854.

30.   Paul, *California Gold*, 69-84.

31.   *Overland Monthly*, 2nd Series, Vol. 25 (Jan. 1895), 62.

32.   *History of Nevada County, California* (Oakland, Cal., 1880), 53.

III: SAN FRANCISCO JOURNALIST

1.   2nd Series, Vol. 25 (Jan. 1895), 62-68.

2.   Franklin Walker, *San Francisco's Literary Frontier* (N.Y., 1939), 24.

3.   Of the ten children of Macdonough, only three had offspring. The only daughter to have children was Charlotte Rosella, who married Henry G. Hubbard in 1844. Rodney Macdonough, *Life of Thomas Macdonough* (Boston, 1909), 246 note.

4.   Ella Sterling Cummings, *The Story of the Files: A Review of California Writers and Literature* (San Francisco, 1893), 16.

5.   John W. Caughey, "Shaping a Literary Tradition," *PHR*, VIII (June 1939), 202-04. The same material is in Caughey, *California* (N.Y., 1940), 392-405.

6.   Issue of Dec. 19, 1852.

7.   *Era*, March 1, Oct. 11, 1857; George R. Stewart, Jr., *Bret Harte, Argonaut and Exile* (N.Y., 1931), 59, 63, 98.

8.   Cummings, *Story of the Files*, 15.

9.   Dec. 19, 1852.

10.   Daggett, "Some of the California Writers of the Early Fifties," *San Francisco Chronicle*, Oct. 24, 1897.

11.   *Era,* Dec. 26, 1852.

12.   *Era,* Jan. 30, 1853.

13.   *Era,* June 5, 19, 1853. The *Era* asserted that it was not possible to change the publication date but that all press work was done before midnight on Saturday so that circulation alone occurred on Sunday.

14.   *Era,* Feb. 27, 1853.

15.   *Era,* Mar. 8, 1853.

16.   *Era,* Mar. 20, 1853.

17.   May 15, 1853.

18.   To Mrs. William Carter, San Francisco, May 27, 1853, Carter Papers.

19.   *Era,* May 28, 1854.

20.   *Era,* July 23, 1854.

21.   *Era,* Oct. 16, 23, 30, 1853, Nov. 6, 13, Dec. 4, 11, 1856. These proved so popular that some were reprinted in other issues.

22.   Issues from Feb. 18 to May 6, 1855, inclusive.

23.   Nov. 19, 26, Dec. 10, 1854, July 1, 1855, Sept. 12, 19, 1858.

24.   Sept. 12, 19, 1858.

25.   Apr. 17, Dec. 11, May 11, 18, 1859, Jan. 1, 1860.

26.   Charles Farrar Browne (Artemus Ward) wrote for the Cleveland *Plain Dealer* and David Ross Locke (Petroleum V. Nasby) for the Toledo *Blade.*

27.   *Era,* Mar. 18, Dec. 23, 1855, Jan. 6, Sept. 28, 1856, Feb. 21, 1858.

28.   *Era,* Aug. 16, Nov. 29, Dec. 6, 1857, and issues of Jan. and Feb. 1858.

29.   *Era,* Dec. 19, 1858. Members of the press announced a "benefit" for Mrs. Pollack and the children. In 1860 Frank Soule visited Pollack's unmarked grave on Lone Mountain and commented: "Fools sneered at his genius. . . . All around him the relatives of the rich and brainless, as well as the worthy, lie within marble and beneath costly shrubs and flowers, and the hand of the water-carrier cherishes their life and beauty. But poor Pollack lies there neglected—no wreath crowning his urn, . . . no friendly hand to twine a chaplet for bust or shaft." San Francisco *Mirror,* Sept. 19, 1860.

30.   Edmond M. Gagey, *The San Francisco Stage: A History* (N.Y., 1950), 3-8.

31.   *Era,* April 24, 1854.

32.   *Era,* Sept. 18, 1853.

33.   *Era,* Oct. 9, 1853.

34.   *Era,* Jan. 1, 1854.

35.   *Era,* Mar. 15, Apr. 16, 1854.

36.   *Era,* Apr. 23, 1854.

37.   *Era,* Apr. 9, 1854.

38.   *Era,* Apr. 16, 1854.

39.   *Era,* Sept. 19, 1858.

40.   *Era,* Mar. 12, 1854. Later issues took readers to similar establishments.

41. *Era,* Apr. 9, 1854.

42. William R. Gillis, *Gold Rush Days with Mark Twain* (N.Y., 1930), 17-27.

43. Dec. 18, 1853.

44. Jan. 8, 1854.

45. Apr. 9, 1854. A long editorial on the human drones of California appeared on Oct. 1, 1854.

46. Apr. 23, 1854.

47. Aug. 20, 1854.

48. Sept. 24, 1854.

49. It survived for two years, until the financial depression of 1856 in San Francisco. Walker, *San Francisco's Literary Frontier,* 25; *Era,* May 13, 1860.

50. Ewer, *The Eventful Nights of August 20th and 21st, and how Judge Edmonds was Hocussed: Or Fallibility of Spiritualism Exposed* (New York, 1855).

51. *Era,* Sept. 3, 1854.

52. *Era,* Oct. 8, 1854.

53. Daggett wrote long afterward:

Just before Mr. Ewer left San Francisco for New York I met him in his study. We were alone and talked freely of the past. A volume of Swedenborg on the table suggested his story of "The Eventful Nights," and we spoke of it. "It was claimed that I wrote the story under spirit influence," he said; "do you remember?" Of course I had not forgotten the charge. "Well," he continued, "we . . . may never meet again in life, and I will say to you that the charge has given me many an hour of anxious thought. I could not conscientiously deny it then, and I cannot deny it now. The story was written under a mental stress and nervous eagerness which I have never been able to understand or satisfactorily account for."

Daggett, "Some of the California Writers of the Early Fifties," in San Francisco *Chronicle,* Oct. 22, 1897.

54. Apr. 5, 1857. Ewer later became a very prominent Anglo-Catholic Episcopalian leader in New York City. *DAB,* VII, 231-32.

55. *Era,* Apr. 26, 1857.

56. July 16, 1854.

57. Sept. 26, 1858.

58. March 8, 1857. Hittell later regretted his action and rigidly repressed the enlarged work. *California Imprints, 1833–1862. A Bibliography,* ed. by Robert Greenwood (Los Gatos, Cal., 1961), 224. For a brief sketch of Hittell's career, see *DAB,* IX, 81-82.

59. Sept. 19, 1858.

60. May 13, 1855.

61. Jan. 29, Apr. 16, 1854.

62. Apr. 16, 1854.

63. Apr. 23, May 14, July 23, 1854.

64. Mar. 5, Aug. 20, 1854.

65. Nov. 26, 1854.

66. May 27, Sept. 2, Jan. 28, 1855.

67. Oct. 1, Sept. 3, 1854.

68. Apr. 23, 1854.

69. Cummings, *Story of the Files,* 14-15; *Era,* Feb. 13, 1853, Mar. 26, Apr. and May issues, 1854.

70. *Era,* May 21, Aug. 6, Sept. 3, 1854. Later the younger Noah was for twenty years editor-in-chief of the *Alta Californian.* Isaac Goldberg, *Major Noah: Life of Mordecai Noah* (New York, 1957), 287.

71. July 2, 1854, Nov. 23, 1856, May 27, 1855.

72. Walker, *San Francisco's Literary Frontier,* 119.

73. *Era,* Sept. 21, 1856, Jan. 18, 1857; *Colville's San Francisco Directory, 1856* (San Francisco, 1856), 249.

74. *Era,* Feb. 1, 1857, Sept. 2, 1860.

75. Cummings, *Story of the Files,* 17; Frank L. Mott, *A History of American Magazines, 1850–1865* (Cambridge, Mass., 1938), 117.

76. From San Francisco, May 27, 1853, Carter Papers.

77. To Betsey Carter, San Francisco, July 19, 1857, Carter Papers.

78. To *id.,* San Francisco, Aug. 12, 1859, Carter Papers.

79. Issue of Sept. 11, 1860. The publication offices were at 166 Montgomery Street, corner of Washington, "opposite the Lyceum."

80. *Mirror,* Sept. 12, Nov. 22, 1860.

81. *Ibid.,* Sept. 13, 1860. Details of the duel are so controversial that accounts of Broderick and of Terry by different authorities in the *DAB* vary as to interpretation.

82. Horace Greeley, *An Overland Journey from New York to San Francisco in the Summer of 1859* (N.Y., 1860), 363.

83. Sept. 27, 1860.

84. Nov. 30, 1860.

85. Dec. 12, 21, 1860.

86. *Herald,* Jan. 9, Feb. 23, Mar. 18, with quotation from issue of Mar. 22, 1861.

87. *Ibid.,* Apr. 25, 1861.

88. *Ibid.,* July 12, Aug. 8, Sept. 24, 1861.

89. Pastors throughout the country were under severe strain. Indicative of their plight, the pastors of the influential First Presbyterian Churches of Cincinnati, Cleveland, and Columbus, Ohio, all had left for other places by February 1862. Cleveland *Leader,* Mar. 19, 1861; Columbus *Gazette,* Feb. 14, 21, 1861.

90. Oscar T. Shuck (ed.), *Sketches of Leading and Representative Men of San Francisco* (San Francisco, 1875), 987-93; *Manual of Calvary Presbyterian Church of San Francisco* (San Francisco, 1863), 3; and *Historical Sketch of Calvary Presbyterian Church* (San Francisco, 1869), 8.

91. Edward F. Cahill, "The Candid Friend," San Francisco *Call,* Feb. 23, 1913.

92. *The Works of Hubert H. Bancroft* (San Francisco, 1890), XXIV, 286.

93. San Francisco *Herald,* Oct. 2, 9, 1861. Scott went to Europe for two years and in 1863 became pastor of the Forty-second Street Presbyterian Church, New York City.

94. *Ibid.,* Oct. 19, 1861; Cahill, "The Candid Friend."

95. *Herald,* Sept. 30, 1861; *Herald and Mirror,* Jan. 29, 1862.

IV: DAGGETT AND THE *TERRITORIAL ENTERPRISE*

1. *The San Francisco Directory, 1861* (San Francisco, 1861), 112; "Notable Men," No. 1, San Francisco *Call* (Nov. 1878), Scrapbook.
2. Clipping in Mark Twain Scrapbook, No. 2, MTP; Mohan, *Pen Pictures,* 58-59.
3. *TE*, Nov. 8, 1863, in Mark Twain Scrapbook, No. 2, MTP.
4. Charles C. Goodwin, *As I Remember Them* (Salt Lake City, 1912), 253.
5. San Francisco *Examiner,* Jan. 22, 1893.
6. Henry N. Smith (ed.), *Twain of the Enterprise,* 5; Fatout, *Twain in Virginia City,* 7-8.
7. Vincent G. Tegeder, "Lincoln and the Territorial Patronage," *MVHR*, XXXV (June 1948), 85-86; Daggett, in San Francisco *Examiner,* Jan. 22, 1893.
8. Henry N. Smith (ed.), *Twain of Enterprise,* 5.
9. *TE*, Jan. 8, 1875; C. Grant Loomis, "Dan De Quille's Mark Twain," *PHR*, XV (Sept. 1946), 336-47.
10. Goodwin, *As I Remember Them,* 253.
11. Henry N. Smith (ed.), *Twain of Enterprise,* 133, citing Twain's report from Carson City, Jan. 13, 1864.
12. Benson, *Twain's Western Years,* 75-77.
13. Fatout, *Twain in Virginia City,* 116-17; Albert B. Paine, *Mark Twain: A Biography* (2 vols., N.Y., 1912), I, 224-27.
14. Fatout, *Twain in Virginia City,* 15-18, 110-11.
15. Fatout in *Mark Twain in Virginia City,* p. 169, maintains that only one issue was ever published, but Franklin R. Rogers presents evidence that there were four in "Washoe's First Literary Journal," *California Historical Society Quarterly,* XXXVI (Dec. 1957), 365-70.
16. "How I Escaped Being in a Duel," *Tom Hood's Comic Almanac for 1873* (London, 1873).
17. Henry N. Smith (ed.), *Twain of Enterprise,* 24-25.
18. De Lancey Ferguson, "Mark Twain's Comstock Duel: The Birth of a Legend," *American Literature,* XIV (Mar. 1942), 66-70; Cyril Clemens, "'Birth of a Legend' Again," *ibid.,* XV (Mar. 1943), 64-65.
19. *TE*, Apr. 28, 29, 1868, Mar. 26, 1869.
20. *TE*, Oct. 17, 1875.
21. *TE*, Jan. 15, 1878.
22. *TE*, Feb. 3, 1878.
23. A fine interpretation of his career is Richard G. Lillard, "Dan De Quille, Comstock Reporter and Humorist," *PHR*, XIII (Sept. 1944), 251-60.
24. A letter written during this period that describes his adventures is printed in part in Oscar Lewis' introduction to the new edition of Dan De Quille (William Wright), *The Big Bonanza* (New York, 1947).
25. San Francisco *Examiner,* Jan. 22, 1893.
26. Lillard, "Dan De Quille," 253-56.
27. *TE*, Jan. 15, 1872, May 16, 1875.
28. *TE*, Feb. 3, 27, 1876.

29. Drury, *Editor,* 217-19.

30. Lillard, "Dan De Quille," 258. See also Fatout, *Twain in Virginia City,* 131.

31. Emrich (ed.), *Comstock Bonanza,* 263; Cummings, *Story of the Files,* 296-97.

32. I, 351.

33. Sam. P. Davis, "The Enterprise Poets," San Francisco *Examiner,* Jan. 22, 1893.

34. *TE,* Dec. 14, 1877. Letters of Goodman to Mark Twain, Fresno, Cal., Mar. 9, Dec. 11, 1881, Jan. 22, 1884, MTP.

35. *Editor and Publisher,* Sept. 1, 1917, p. 30.

36. *Mark Twain's America,* 135 note.

37. *As I Remember Them.*

38. *TE,* June 14, 1877; *Salt Lake Tribune,* Nov. 22, 1901; *New International Year Book, 1918,* p. 480.

39. *Utah Historical Quarterly,* XXV (1957), 95-117; XXVI (1958), 374; XXVIII (1960), 57-71.

40. *Mark Twain's America,* 135 note; *American Yearbook, 1918,* 788.

41. Daggett to Twain, Oct. 24, Dec. 11, 1881, Dec. 19, 1885, MTP.

42. Goodman to Twain, Mar. 9, 1881, MTP; Sonora *Union Democrat,* Mar. 9, 1918, Clipping in John Daggett Scrapbook, California State Library.

43. Sam P. Davis (ed.), *History of Nevada* (2 vols., Los Angeles, 1913), I, 391-98; *TE,* May 18, 1878.

44. Goodwin, *As I Remember Them,* 185 ff.

45. *Ibid.*

46. Clipping in Daggett Scrapbook. The Custer statue has been considered McDonald's masterpiece. Dedicated with appropriate ceremony at West Point, August 30, 1879, it received "much celebrity and national praise," but the statue itself "has met an unknown fate," for "in its place is an obelisk-like shaft," Edna Marie Clark, *Ohio Art and Artists* (Richmond, Va., 1932), 143; H. P. Caemmerer (ed.), *Washington: The National Capital* (Washington, D.C., 1932).

47. Goodwin, *As I Remember Them,* 185-91. For the origin of Williams' fortune, see Oscar Lewis, *Silver Kings,* 146.

48. A sketch of both is found in *DAB.*

49. Goodwin, *As I Remember Them.*

50. *Ibid.,* 188.

51. Virginia City *Chronicle,* 1880, clipping in Scrapbook.

52. Goodwin, *As I Remember Them.*

53. *Mark Twain's Western Years,* 71.

54. Clipping, Scrapbook.

55. There are ninety-one more lines, Scrapbook.

56. May 31, 1876.

57. Issues of May 31, 1876.

58. *TE,* July 6, 1878.

59. Daggett to R. B. Hayes, Virginia City, July 7, 1878, Hayes Papers, HML.

V: DAGGETT'S VIRGINIA CITY

1. *TE,* June 27, July 7, 1872, Mar. 25, June 15, 1875.
2. Personal Files, California State Library, Sacramento.
3. Daggett still lived there in 1878 after his wife's death. Bishop's *Virginia City Directory, 1878-9* (San Francisco, 1878). Copy in Storey County Court House, Virginia City.
4. *TE,* Nov. 30, 1870, Apr. 20, Sept. 21, 1873, Mar. 22, 1877.
5. Angel (ed.), *History of Nevada,* 321-22.
6. Lewis, *Silver Kings,* 5-6; Mack, "Stewart," 105 ff.
7. *TE,* Jan. 15, Oct. 13, 1874.
8. *TE,* Apr. 29, 1869.
9. *TE,* Feb. 17, 1875.
10. Mack, "Stewart," 105 ff; Lewis, *Silver Kings,* 35.
11. *TE,* May 9, 10, 1872; account in *DAB,* X, 188-89.
12. Lewis, *Silver Kings,* 47-101. On one of Mackay's trips abroad he left Virginia City on June 28, 1871, returning on October 3, *TE,* June 29, Oct. 4, 1871. Again, in August 1876, he returned from two or three months in Europe, *TE,* Aug. 11, 1876.
13. *TE,* Apr. 20, 1877, May 15, 1876. One daughter, Clara, became the wife of Frederick Newlands, long U.S. Senator from Nevada. See also Oscar Lewis and Carroll Hall, *Bonanza Inn* (N.Y., 1939), 119-214.
14. *TE,* Mar. 3, 1875, July 10, 12, 1876; *DAB,* VI, 246-47.
15. *TE,* July 10, 12, 1878; Lewis, *Silver Kings,* 161-99. After his death a school teacher, Mrs. Nettie Craven, claimed to have had a marriage contract with Fair, dated May 23, 1892. The resulting law suit cost the Fair family possibly two million dollars and ended in a small settlement for Mrs. Craven.
16. Lewis, *Silver Kings,* 217-23.
17. Fatout, *Twain in Virginia City,* 56-60; Rodman Paul, *Mining Frontiers of the Far West, 1848-1880* (N.Y., 1963), 36-86; Greever, *Bonanza West.* For the story, covering many decades, see Grant E. Smith, *The History of the Comstock Lode* (Reno, 1943).
18. Virginia City had survived earlier only by the use of huge freight wagons from Sacramento, bringing food and mining equipment and taking back ore to be reduced in California. Oscar O. Winther, *The Transportation Frontier—Trans-Mississippi West, 1865-1890* (N.Y., 1964), 30.
19. *TE,* Jan. 29, Feb. 4, 6, Aug. 28, Sept. 5, Oct. 1, 2, 3, 5, 1875; George D. Lyman, *Ralston's Ring* (N.Y., 1937).
20. *TE,* Apr. 8, 1869.
21. Paul, *Mining Frontiers,* 70-71; *TE,* Apr. 30, 1875.
22. For Sutro's career, see Robert E. Stewart, Jr., and Mary F. Stewart, *Adolph Sutro;* Paul, *Mining Frontiers,* 81-85; Greever, *Bonanza West,* 116-20; *TE,* June 12, 1878.
23. *TE,* Aug. 26, 1873, Jan. 20, Aug. 10, 1876, June 21, 1877, Dec. 18, 1868; De Quille, *Big Bonanza,* 116.
24. *TE,* June 21, 1877.
25. *TE,* Apr. 16, June 15, 1875, July 10, 1872. De Quille, *Big Bonanza,* 297-99.
26. *TE,* Aug. 24, 1871.

27. *TE*, May 5, 1875.

28. *TE*, Feb. 1, Mar. 22, 1868.

29. To President R. B. Hayes, Washoe Club, Virginia City, Nevada, Oct. 6, 1877, Hayes Papers, HML.

30. *TE*, Dec. 11, 1872, June 25, 1873.

31. George Lyman, *The Saga of the Comstock Lode* (New York, 1934), 196.

32. *TE*, Dec. 12, 1873.

33. *TE*, May 6, 1877.

34. Quoted in *TE*, Mar. 15, 1877.

35. *TE*, May 8, 1868.

36. *TE*, Oct. 27, 1880.

37. *TE*, Mar. 26, 1872.

38. *TE*, Nov. 2, 1870.

39. *TE*, Jan. 27, May 30, 1871.

40. *TE*, Sept. 5, 1869, July 6, 1875.

41. *Compendium of the Tenth Census, 1880* (Washington, 1883), 520.

42. *TE*, Jan. 8, 1867, Mar. 18, 1868, July 9, 1871, Mar. 19, 1872.

43. *TE*, Feb. 10, Sept. 10, 1870, Feb. 1, 1871, Feb. 16, 1875.

44. *TE*, Oct. 18, 1870, Sept. 22, 1874.

45. *TE*, Mar. 17, 1869.

46. *TE*, Apr. 29, 1875.

47. *TE*, June 19, 1871, June 25, 1872.

48. *TE*, Sept. 9, 1873.

49. *TE*, Sept. 16, June 6, 1872.

50. *TE*, Aug. 6, 1868, Oct. 11, 1872.

51. *TE*, Mar. 15, 28, 1871, Aug. 1, 1873.

52. *TE*, July 15, Aug. 23, Sept. 23, 1871.

53. *TE*, Feb. 6, 1868, Sept. 5, 1869, July 10, 1872.

54. *TE*, Oct. 28, 1875.

55. *TE*, Oct. 30, Nov. 2, 4, 1875.

56. *TE*, Nov. 5, 1875; De Quille, *Big Bonanza*, 430.

57. *TE*, Feb. 1, 1876.

58. *TE*, May 1, 1875.

59. Fatout, *Twain in Virginia City*, 75; Greever, *Bonanza West*, 137.

60. Mack, *Mark Twain in Nevada*, 299-306.

61. *TE*, Jan. 9, July 18, 1867, Oct. 6, 17, 1877.

62. *TE*, Dec. 5, 1867, Jan. 18, 1868.

63. *TE*, Apr. 30, June 16, 21, 23, 1868.

64. *TE*, Aug. 5, 1869.

65. *TE*, Jan. 20, 21, Apr. 13, 1870.

66. *TE*, June 21, July 1, 28, 29, 1870.

67. *TE*, Feb. 4, June 11, 1871.

68. *TE*, Oct. 26, 27, 1871, Nov. 11, Dec. 24, 1873, Aug. 25, 1875.

69. *TE*, Oct. 17, Dec. 19, 1877.

70. *TE*, Jan. 29, Dec. 21, 29, 1878.

71. Printed by the authors for private circulation, 1871. Copies are in Huntington Library, Nevada Historical Society Library, and Library of Congress.

72. *TE*, Aug. 16, 17, 18, 1872.

73. Fatout, *Twain in Virginia City*, 118-34.
74. *TE*, Apr. 20, Oct. 14, 15, 1869.
75. *TE*, June 21, 1873, Aug. 4, 1878.
76. *TE*, Aug. 8, 16, 17, 18, 1878.
77. *TE*, June 29, 1869.
78. *TE*, July 22, 23, 1870, Aug. 22, Dec. 22, 1871.
79. *TE*, Oct. 28, Nov. 5, 1871.
80. *TE*, May 20, 25, 1874, Sept. 27, 29, 30, 1872.
81. *TE*, Dec. 2, 1873; William G. McLoughlin, Jr., *Modern Revivalism: Charles G. Finney to Billy Graham* (N.Y., 1959), 154-55.
82. *TE*, Oct. 21, 22, 28, 29, 1874.
83. Robert D. Clark, *The Life of Matthew Simpson* (N.Y., 1956); *TE*, Aug. 29, 1878, Feb. 12, 13, Mar. 20, 1875.
84. *TE*, June 13, 15, 1875.
85. *TE*, Jan. 27, 1867.
86. *TE*, Aug. 3, Aug. 17, 19, 1873.
87. *TE*, Apr. 18, 1871.
88. *TE*, June 12, 1868.
89. *TE*, Dec. 24, 1868.
90. *TE*, May 21, 1871, Mar. 17, July 21, 1874.
91. *TE*, Dec. 10, 1875, Aug. 11, 1878.
92. *TE*, Oct. 19, 20, 21, 1875.
93. *TE*, Oct. 19, 1870, Aug. 8, 1878.
94. *TE*, Feb. 5, 7, 1874.
95. *TE*, Aug. 3, 1867, Oct. 20, 1868, June 29, Dec. 19, 1869.
96. *TE*, Dec. 5, 8, 1869; Lewis, *Silver Kings*, 35.
97. *TE*, Oct. 7, 1869.
98. *TE*, Oct. 7, 1872.
99. Davis (ed.), *Nevada*, I, 420 ff.
100. Mack, "Stewart."
101. *TE*, Nov. 10, 1873, Nov. 13, 1874.
102. *TE*, Oct. 27, 1874.
103. *Big Bonanza*, 403, 435.
104. *TE*, Oct. 25, Nov. 5, 1874.
105. Davis (ed.), *Nevada*, I, 420 ff.
106. *TE*, Oct. 21, 29, Nov. 5, 17, 1874, Jan. 6, 8, 13, 1875.
107. San Francisco *Examiner*, quoted in *TE*, Jan. 16, 1875.
108. *TE*, Aug. 1, 1876.
109. *TE*, Aug. 22, Dec. 6, 7, 13, 14, 1876.
110. Defiance, Ohio, *Democrat*, Dec. 21, 1876.
111. *TE*, Jan. 10, 1877.
112. *TE*, Mar. 22, Apr. 19, 1877. Fortunately, Mrs. Daggett's aunt, Mrs. Tompkins, was willing and able to care for the young Daggett daughters, and Daggett's friends took him on diverting trout fishing expeditions, *TE*, June 30, 1877.

VI: LONE CONGRESSMAN FROM NEVADA

1.   Clippings in Daggett Scrapbook.

2.   Eureka (Nevada) *Sentinel,* Dec. 4, 1877; San Francisco *Alta,* Dec. 9, 1877.

3.   *TE,* Aug. 27, Oct. 6, 1878.

4.   *Works of Bancroft,* XXV, 172-75, 189-90, 203; Effie M. Mack, *A History of the State of Nevada* (Glendale, Cal., 1937), 247-48, 253-58. See also, Earl S. Pomeroy, "Lincoln, The Thirteenth Amendment, and the Admission of Nevada," *PHR,* XII (Dec. 1943) 362-69.

5.   *TE,* Oct. 6, 12, 1878.

6.   *TE,* Oct. 15, 29, 1878.

7.   Mohan, *Pen Pictures,* 58-59.

8.   *The Tribune Almanac and Political Register for 1879* (N.Y., 1879), 83.

9.   Mohan, *Pen Pictures,* 5-6, 63; *TE,* Dec. 11, 1878.

10.   Clipping, Scrapbook.

11.   Daggett to Hayes, Virginia City, Oct. 6, 1877, Hayes Papers, HML.

12.   *Id.* to *id.,* Virginia City, July 7, 1878, Hayes Papers, HML.

13.   Complete poem is in Scrapbook.

14.   Pacific Coast Dispatch from Washington, D.C., Scrapbook.

15.   Clipping in *ibid.*

16.   July 7, 1879.

17.   Story, told by Daggett in Carson City, as reported in Carson City *Appeal,* August 1881, clipping in Scrapbook.

18.   *Congressional Directory,* 46th Cong., 1st Sess., First Edition (Washington, 1879), 152-58; *ibid.,* 2d Sess., First Edition, 152, and Third Edition (1880), 154; *ibid.,* 3d Sess., Second Edition (1881), 163.

19.   *Cong. Record,* 46th Cong., 1st Sess. (Washington, 1879), 3, 5.

20.   *Ibid.,* 397.

21.   Watt P. Marchman, "Thomas L. Young," in *Governors of Ohio* (Columbus, 1954), 105-07.

22.   Eulogy of Young by former Governor Edward F. Noyes of Ohio at Young's funeral in July 1888. Cincinnati *Commercial Gazette,* July 24, 1888.

23.   Nevada *Democrat,* Dec. 25, 1914.

24.   *Cong. Record,* 46th Cong., 1st Sess., Vol. 9, Part 1.

25.   *Ibid.,* Part 2, pp. 1569, 1572.

26.   *Ibid.,* 1574.

27.   *Appleton's Annual Encyclopaedia, 1878* (N.Y., 1879), 598-99.

28.   Shirley W. Smith, *James Burrill Angell* (Ann Arbor, Mich., 1954), 127-39; *Executive Document,* No. 1, 47th Cong., 1st Sess., *Foreign Relations, Part I; U.S. Statutes-at-Large,* XXII, 47th Cong., 1881-83 (Washington, 1883), 58-61.

29.   *Tribune Almanac and Political Register, 1883,* 95.

30.   Chester McArthur Destler, "The Opposition of American Businessmen to Social Control during the Gilded Age," *MVHR,* XXXIX (March 1953), 661-62.

31.   Ralph L. Dewey, *The Long and Short Haul Principle of Rate*

Regulation (Columbus, Ohio, 1935), 59-60. Some insight into railroad procedures is indicated by the fact that in 1884 McCrary resigned as U.S. Circuit Judge to serve for the rest of his life as general counsel for the Atchison, Topeka, and Santa Fe Railroad, *DAB*, XII, 2-3.

32. William Z. Ripley, *Railroads: Rate and Regulation* (N.Y., 1912), 611-13.

33. *DAB*, XV, 432-33; Ben H. Proctor, *Not Without Honor: The Life of John H. Reagan* (Austin, 1962).

34. *Cong. Record*, 46th Cong., 3d Sess., Appendix, 181-98.

35. *Ibid.*, Part 3, 2087.

36. *Ibid.*, Appendix, 181-98.

37. Clippings from *N.Y. Times*, *Gold Hill News*, and Salt Lake City *Tribune* in Scrapbook.

38. Lee Benson, *Merchants, Farmers, and Railroads: Railroad Regulation and New York Politics, 1850-1887* (Cambridge, Mass., 1955), 214-17.

39. Thomas C. Cochran, *Railroad Leaders, 1845-1890* (Cambridge, 1953), 191.

40. Benson, *Merchants*, 219.

41. Proctor, *Reagan*, 240-61; Cullom, *Fifty Years of Public Service: Personal Recollections* (Chicago, 1911).

42. *U.S. Statutes at Large*, XX, 25 ff.; Richardson (ed.), *Messages and Papers of the Presidents*, VII, 486 ff.; for Hayes's problem in the matter, see Harry Barnard, *Rutherford B. Hayes and His America* (Indianapolis, 1954), 461-62.

43. Clippings dated July 20, 1878, in Scrapbook.

44. *Appleton's Annual Encyclopaedia, 1878*, 599.

45. *Cong. Record*, 46th Cong., 1st Sess., 1600, 1561.

46. *Appleton's Annual Encyclopaedia, 1878*, 599.

47. *Cong. Record*, 46th Cong., 2d Sess., Vol. 10, 3597.

48. *Ibid.*, 417, 2169.

49. *Ibid.*, Part 4, 3633; *U.S. Statutes-at-Large*, 46th Cong., Vol. 21, 287-88.

50. *Cong. Record*, 46th Cong., 1st Sess., 644. These bills were read a second and third time and then referred to the committee on claims.

51. *Ibid.*, 2d Sess., 101, 112, 2629, 767, 2341; 3d Sess., 338, 2228, 773.

52. *Ibid.*, 1564.

53. *Appleton's Annual Encyclopaedia, 1880*, 556. The proposed change embodied in the "Square Location Bill" was widely discussed. Some Nevadans claimed that Daggett was right in opposing the change which would have aided Colorado to the disadvantage of other mining interests. Gold Hill *Evening News*, July 21, 1880.

54. *TE*, Oct. 1, Oct. 2, Oct. 21, 1880.

55. Carson *Morning Appeal*, June 5, 1880. Out of personal friendship, Davis later, at Pioche, said some complimentary things about Daggett and drew hisses from a Democratic audience, *TE*, Oct. 26, 1880.

56. *TE*, Oct. 30, Nov. 2, 1880.

57. *The Tribune Almanac, 1883*, 64; *Appleton's Annual Encyclopaedia, 1880*, 556.

58. Interview of Nov. 1880, in N.Y. *Herald*, clipping in Scrapbook.

59. Clippings in Scrapbook.
60. *TE,* Oct. 28, 1880; Davis (ed.), *Nevada,* I, 422.
61. Carson City *The Nevada Tribune,* Aug. 25, 1883; *TE,* Dec. 1, 1880.
62. Carson City *Appeal,* clipping in Scrapbook. The element of exaggeration, characteristic of Nevada journalism of the time, seems almost obvious.
63. Nov. 26, 1870.
64. Davis (ed.), *Nevada,* I, 422-23; *Tribune Almanac, 1882,* 33; *Tribune Almanac, 1883,* 64.
65. Letter of June 17, 1881, from Carson City, in Garfield Papers Vol. 144, LC.
66. *TE,* Nov. 9, 16, Dec. 1, 1880.
67. *TE,* Dec. 14, 1880.
68. Letter dated Washington, Dec. 13, 1880, in *TE,* Dec. 21, 1880.
69. Letter from Daggett, Washington, Jan. 24, 1881, in Virginia City, *The Evening News,* Feb. 1, 1881.
70. Clipping, 1881, Scrapbook.
71. *Works of Bancroft,* XXIV, 203.

VII: POLITICAL MANEUVERING AND
THE HAWAIIAN MISSION

1. *TE,* Sept. 27, 1881.
2. Clipping from unidentified paper, May 1881, Scrapbook.
3. Clipping from unidentified Carson City paper, Scrapbook.
4. Undated clipping in Scrapbook.
5. *TE,* Sept. 27, 1881.
6. *TE,* Sept. 27, 1881.
7. The story of Cox's life is told by David Lindsey in his *"Sunset" Cox: Irrepressible Democrat* (Detroit, 1959).
8. Undated clippings from *Enterprise,* Scrapbook.
9. Cox to Daggett, Washington, Apr. 8, 1882, unidentified clipping in Scrapbook.
10. Published by George W. Carleton and Company, New York City, 1882.
11. Franklin Walker, *San Francisco's Literary Frontier* (New York, 1939), 24.
12. Issue of Nov. 1882, Scrapbook.
13. *Works of Bancroft,* XXXVII, 633.
14. XI, No. 20, Nov. 11, 1882.
15. Clippings dated Nov. 1882, in Scrapbook.
16. Oct. 18, 1882.
17. Eureka *Leader,* Dec. 1881; Carson City *Daily Index,* Dec. 28, 1881, Scrapbook.
18. Eugene H. Kleinpell, "James M. Comly, Journalist-Politician," Ph.D. dissertation, The Ohio State University, 1936, pp. 2-3, 27, 81-2.

19. Barnard, *Rutherford B. Hayes,* 270-76; Reginald C. McGrane, *William Allen: A Study in Western Democracy* (Columbus, Ohio, 1925), 208-45.

20. Kleinpell, "Comly," 159-61; C. Vann Woodward, *Reunion and Reaction* (Second ed., Garden City, N.Y., 1956), 113-16, 127-28.

21. His old-time friend, William Dean Howells, in letters of May 16 and 27, 1881, explained to Comly why he had been unable to secure publication of Comly's manuscripts in the *Atlantic Monthly,* Comly MSS.

22. *Foreign Relations, Hawaiian Despatches,* XVII (Oct. 1877), No. 2; letters of Sept. 30, 1878, Apr. 12, March 19, 1880, in Comly MSS.

23. *Ohio State Journal,* Nov. 24, 1877, Jan. 21, 1878.

24. Kleinpell, "Comly," 238-39, 244, 274.

25. Andy W. Francisco to R. B. Hayes, Columbus, Ohio, Apr. 20, 1881, Hayes MSS., HML.

26. H. F. Page to Garfield, Washington, D.C., Mar. 1, 1881, Garfield Papers, Vol. 133, Part 1, LC.

27. Jones and Fair to Garfield, Mar. 15, 1881, Dept. of State Letters, NA.

28. Garfield Papers, Vol. 134, Part 2, LC.

29. Francisco to Comly, Columbus, May 26, 1881, Comly MSS, OSM.

30. *Id.* to *id.,* July 18, 1881, *ibid.*

31. Alfred E. Lee, *History of the City of Columbus, Ohio* (2 vols., N.Y., 1892), I, 480-81, 900-02.

32. Francisco to Comly, July 18, 1881, Comly MSS., OSM.

33. Letters of June 16, 20, 1881, printed in *Garfield-Hinsdale Letters,* ed. by Mary L. Hinsdale (Ann Arbor, 1949), 500-04.

34. Francisco to Comly, July 18, 1881, Comly MSS, OSM.

35. To President Arthur, Honolulu, May 8, 1882, Despatches, NA.

36. To President Arthur, Dept. of State Letters, NA. The Letter carries the notation "Referred to Dept. of State by Direction of the President . . . , April 25, 1882."

37. Carson City *Nevada Tribune,* Aug. 25, 1883; Comly to Frelinghuysen, May 15, 1882, Despatches, NA.

38. Letters in Instructions, NA.

39. Daggett to Sec. of State, Virginia City, Aug. 4, 1882, Despatches, NA; *TE,* Aug. 13, 1882.

40. Clippings, Scrapbook.

41. Alice Felt Tyler, *The Foreign Policy of James G. Blaine* (Minneapolis, 1927); David M. Pletcher, *The Awkward Years: American Foreign Relations Under Garfield and Arthur* (Columbia, Mo., 1962), 61-2.

42. Autographed letter of Gibson, Aug. 17, 1882, Comly MSS, OSM.

43. Comly to Frelinghuysen, Aug. 21, 1882, and Daggett to Frelinghuysen, Aug. 26, 1882, Despatches, NA.

44. Clipping, Aug. 18, 1882, Scrapbook.

45. Clipping, Scrapbook. A program of the dinner is in Comly MSS, OSM.

46. Honolulu *Saturday Press,* Sept. 2, 1882; Ethel M. Damon, *Sanford Ballard Dole and His Hawaii* (Palo Alto, Cal., 1957), 153-95.

47. Letters of Sept. 6, 20, 1882, in Despatches, and Cartwright to Daggett, Sept. 9, 1882, in Miscellaneous Letters Received, NA.

48. Inventory signed by Comly and Daggett, Aug. 21, 1882; Daggett to Frelinghuysen, Aug. 26, Dec. 31, 1882, Despatches, NA.

49. Daggett to Frelinghuysen, Sept. 20, 1882, Despatches, NA.

50. Ralph S. Kuykendall and A. Grove Day, *Hawaii: A History* (N.Y., 1948), 167.

51. Honolulu *Pacific Commercial Advertiser*, Sept. 13, 1882.

52. Princess Likelike was the title of the King's younger sister.

53. Honolulu *Daily Advertiser*, Oct. 30, 1882; Daggett to Frelinghuysen, Nov. 18, 1882, Despatches, NA.

54. Daggett to Frelinghuysen, Dec. 10, 1882, Despatches, NA.

55. Ralph S. Kuykendall, *The Hawaiian Kingdom, 1854-1874* (Honolulu, 1953); Kuykendall, "Introduction of the Episcopal Church into the Hawaiian Islands," *PHR*, XV (June 1946), 133-47.

56. *Pacific Commercial Advertiser*, Dec. 2, 1882.

57. Daggett to Frelinghuysen, Nov. 30, 1883, Despatches, NA.

58. *Id.* to *id.*, Dec. 31, 1882, Despatches, NA; Damon, *Dole*, 167-68.

59. *Id.* to *id.*, Sept. 15, 24, Nov. 18, 1882, Feb. 10, 1883, Despatches, NA.

60. Kuykendall and Day, *Hawaii*, 165-66.

61. Daggett to Frelinghuysen, Feb. 12, 15, 26, 1883, Despatches, NA; *Daily Pacific Advertiser*, Feb. 15, 1883.

62. Daggett to Frelinghuysen, Apr. 6, 17, June 1, 30, 1883, Despatches, NA.

63. *Id.* to *id.*, May 31, 1883, Despatches, NA; *Hawaiian Almanac and Annual, 1885* (Honolulu, 1884), 4.

64. Daggett to Frelinghuysen, July 7, 1883, Despatches, NA.

65. July 7, 1883.

66. Daggett to Frelinghuysen, May 7, 1883, Despatches, NA; clipping from *Enterprise*, Sept. 1883, Scrapbook.

67. San Francisco *Call*, Oct. 9, 1883; San Francisco *Chronicle*, Oct. 16, 1883; San Francisco *Examiner*, Sept. 30, 1883.

68. Daggett to Frelinghuysen, Oct. 12, 1883, Despatches, NA; *Hawaiian Almanac and Annual, 1883*, 75, *Hawaiian Almanac and Annual, 1884*, 77.

69. For the earlier years see Kuykendall, *The Hawaiian Kingdom;* William D. Alexander, *History of the Later Years of the Hawaiian Monarchy and the Revolution of 1893* (Honolulu, 1896), 1-2.

70. Kuykendall and Day, *Hawaii*, 144.

71. Damon, *Dole*, 125-27; Alexander, *History*, 2.

72. For aspects of Spreckels' life, see Damon, *Dole*, 157, 164-65.

73. Damon, *Dole*, 101, 167; Alexander, *History*, 5-6.

74. For the embarrassment caused by Moreno in Italy, see Damon, *Dole*, 161.

75. Kuykendall and Day, *Hawaii*, 167.

76. Daggett to Frelinghuysen, July 14, 1883, Despatches, NA.

77. Gibson served as Minister of Foreign Affairs, President of the Board of Education, member of the Board of Immigration, and Commissioner of Crown Lands, *Hawaiian Almanac and Annual, 1884*, 76-79.

78. Judd to S. C. Armstrong, Mar. 13, 1883, enclosed in Armstrong to Chester Arthur, Apr. 21, 1883, State Dept. Letters, NA.

79. Daggett to Frelinghuysen, Dec. 16, 1883, Despatches, NA; Damon, *Dole*, 179.

80. Daggett to Frelinghuysen, Feb. 14, June 30, 1884, Despatches, NA.

81. *Id.* to *id.*, June 30, 1884, Despatches, NA.

82. *Id.* to *id.*, May 7, Dec. 22, 1883, Jan. 15, 1884, Despatches, NA.

83. Daggett to Gibson, May 31, June 5, 1884, Hawaiian Govt. letters; Gibson to Daggett, June 3, 5, 1884, Notes; Daggett to Frelinghuysen, May 31, 1884, Despatches; all in NA.

84. Kuykendall and Day, *Hawaii*, 169.

85. Daggett to Frelinghuysen, Jan. 15, Feb. 25, 28, 1885, Despatches, NA.

VIII: RECIPROCITY AND RETURN TO PRIVATE LIFE

1. For relations during the formative period, see Harold W. Bradley, *The American Frontier in Hawaii, 1789-1843* (Stanford University, Cal., 1942).

2. Kuykendall, *The Hawaiian Kingdom*, II, 44-47, 209-30; O. E. Hooley, "Hawaiian Negotiations for Reciprocity, 1855–1857," *PHR*, VII (1938), 128-46.

3. William M. Malloy (Comp.), *Treaties, Conventions, International Acts, Protocols and Agreements between the United States of America and Other Powers* (Washington, 1910), I, 915-17.

4. The Senate had insisted on adding an amendment which bound the Hawaiian King not to lease or alienate in any way any part of his territory nor to extend reciprocity to any other government.

5. John Patterson, "The United States and Hawaiian Reciprocity, 1867–1870," *PHR*, VII (Feb. 1938), 14-27.

6. Pletcher, *Awkward Years*, 173-77.

7. Donald M. Dozer, "The Opposition to Hawaiian Reciprocity, 1876–1888," *PHR*, XIV (June 1945), 158.

8. Pletcher, *Awkward Years*, 175-76.

9. Dozer, "Opposition," 158-72.

10. Daggett to Frelinghuysen, Dec. 11, Sept. 18, 1882, Nov. 1, 1883, Jan. 31, 1884, Despatches; Daggett to George A. Jackson, Feb. 4, 1884, Miscellaneous Letters Sent; all in NA.

11. *Papers Relating to Foreign Relations, 1883*, 545-46, 552-55.

12. *Ibid.*, 558-63.

13. Dozer, "Opposition," 171.

14. Daggett to Frelinghuysen, Dec. 21, 1882, in *FR, 1883*, 546-47.

15. Dozer, "Opposition," 172; Pletcher, *Awkward Years*, 330-40.

16. Kuykendall and Day, *Hawaii*, 156; letter of Daggett, Nov. 14, 1884, in *FR, 1884*, 265.

17. Alex Ladenson, "The Background of the Hawaiian-Japanese Labor Convention of 1886," *PHR*, IX (Dec. 1940), 389-400; Kuykendall, *The Hawaiian Kingdom*, 178-91.

18. Blaine to Comly, Dec. 1, 1881, Diplomatic Instructions, NA; Donald Rowland, "The United States and the Contract Labor Question in Hawaii, 1862–1900," *PHR*, II (Aug. 1933), 249-70.

19. Daggett to Frelinghuysen, Apr. 6, 1883, in *FR, 1883*, 555-56. Daggett underestimated the number of Chinese. By the census of Dec. 1884, in a total population of 80,578, Chinese numbered 17,937, of whom 871 were females. As he indicated, the number of full-blooded Hawaiians was declining, from 44,078 in 1878 to 40,014 in 1884.

20. Daggett to Frelinghuysen, Oct. 13, 1883, *FR, 1883*, 564-65.

21. Frelinghuysen to Daggett, Nov. 15, 1883, *FR, 1833*, 567-68.

22. *FR, 1883*, 265-66, 279, 282.

23. Hilary Conroy, *The Japanese Frontier in Hawaii, 1868–1898* (Berkeley, Cal., 1953), 54; William A. Russ, Jr., "Hawaiian Labor and Immigration Problems Before Annexation," *Journal of Modern History*, XV (Sept. 1943), 207.

24. Daggett to Frelinghuysen, Feb. 14, 1885, *FR, 1885*, 470; Ladenson, "Background . . . 1886," 394-400.

25. Kuykendall, *Hawaiian Kingdom*, 71-75, 257-59.

26. Letter of Feb. 15, 1884, U.S. Legation, Miscellaneous Letters Received, NA.

27. Daggett to Frelinghuysen, Feb. 27, Apr. 24, 1884, Despatches, NA; Kuykendall and Day, *Hawaii*, 167-68.

28. Bayard to Daggett, Mar. 25, Apr. 7, 1885, Instructions, NA. Daggett resigned on April 10, Daggett to Bayard, Apr. 10, 1885, Despatches, NA.

29. June 15, 1885, clipping in Scrapbook.

30. Honolulu *Bulletin*, Feb. 16, 1887, clipping in Scrapbook.

31. Daggett to Frelinghuysen, Aug. 26, 1882, June 30, Oct. 12, 1883, Despatches, NA; John Davis, Acting Sec. of State, to Daggett, May 24, July 28, 1883, Instructions, NA.

32. She died of apoplexy, Apr. 25, 1885, leaving no heirs and no one to contest, on the score of lineage, the sovereign rights of the existing dynasty. Daggett to Bayard, Apr. 25, 1885, *FR, 1885*, 473.

33. Born May 20, 1858, he died Aug. 27, 1862. Kuykendall, *Hawaiian Kingdom*, 83-95.

34. Glenn D. Hurst in Nevada *Democrat*, Dec. 25, 1914.

35. Clipping of Sept. 1883, Scrapbook.

36. Kuykendall and Day, *Hawaii*, 162-63; Damon, *Dole*, 170.

37. Edith Armstrong Talbot, *Samuel C. Armstrong* (New York, 1904).

38. Armstrong to President Arthur, Hampton, Va., Apr. 13, 1883, Dept. of State Letters, NA.

39. Hyde to S. C. Armstrong, Honolulu, Mar. 10, 1883, cited in Armstrong to Arthur, Apr. 21, 1883, Dept. of State Letters, NA. A programme of the phallic ritual, printed in Hawaiian, was the basis for the charges.

40. Letter of Judd to Armstrong, Honolulu, Mar. 13, 1883, enclosed in Armstrong to Arthur, Apr. 13, 1883, Dept. of State Letters, NA.

41. Julius W. Pratt, "The Hawaiian Revolution, A Reinterpretation," *PHR*, I (Aug. 1932), 273-95. Much evidence tended to indicate that the

Queen was guiltless of many of the charges but that they were difficult to refute. Pratt, "Revolution," 277-78 note, 281-82.

42.   *Ibid.*, 294; Donald Rowland, "The Establishment of Hawaii," *PHR*, IV (Aug. 1935), 201-21.

43.   Charles W. Stoddard, *Hawaiian Life* (Chicago, 1894).

44.   Dated Honolulu, Mar. 30, 1883, copy in Scrapbook.

45.   Clipping with forty-two additional lines, Scrapbook.

46.   Clipping, Scrapbook.

47.   Waikiki has been Hawaii's favorite summer retreat and seaside resort.

48.   Cummings, *The Story of the Files*, 294-95.

49.   To Mark Twain, Fresno, Cal., Dec. 8, 1883, MTP.

50.   For Webb's career, see Walker, *San Francisco Literary Frontier*, 132-33, 178-84.

51.   Goodman to Mark Twain, Dec. 8, 1883, Jan. 22, 1884, MTP.

52.   *Id.* to *id.*, Feb. 10, 1884, MTP.

53.   Mack, *Mark Twain in Nevada*, 104-10, a discussion based in part on Mark Twain's account, reprinted in *Sacramento Daily Record-Union*, March 25, 1885.

54.   *The San Franciscan*, I (1885). The first number also included Tom Fitch's "The Crime of England Against Ireland"; C. C. Goodwin's "California; A Pioneer's Lecture to the People on their Duties"; Sam Davis's "The Reporter's Revenge"; and Arthur McEwen's "Why the Gold Gulch 'News' was Suspended." Microfilm copy, Bancroft Library. Professor G. M. Nelson in a later issue of the *San Franciscan* presented evidence that the Hawaiians came from Phoenician rather than Jewish stock. Clipping, Scrapbook.

55.   Joseph Goodman to Mark Twain, Dec. 8, 1883, MTP.

56.   *Mark Twain–Howells Letters, 1872–1900* (2 vols, Cambridge, Mass., 1960), ed. by Henry Nash Smith and William M. Gibson, I, 307-08; Daggett to Mark Twain, Washington, D.C., May 3, 1880, MTP.

57.   Daggett to Mark Twain, Washington, Nov. 5, 1885, MTP.

58.   *Mark Twain, Business Man*, ed. by Samuel C. Webster (Boston, 1946), 341-42, containing letter of Mark Twain to Webster, Hartford, Nov. 11, 1885.

59.   Daggett to Mark Twain, Washington, Nov. 13, 1885, and from San Diego, Cal., Nov. 28, 1885, MTP.

60.   *TE*, Nov. 16, 21, Dec. 1, 1880, sheds light on their friendship. In November 1880 Mackay had Daggett as his guest on a private car from Reno to New York. Perhaps at that time Mackay agreed to help. In New York Daggett told reporters that Mackay was "one of the most unselfish men" he had ever known, one "of marvelous liberality."

61.   Daggett to Mark Twain, San Diego, Dec. 19, 1885, MTP.

62.   New York, C. L. Webster and Co.

63.   Review in San Francisco *Chronicle*, Scrapbook.

64.   May 7, 1889, Scrapbook.

65.   Undated clippings from the *Bulletin* and *Tribune*, Scrapbook.

66.   *Mark Twain, Business Man*, ed. by S. C. Webster, 342-43, 378.

IX: CLOSING YEARS

1. Hugh J. Mohan, *Pen Pictures*, 58-59.
2. Goodman to Mark Twain, Fresno, Cal., Dec. 8, 1883, MTP.
3. Davis (ed.), *History of Nevada*, I, 425.
4. The poem in all consists of thirty-eight lines. Clipping, Scrapbook.
5. Daggett to Mark Twain, San Diego, Cal., Nov. 28, 1885, MTP.
6. Manuscript poem, Scrapbook.
7. Scrapbook.
8. Letter of Dec. 19, 1885, MTP.
9. Scrapbook.
10. *History of Solano County* (San Francisco, 1879), 317-19; *History of Solano and Napa Counties*, ed. by Tom Gregory et al. (Los Angeles, 1912), 75, 124-25.
11. Magazine clipping, Scrapbook.
12. To Betsey Carter, Vacaville, Aug. 6, 1887, Carter Papers.
13. Poem of June 1889 in Scrapbook. For the Samoan situation, see George H. Ryden, *The Foreign Policy of the United States in Relation to Samoa* (New Haven, 1933).
14. Dated Vacaville, Cal., Dec. 27, 1889.
15. Jan. 25, 1890.
16. Letter, Sept. 4, 1892, in Sacramento *Union*, clipping in Scrapbook. The editor replied that the error originated in *Lippincott's Magazine* in a short biographical sketch of Mrs. Atherton.
17. Clipping, dated San Diego, Sept. 28, 1892, Scrapbook.
18. Clipping from San Francisco *Call*, Scrapbook; Kuykendall and Day, *Hawaii*, 173.
19. To Betsey Daggett, Holly Mount, Aug. 6, 1887, Carter Papers.
20. To *id.*, Vacaville, Oct. 20, 1895, *ibid.*
21. Walker, *San Francisco's Literary Frontier*, 77, 106.
22. Mott, *History of American Magazines, 1865-1885*, 56-57.
23. Carey McWilliams, *Ambrose Bierce* (New York, 1929), 167.
24. Copy in Scrapbook.
25. Mott, *History of American Magazines, 1865-1885*, 56.
26. *Overland Monthly*, Second Series, Vol. 24 (Nov. 1894), 491-98.
27. *Ibid.*, Vol. 25 (Jan. 1895), 62-68.
28. *Ibid.*, Vol. 26 (Dec. 1895), 614-17.
29. *Ibid.*, 337.
30. Lewis, *Silver Kings*, 63-64; obituary of Mackay in *N.Y. Times*, July 21, 1902.
31. For further comment, see Lewis, *Silver Kings*, 109.
32. Two copies in Scrapbook.
33. San Francisco *Examiner*, Aug. 29, Aug. 30, 1895; San Francisco *Chronicle*, Aug. 29, 1895. A formal invitation to the Roelofsz ceremony is in the Carter Papers.
34. Clipping, account by Virginia City correspondent of San Francisco *Call*, Scrapbook.
35. Clipping from *Call*, Jan. 8, 1896, Scrapbook.
36. Oct. 24, 1897.

37. Clipping, Scrapbook.

38. No mention of her death is found in the extensive Scrapbook, and her name is not included in any of the obituaries of Daggett. The present author has searched San Francisco newspapers and has sought the aid of the local newspaper and librarians without success. The county recorder of Solano County, where Vacaville is located, finds no record of her death there. Letter to the present author, June 15, 1964.

39. Copies in longhand, Scrapbook.

40. San Francisco *Chronicle,* Nov. 13, 1901.

41. *Ibid.,* Nov. 15, 1901; San Francisco *Call,* Nov. 13, 1901. Some of the obituaries were incorrect, stating that he was born in Piqua, Ohio, and that he had been a widower for twenty-eight years.

42. The bodies in Laurel Hill Cemetery were later removed, but there is no record of Daggett in *Records From Tombstones in Laurel Hill Cemetery, 1853–1937* (San Francisco, 1935), copy in State Library, Sacramento, and the cemetery organization that succeeded the Laurel Hill association has no record of his burial.

43. Francis P. Weisenburger, *Ordeal of Faith: The Crisis of Church-Going America, 1865–1900* (N.Y., 1959), 285-87.

44. Edward Wagenknecht, *Mark Twain: The Man and His Work* (Norman, Okla., 1961), 174-75, 198.

45. Dixon Wecter, "Mark Twain and the West," *The Huntington Library Quarterly,* VIII (Aug. 1945), 359.

46. Richard D. Altick, "Mark Twain's Despair: An Explanation in Terms of His Humanity," *The South Atlantic Quarterly,* XXXIV (Oct. 1935), 366.

47. To Betsey Carter, San Francisco, Aug. 12, 1859, Carter Papers.

48. Carson City (Nevada) *Appeal,* Oct. 1880, clipping in Scrapbook.

49. Daggett to Betsey Carter, Honolulu, Apr. 14, 1883, original in the possession of Daggett's great grandniece, Mrs. Welles Bedford, San Nuys, California.

Selected Bibliography

Brief but tantalizing comment regarding Daggett is found in works dealing with the early Western mining communities, the San Francisco literary frontier of the 1850's, Nevada state history, Mark Twain, and Hawaii during the 1880's. Yet he has remained an elusive, shadowy figure. The present volume brings together the results of careful research regarding the various aspects of his life.

A small but significant collection of letters and papers in the possession of the author's sister-in-law, Miss Maude M. Carter, Daggett's grandniece, of Defiance, Ohio, has been of basic assistance. Dust-covered files of the Defiance *Democrat,* the paper where Daggett learned the printer's trade, have been used to reconstruct the life of the village in which he spent his boyhood. The sermons preached during Daggett's youth in the church at Defiance attended by the family are in the Ohio Historical Society Library, Columbus, and have been carefully perused for light on ideological influences of his early years. Local church records have been consulted in the Synod Room, College of Wooster Library, Wooster, Ohio. Ohio newspapers dealing with the Gold Rush from Ohio to California have been used in the Ohio Historical Society Library. Files of the *Golden Era* in the Huntington Library, San Marino, California, those of the San Francisco *Mirror* and of the Virginia City *Territorial Enterprise* in the Bancroft Library, Berkeley, letters of Daggett and his friends to Mark Twain in the Mark Twain Collection, University of California Library, Berkeley, and other contemporary materials have been used.

No files of the *Territorial Enterprise* for 1865 are known to be extant. Clippings from the *Enterprise* for December 5, 1862, to May 31, 1864, are in four scrapbooks, Mark Twain Papers, University of California Library, Berkeley. Some material from these is presented in Henry Nash Smith (ed.), *Mark Twain of the Enterprise.*

Files of the *Territorial Enterprise* for January 1, 1867, to January 1, 1881, in the Bancroft Library have been carefully perused by the present author. Material in relation to the Comstock is found in Effie M. Mack, "Life and Letters of William Morris Stewart, 1827-1909"; Oscar Lewis, *Silver Kings;* George Lyman, *The Saga of the Comstock Lode;* Wells Drury, *An Editor on the Comstock;* Duncan Emrich (ed.), *Comstock Bonanza;* and William Wright (Dan De Quille), *The Big Bonanza.* The story of the noted *Territorial Enterprise* journalists is told in Henry Nash Smith (ed.), *Twain of the Enterprise;* Paul Fatout, *Mark Twain in Virginia City;* Ivan Benson, *Mark Twain's Western Years;* and Effie M. Mack, *Mark Twain in Nevada.*

Additional sources are in the California State Library at Sacramento, the California Historical Society Library and that of the Society of California Pioneers at San Francisco, and the Nevada Historical Society Library and the University of Nevada Library at Reno. Newspapers and collections of letters in the Library of Congress; diplomatic correspondence in the National Archives; letters in the Hayes Memorial Library, Fremont, Ohio; newspapers in the Pennsylvania Historical Society Library at Philadelphia; and the correspondence of James M. Comly, Daggett's predecessor as Minister to Hawaii, in the Ohio Historical Society Library have been of great assistance. During his last thirty years, Daggett kept a scrapbook, a microfilm copy of which, in the Bancroft Library, has proved invaluable. The many published histories, biographies, and government records, have of course been consulted. The author has also visited the scenes of Daggett's life in Ohio, San Francisco, Virginia City, and Washington, D.C.

MANUSCRIPTS AND SCRAPBOOKS

Abaijian, Elizabeth E. Scrapbook. California Historical Society Library, San Francisco.

Carter, Betsey Daggett. Papers. Defiance, Ohio.

Comly, James M. Papers, 1877-82. OSM.

Daggett, John. Scrapbook. California State Library. (Rollin and he were not related.)

Daggett, Rollin Mallory. Scrapbook, Microfilm copy. BL.

Garfield, James A. Papers, Vol. 144. LC, BL. (Other Garfield Papers used have been printed in *The Garfield-Hinsdale Letters, Correspondence Between James Abram Garfield and Burke Aaron Hinsdale,* ed. by Mary L. Hinsdale [Ann Arbor, U. of Michigan Press, 1949].)

Giddings, Joshua R. Papers. OSM.

Hayes, Rutherford B. Papers. HML.

"Personal Files." California State Library. Sacramento.

Records, First Presbyterian Church, Defiance, Ohio, Vol. I. Synod Room, College of Wooster Library, Wooster, Ohio.

Tucker, Edwin R. Manuscript sermons, 1841–63. OSM.

Twain, Mark. Papers. University of California Library. (Some of Twain's correspondence has been published in *Mark Twain–Howells Letters, 1872–1900,* ed. by Henry Nash Smith and William M. Gibson, 2 vols., Cambridge, Mass., Harvard University, 1960; and in *Mark Twain, Business Man,* ed. by Samuel C. Webster. Boston, Little, Brown and Co., 1946.)

DAGGETT'S PUBLISHED WRITINGS

Daggett's published writings include numerous articles in the *Golden Era;* some he initialled and others he published under the pseudonyms

"Blunderbuss," "Korn Kob," and "Old Zeke." The files for 1852 to 1860, HL, have been carefully perused. He also contributed numerous editorials to the San Francisco *Mirror* and a variety of prose and poetry to the Virginia City *Territorial Enterprise.* He presented in the *Wasp,* the *San Franciscan,* and the *Overland Monthly* literary efforts which are discussed in the appropriate chapters in this volume. Many of his official letters as Minister to Hawaii are published in *Foreign Relations of the United States.* Two volumes came from his pen: a novel, *Braxton's Bar* (New York, George W. Carleton and Co., 1882), and *The Legends and Myths of Hawaii. The Fables and Folklore of a Strange People. By His Hawaiian Majesty, Kalakaua, Edited and with an Introduction by Hon. R. M. Daggett* (New York, C. L. Webster and Co., 1888). With Joseph Goodman he wrote a play, *The Psychoscope: A Sensational Drama in Five Acts* (Virginia City, Privately printed, 1871). In his later years, his significant contributions to San Francisco newspapers included, "Daggett's Recollections," *Examiner,* Jan. 22, 1893; "Brisk Days on the Comstock," *Morning Call,* Sept. 10, 1893; and "Some of the California Writers of the Early Fifties," *Chronicle,* Oct. 24, 1897.

MANUSCRIPT GOVERNMENT RECORDS

"Department of State Records," Letters Received, cited as Dept. of State Letters. An unpublished index is available in National Archives.
"Despatches from U.S. Ministers to Hawaii": Vol. 20, Feb. 14, 1881—Nov. 1882; Vol. 21, Dec. 10, 1882—June 30, 1884; Vol. 22, July 5, 1884—Dec. 27, 1886, cited as Despatches.
"Diplomatic Instructions of the Department of State, Hawaii, 1801–1906": Aug. 28, 1848—Mar. 25, 1885; Mar. 6, 1885—June 14, 1900, cited in this volume as Instructions.
"Hawaii, U.S. Legation Archives, Correspondence with Hawaiian Government, 1877–1900," cited as Hawaiian Govt. letters, NA.
"Hawaii, U.S. Legation Archives, Miscellaneous Letters Received, 1879–1886," cited as Miscellaneous Letters Received.
"Hawaii, U.S. Legation Archives, Miscellaneous Letters Sent, 1865–1897," cited as Miscellaneous Letters Sent.
"Hawaii, U.S. Legation Archives, Notes From Hawaiian Government, Aug. 21, 1882—Nov. 21, 1890," cited as Notes, NA.

UNPUBLISHED Ph.D. DISSERTATIONS AND MASTER'S THESES

Johnson, Oliver N. "Ohio in the Mexican War." Master's thesis, The Ohio State University, 1926.
Kleinpell, Eugene H. "James M. Comly, Journalist-Politician." Ph.D. dissertation, The Ohio State University, 1936.

Mack, Effie Mona. "Life and Letters of William Morris Stewart, 1827–1909: A History of His Influence on State and National Legislation." Ph.D. dissertation, University of California, Berkeley, 1930.

Thomas, Melvin R. "The Impact of the California Gold Rush on Ohio and Ohioans." Master's thesis, The Ohio State University, 1949.

PUBLISHED GOVERNMENT RECORDS

I. *United States*

Compendium of the Tenth Census, 1880 (Washington, 1883).

Congressional Directory, 46th Cong. 1st Sess., First Edition (Washington, 1879); 46th Cong. 2d Sess., First Edition and Third Edition (Washington, 1880); 46th Cong. 3d Sess., Second Edition (Washington, 1881).

Congressional Record, 46th Cong. 1st Sess.; 46th Cong. 2d Sess.; 46th Cong. 3d Sess. (Washington, 1879-81).

Malloy, William M. (Comp.). *Treaties, Conventions, International Acts, Protocols, and Agreements between the United States and Other Powers* (Washington, 1910), I.

Papers Relating to the Foreign Affairs of the United States, Hawaii, 1877, 1878, 1879, 1880, 1881, 1882, 1883, 1884, 1885 (Washington, 1878-86).

Richardson, James D. *Messages and Papers of the Presidents*, VII (Washington, 1896).

Statutes-at-Large of the United States, 1879–1881 (Washington, 1880-82).

II. *Ohio*

Ohio Executive Documents, XI, Part I (Columbus, 1846).

NEWSPAPERS

Cincinnati *Gazette*. Jan. 22, 1837; Jan. 1—Dec. 31, 1849.

Cincinnati *Commercial Gazette*. July 24, 1888.

Columbus *Ohio State Journal*. Nov. 24, 1877, Jan. 21, 1878.

Columbus *Ohio Statesman*. Apr. 1, 1849—May 1, 1850.

Defiance (Ohio) *Crescent News*. Oct. 9, 1903.

Defiance *Democrat*. July 18, 1844—Aug. 23, 1851, Dec. 21, 1876, Jan. 30, 1881.

Defiance *Express*. July 1, 1886, Nov. 21, 1901.

Defiance *Northwestern*. June 15, 1843—May 23, 1844.

New York Times. July 21, 1902.

Piqua (Ohio) *Register*. Mar. 24, 1849—Dec. 12, 1850.

Salt Lake (Utah) *Tribune*. July 21, 1902.

San Francisco *Call*. Oct. 9, 1883, Nov. 1—Nov. 30, 1901, Feb. 23, 1913.

San Francisco *Chronicle*. Oct. 16, 1883, Aug. 1—Oct. 1, 1895, Oct.—Dec. 31, 1897, Jan. 1—Oct. 31, 1899, Nov. 1—Nov. 30, 1901.

Articles 205

San Francisco *Examiner.* Sept. 30, 1895.
San Francisco *Herald.* Aug. 1, 1860, Dec. 31, 1861.
San Francisco *Herald and Mirror.* Jan. 1, 1862—Jan. 1, 1863.
Virginia City (Nevada) Daily *Territorial Enterprise.* Jan. 1, 1867—Jan. 1, 1881, Jan. 1, 1881—Oct. 12, 1900, scattered copies.

ARTICLES

Adler, Jacob. "The Oceanic Steamship Company: A Link in Claus Spreckels' Hawaiian Sugar Empire," *PHR,* XXIX (Aug. 1960) 257-69.
Altick, Richard D. "Martin Twain's Despair: An Explanation in Terms of His Humanity," *The South Atlantic Quarterly,* XXXIV (Oct. 1935), 359-68.
Bieber, Ralph P. "California Gold Mania," *MVHR,* XXXV (June 1948), 3-28.
Boase, Paul H. "In Cases of Extreme Necessity," *Historical and Philosophical Society of Ohio Bulletin,* XVI (July 1958), 191-205; "Let the Men and Women Sit Apart," *HPSOB,* XV (Jan. 1957), 33-48; "Moral Policemen on the Ohio Frontier," *OHQ,* XLVII (Jan. 1959), 38-53.
Caughey, John W. "Shaping a Literary Tradition," *PHR,* VIII (June 1939), 202-15.
Clemens, Cyril. "'Birth of a Legend,' Again," *American Literature,* XV (March 1943), 64-65.
Creer, Leland H. "Report of President of the Historical Society," *Utah Historical Quarterly,* XXVI (Oct. 1958), 373-81.
De Quille, Dan. See Wright, William.
Dozer, Donald M. "The Opposition to Hawaiian Reciprocity, 1876–1888," *PHR* (June 1945), 157-84.
Ferguson, De Lancey. "Mark Twain's Comstock Duel: The Birth of a Legend," *American Literature,* XIV (Mar. 1942), 66-70.
Hockman, David. "Reminiscences," *Maumee Valley Pioneer* (Grand Rapids, Ohio, 1890), I, 2-8.
Hooley, O. E. "Hawaiian Negotiations for Reciprocity, 1867–1870," *PHR,* VII (June 1938), 128-46.
Ivans, Stanley S. "A Constitution for Utah," *Utah Historical Quarterly,* XXV (Apr. 1957), 95-117.
Kemble, John H. "The Panama Route to the Pacific Coast," *PHR,* VII (March 1938), 1-13.
Kuykendall, Ralph S. "Introduction of the Episcopal Church into the Hawaiian Islands," *PHR,* XV (June 1946), 133-47.
Ladenson, Alex. "The Background of the Hawaiian-Japanese Labor Convention of 1886," *PHR,* IX (Dec. 1940), 389-400.
Loomis, C. Grant. "Dan De Quille's Mark Twain," *PHR,* XV (Sept. 1946), 336-47.
Lye, William F. "Edward W. Tullidge," *Utah Historical Quarterly,* XXVIII (Jan. 1960), 57-71.

McKee, Irving. "Artemus Ward in California and Nevada, 1863-1864,"
    PHR, XX (Feb. 1951), 11-24.
Marshall, Schuyler C. "Four Ohio Argonauts in California," *OHQ,* LXII
    (Oct. 1953), 368-73.
Patterson, John. "The United States and Hawaiian Reciprocity, 1867–1870,"
    PHR, VII (Feb. 1938), 14-27.
Pomeroy, Earl S. "Lincoln, The Thirteenth Amendment, and the Admission
    of Nevada," *PHR,* XII (Dec. 1943), 362-69.
Pratt, Julius W. "The Hawaiian Revolution: A Reinterpretation," *PHR,* I
    (Aug. 1932), 273-95.
Rogers, Franklin R. "Washoe's First Literary Journal," *Cal. Historical Soc.
    Quarterly,* XXXV (Dec. 1957), 365-70.
Rowland, Donald. "The United States and the Contract Labor Question in
    Hawaii, 1862–1900," *PHR,* II (Aug. 1933), 249-70.
Russ, William A., Jr. "Hawaiian Labor and Immigration Problems Before
    Annexation," *Journal Modern History,* XV (Sept. 1943), 207-23.
Tedeger, Vincent G. "Lincoln and the Territorial Patronage," *MVHR,* XXXV
    (June 1948), 85-86.
Thomas, Robert. "Buckeye Argonauts," *OHQ,* LIX (July 1950), 256-69.
Wecter, Dixon. "Mark Twain and the West," *The Huntington Library
    Quarterly,* VIII (Aug. 1945), 359-78.
Weisenburger, Francis P. "Northwestern Ohio a Hundred Years Ago,"
    Northwest Ohio Quarterly, XVI (Jan. 1944), 12-21; (ed.) "Memoirs
    of Edwin Phelps," *NOQ,* XVII (Apr.–July, 1945), 72-125.
Wyman, Walker D. "The Outfitting Posts," *PHR,* XVIII (Feb. 1949), 14-23.

BOOKS

Alexander, William D. *History of the Later Years of the Hawaiian Monarchy
    and the Revolution of 1893.* Honolulu, Hawaiian Gazette Co., 1896.
Bancroft, Hubert H. *Works.* 39 vols., San Francisco, A. L. Bancroft & Co.,
    1882-90.
Barnard, Harry. *Rutherford B. Hayes and His America.* Indianapolis, Bobbs-
    Merrill, 1954.
Bateman, Alan M. *Economic Mineral Deposits.* 2nd edition, New York,
    Wiley and Sons, 1950.
Benson, Ivan. *Mark Twain's Western Years.* Stanford, Cal., Stanford Uni-
    versity Press, 1938.
Benson, Lee. *Merchants, Farmers, and Railroads: Railroad Regulation and
    New York Politics, 1850–1887.* Cambridge, Mass., Harvard University
    Press, 1955.
Bieber, Ralph. *Southern Trails to California in 1849.* Glendale, Cal., Arthur
    H. Clark Co., 1937.
Bradley, Harold W. *The American Frontier in Hawaii, 1789–1843.* Stan-
    ford, Cal., Stanford University Press, 1942.
Caemmerer, H. P. (ed.). *Washington: The National Capital.* Washington,
    D.C., Govt. Printing Office, 1933.
Caughey, John W. *California.* New York, Prentice-Hall, 1940.

————. *Gold is the Cornerstone.* Berkeley, Cal., University of California Press, 1949.

Clark, Edna Marie. *Ohio Arts and Artists.* Richmond, Va., Garrett and Massie, 1932.

Clark, Robert D. *The Life of Matthew Simpson.* New York, Macmillan, 1956.

Cochran, Thomas C. *Railroad Leaders, 1845-1890.* Cambridge, Mass., Harvard University Press, 1953.

Conroy, Hilary. *The Japanese Frontier in Hawaii, 1868-1898.* Berkeley, Cal., University of California Press, 1953.

Coy, Owen C. *The Great Trek.* Los Angeles, Powell Publishing Co., 1931.

Cullom, Shelby. *Fifty Years of Public Service: Personal Recollections.* Chicago, A. C. McClurg and Co., 1911.

Cummings, Ella Sterling. *The Story of the Files: A Review of California Writers and Literature.* San Francisco, Cooperative Printing Co., 1893.

Damon, Ethel M. *Sanford Ballard Dole and His Hawaii.* Palo Alto, California. Pacific Books, 1957.

De Voto, Bernard. *Mark Twain's America.* Cambridge, Mass., Harvard University Press, 1932.

Dewey, Ralph L. *The Long and Short Haul Principle of Rate Regulation.* Columbus, Ohio State University Press, 1935.

Drury, Wells. *An Editor on the Comstock Lode.* New York, Farrar and Rinehart, 1936.

Emrich, Duncan (ed.). *Comstock Bonanza.* New York, Vanguard Press, 1950.

Ewer, Frederick C. *The Eventful Nights of August 20th and 21st, and how Judge Edmonds was Hocussed.* New York, S. Hueston, 1855.

Fatout, Paul. *Mark Twain in Virginia City.* Bloomington, Indiana University Press, 1964.

Fletcher, Robert S. *Eureka: From Cleveland by Ship to California, 1849–1850.* Durham, N.C., Duke University Press, 1959.

Gagey, Edmond M. *The San Francisco Stage: A History.* New York, Columbia University Press, 1950.

Gillis, William R. *Gold Rush Days with Mark Twain.* New York, A. and C. Boni, 1930.

Goldberg, Isaac. *Major Noah: Life of Mordecai Noah.* New York, Jewish Historical Publication Society, 1957.

Goodwin, Charles C. *As I Remember Them.* Salt Lake City, Salt Lake Commercial Club, 1913.

Governors of Ohio. Columbus, Ohio Historical Society, 1954.

Greeley, Horace. *An Overland Journey From New York to San Francisco in the Summer of 1859.* New York, C. M. Saxton, Barker and Co., 1860.

Greever, William S. *The Bonanza West.* Norman, University of Oklahoma Press, 1963.

Hittell, John S. *Mining in the Pacific States of North America.* San Francisco, H. H. Bancroft and Company, 1861.

Holbrook, Stuart. *The Yankee Eoxdus: An Account of the Migration from New England.* New York, Macmillan, 1950.

Kuykendall, Ralph S. *The Hawaiian Kingdom, 1854–1874.* Honolulu, University of Hawaii Press, 1953.

———— and A. Grove Day. *Hawaii: A History.* Englewood Cliffs, New Jersey, Prentice-Hall, 1961.

Lewis, Oscar. *Silver Kings.* New York, Knopf, 1947.

———— and Carroll Hall. *Bonanza Inn.* New York, Knopf, 1939.

Lindley, David. *"Sunset Cox": Irrepressible Democrat.* Detroit, Wayne State University Press, 1959.

Lord, Eliot. *Comstock Mining and Miners.* Washington, D.C., Government Printing Office, 1883.

Lyman, George D. *The Saga of the Comstock Lode.* New York, Charles Scribner's Sons, 1934.

————. *Ralston's Ring.* New York, Charles Scribner's Sons, 1937.

Macdonough, Rodney. *Life of Thomas Macdonough.* Boston, Fort Hill Press, 1909.

McGrane, Reginald C. *William Allen. A Study in Western Democracy.* Columbus, Ohio Historical Society, 1925.

McLoughlin, William G., Jr. *Modern Revivalism: Charles G. Finney to Billy Graham.* New York, Ronald Press, 1959.

McWilliams, Carey. *Ambrose Bierce.* New York, A. and C. Boni, 1929.

Mathews, Lois K. *The Expansion of New England.* New York, Houghton Mifflin, 1909.

Mott, Frank L. *A History of American Magazines, 1850–1865; 1885–1905.* Cambridge, Mass., Harvard University Press, 1938-57.

Paine, Albert B. *Mark Twain: A Biography.* 2 vols., New York, Harper and Brothers, 1912.

Paul, Rodman W. *California Gold: The Beginnings of Mining in the Far West.* Cambridge, Mass., Harvard University Press, 1947.

————. *Mining Frontiers of the Far West, 1848–1880.* New York, Holt, Rinehart, and Winston, 1963.

Pletcher, David M. *The Awkward Years: American Foreign Relations Under Garfield and Arthur.* Columbia, Mo., University of Missouri Press, 1962.

Proctor, Ben H. *Not Without Honor: The Life of John H. Reagan.* Austin, University of Texas Press, 1962.

Ripley, William Z. *Railroads: Rate and Regulation.* New York, Longmans, Green and Company, 1912.

Rogers, Franklin R. *Mark Twain's Burlesque Patterns.* Dallas, Texas, Southern Methodist University Press, 1960.

Rosenberg, Charles R. *The Cholera Years.* Chicago, University of Chicago Press, 1962.

Ryden, George H. *The Foreign Policy of the United States in Relation to Samoa.* New Haven, Yale University Press, 1933.

Shinn, Charles H. *The Story of the Mine, as Illustrated by the Great Comstock Lode of Nevada.* New York, D. Appleton and Company, 1896.

Smith, Grant H. *The History of the Comstock Lode, 1850–1920.* Reno, Mackay School of Mines, 1943.

Smith, Henry Nash (ed.). *Mark Twain of the Enterprise.* Berkeley and Los Angeles, University of California Press, 1957.

Stewart, George R., Jr. *Bret Harte, Argonaut and Exile.* Boston, Houghton, Mifflin, 1931.

Stewart, Robert E., and Mary F. Stewart. *Adolph Sutro.* Berkeley, Cal., Howell-North, 1962.

Stoddard, Charles W. *Hawaiian Life.* Chicago, F. T. Neely, 1894.

Talbot, Edith Armstrong. *Samuel C. Armstrong.* New York, Doubleday, Page, and Company, 1904.

Tyler, Alice Felt. *The Foreign Policy of James G. Blaine.* Minneapolis, University of Minnesota Press, 1927.

Wagenknecht, Edward. *Mark Twain: The Man and his Work.* Norman, University of Oklahoma Press, 1961.

Walker, Franklin. *San Francisco's Literary Frontier.* New York, Knopf, 1939.

Webster, Samuel C. (ed.). *Mark Twain: Business Man.* Boston, Little, Brown, and Company, 1946.

Weisenburger, Francis P. *Ordeal of Faith: The Crisis of Church-Going America, 1865–1900.* New York, Philosophical Library, 1959.

Winther, Oscar. *The Transportation Frontier—The Trans-Mississippi West, 1865–1900.* New York, Holt, Rinehart, and Winston, 1964.

Woodward, C. Vann. *Reunion and Reaction.* Second edition, Garden City, New York, Doubleday, 1956.

Wright, William (Dan De Quille). *History of the Big Bonanza.* Second edition, New York, Knopf, 1947.

Zollinger, James P. *Sutter: The Man and his Empire.* New York, Oxford University Press, 1939.

STATE AND LOCAL HISTORIES, DIRECTORIES, AND RELATED WORKS

Angel, Myron. *History of Nevada,* Oakland, Cal., Thompson and West, 1881.

Crocker-Langley San Francisco Directory, 1899, 1900, 1901. San Francisco, 1899, 1900, 1901.

Davis, Samuel P. (ed.). *History of Nevada.* 2 vols., Reno and Los Angeles, Elmo Publishing Co., 1913.

Greenwood, Robert (ed.). *California Imprints, 1833–1862: A Bibliography.* Los Gatos, California, Talisman Press, 1961.

Historical Sketch of Calvary Presbyterian Church. San Francisco, Privately printed, 1869.

History of Defiance County, Ohio. Chicago, Warner Beers and Company, 1883.

History of Nevada County, California. Oakland, California, 1880.

History of Solano County, California. San Francisco, Wood, Alley and Co., 1879. Tom Gregory *et al.* (eds.). *History of Solano and Napa Counties.* Los Angeles, Historical Record Company, 1912.

Hough, Franklin B. *A History of St. Lawrence and Franklin Counties, New York.* Albany, Little and Company, 1853.

Knapp, Horace S. *History of the Maumee Valley.* Toledo, Blade Publishing House, 1872.

Lee, Alfred E. *History of the City of Columbus, Ohio.* 2 vols., New York, Munsell and Co., 1892.

Mack, Effie M. *Nevada, a History of the State From the Earliest Times Through the Civil War.* Glendale, Cal., Arthur H. Clark and Co., 1936.

Manual of Calvary Presbyterian Church of San Francisco. San Francisco, Privately printed, 1863.

Mohan, Hugh J. *Pen Pictures of State Officers, Legislators, Public Officials and Newspaper Men.* Virginia City, 1879.

Records From Tombstones in Laurel Hill Cemetery, 1853–1937, San Francisco, Cal. 1935. Mimeographed copy in California State Library.

San Francisco City Directory, 1861. San Francisco, 1861.

Shuck, Oscar T. (ed.). *Sketches of Leading and Representative Men of San Francisco.* San Francisco, Privately printed, 1863.

Slocum, Charles E. *History of the Maumee Valley.* Defiance, Ohio, Bowen and Slocum, 1905.

BIOGRAPHICAL DICTIONARIES, ENCYCLOPEDIAS, AND YEAR BOOKS

Appleton's The Annual Encyclopaedia, 1878, 1880, 1882. New York, 1879, 1881, 1883.

Dictionary of American Biography, ed. by Allen Johnson, Dumas Malone, et al., 22 vols. and supplements. New York, Charles Scribner's Sons, 1928-58.

Hawaiian Almanac and Annual, 1883, 1884. Honolulu, 1883, 1884.

New International Year Book, 1918. New York, Dodd, Mead & Co., 1919.

Tribune Almanac and Political Register for 1879; 1883. New York, 1879, 1883.

Index

"Ada Clare": contributor to *Golden Era*, 28

Aldrich, Nelson W.: congressional colleague of Daggett, 105

Allen, Elisha H.: Hawaiian representative in Washington, 141, 146

Amusements: in Virginia City, 79-83

Anthony, Susan B.: woman's rights lecturer, 91

Argonaut: a leading California journal, 127-59

Armstrong, Samuel C.: head of Hampton Institute, 156; asserts that Daggett is "licentious" and asks his removal, 157-58

Arthur, Chester A.: president, 131-32, 147-49, 156-57

Baldwin, Alexander: member of Nevada territorial council, 53; career of, 93-94

Bancroft, Hubert H. (historian of the West): comments on Daggett, 122, 127

Bank of California: 77; influence in Nevada, 78, 94-95, 118

Baptists: in Nevada, 81, 121

Barrett, Lawrence: theatrical star in Nevada, 87-88

Bayard, Thomas F.: Cleveland's secretary of state, 154

Beecher, Henry Ward: lecturer in Nevada, 90-91

Belcher mine: Daggett's investments in, 79

Belknap, George E. (naval commander in Hawaii): 141; Daggett's relations with, 136

Benson, Ivan: comments on Daggett's influence, 66

Bernicia (U.S. naval vessel in Hawaii): 141

Bible in the schools: attitude of *Golden Era* toward, 42

Blackman, Sylvester: early northwestern Ohio pioneer, 7

Blaine, James G.: political friend of Daggett, 129; secretary of state, 133, 150-51

Blaisdell's Bell Ringers: attraction in Virginia City, 87

Bland, Richard: sponsor of silver legislation, 114

"Bloody Massacre of Empire City": hoax of Mark Twain on *Enterprise*, 56

"Blunderbuss": pseudonym of Daggett, 24, 33-34

Boers: Daggett's opinion of war in Africa, 171

Booth, Edwin: theatrical attraction in Nevada, 36

Bowles, Samuel: Massachusetts editor visits Nevada, 93

Braxton's Bar (novel by Daggett): 126-27, 163

Broderick, David C.: political leader in California, 47, 110; Daggett's admiration for, 110

Brooks, James: publisher of *Pioneer*, 40; a publisher of *Golden Era*, 45

Brown, Henry A.: lobbyist for American sugar interests, 147

Brown, William A.: northwestern Ohio pioneer, 7

Browne, Charles Farrar (Artemus Ward): lecturer in Virginia City, 90

Brunersburg, Ohio: Daggetts settled in, 10, 11

gland settlers in, 5; living conditions
in, 5
Ridge, John R. ("Yellow Bird"): contributor to *Golden Era,* 29; Daggett's
appraisal of, 30, 171; edits San Francisco *Herald,* 49
Rising, Judge Richard: condemns vigilantes, 85; drunkenness of, 85
Roelofsz, John P.: Dutch-born fruit
rancher, 171; Daggett's son-in-law,
171, 198 note 33
Roughing It: Mark Twain's account of
Virginia City life, 56, 57
Royal Agricultural Society: activities of,
150

Sacramento: appearance in 1850, 23-24;
Daggett's sojourn there, 24
San Diego: Daggett and his wife spend
winter in, 166
San Franciscan: receives contributions
from De Quille, 59; launched by
Goodman, 159-60; Mark Twain con-
tributes to under pressure, 160; Daggett writes for, 160-61
San Francisco: Daggett locates in, 27;
Golden Era established in, 27-28;
early newspapers in, 29; advocacy of
Sunday observance laws in, 30-31;
theatre in, 35-37; social conditions in,
37-39; vice in, 39-40; gas monopoly
in, 42; Chinese in, 43; Know-Nothingism as political issue in, 43; changes
in *Era* location and personnel, 44-45;
decline of *Era,* 45; Daggett and
Foard sell the *Era,* 47; Daggett and
Foard establish *Mirror* in, 47; attitudes toward secession in, 48-49;
Daggett crusades against Calvary
Church pastor in, 49-51; Daggett en-
gages in other controversies in, 50;
Daggett disposes of interests in
Mirror, 51; Daggett leaves city, 52;
Comstock journalists seek vacations
in, 54; much of Nevada wealth held
in, 73, 75; Spreckels profits by Hawaiian coins minted in, 143; as liter-
ary and publishing center, 168; Dag-
gett's retirement in, 171; Daggett's
death and burial in, 172
San Francisco *Alta*: 48
San Francisco *Bulletin*: 48, 163
San Francisco *Chronicle*: 48-49; comments on Daggett, 132-33
San Francisco *Herald*: 48-49

San Francisco *Mirror*: Daggett, publisher of, 47-51
San Francisco *Times*: 48
San Francisco *Tribune*: comments on
Daggett, 132
Saxe, John G.: lyceum lecturer, 90
Scott, William A.: leading San Francisco Presbyterian minister, 49; op-
poses vigilantes, 49; tries to avoid
political involvements, 49; arouses
Daggett's opposition and fury, 50;
resigns pastorate, 50; is supported by
congregation and Governor John
Downey, 50; leaves for England and
later accepts New York pastorate, 184
note 93
Searles, John E., Jr.: member of commission to investigate sugar smuggling, 149
Secession: attitude of Californians
toward, 48-51; views of in Nevada,
53, 54
Shannon, Wilson (former Governor of
Ohio): 20; leader of California gold
seekers, 20
Sharon, William: buys *Territorial Enterprise,* 61, 95-96; friendly toward
Daggett, 66, 95-96; silver tycoon in
Nevada, 73, 83-84, 94; summary of
career of, 75; manager of Nevada
branch of Bank of California, 77, 94-
95, 118-19; theatre patron, 88; defeated for Republican nomination for
U.S. Senate, 95; builder of Virginia
and Truckee Railroad, 96; manipulator of votes to secure U.S. Senate
seat, 96-97, 118; elected senator, 97;
defeated for reelection, 118-20
Sheridan, Philip (Civil War general):
63-64, 92, 128
Sherman, John: as mediating force in
Ohio Republicanism, 131; concern
over practical aspects of Hawaiian
reciprocity, 147
Silver, coinage of: Nevada's interest in,
74, 100, 114-15, 144-45
Simpson, Matthew (Methodist bishop):
popular speaker in Nevada, 92
Snook, Ann Daggett (Rollin's cousin):
early impressions of Ohio frontier,
9-10
Sparks, William A. J.: congressional
opponent of Daggett's school land
bill, 115-16
Spaulding, O. L.: member of commis-

Virginia City, Nevada: earliest settlements in, 52; Daggett establishes brokerage house in, 52; Mark Twain resides in, 54; Confederate element in, 54; early journalism in, 54 ff.; Memorial Day celebrations in, 67-68; living conditions in, 71-73; business leaders of, 73-76; mining conditions in, 76-79; amusements in, 79-81; prostitution in, 81-82; immigrant groups in, 83-84; vigilantes in, 84-85; theatre in, 86-90; lecturers in, 90-91; churches in, 92; lodges, 93; as declining community, 166; early freighting facilities, 187 note 18

Virginia City *Chronicle*: competitor of the *Enterprise*, 62, 63, 82

Virginia City *Enterprise*: pioneer paper at Genoa and Carson City, 53; removed to Virginia City, 53; remarkable staff, including Mark Twain, Daggett, and Dan De Quille, 53; activities of journalistic cronies, 54-56; De Quille's contributions to, 58-59; decline of, 59; rivalry between Goodman and Daggett as poets, 60-61; Sharon becomes owner, 61; Daggett as editor, 61-62; Goodman as editor, 61-62; contributions of Denis Driscoll and Dennis E. McCarthy, 62-63; attacks on Chief Justice Turner, 63; attitude toward General Philip Sheridan, 63; opposition to prize fighting, 64; attack on General Thomas Williams, 65; denunciation of Mr. and Mrs. Frank Leslie, 65; comments on Daggett's poems, 68, 104; burned in disastrous fire, 85-86; reports on life in Virginia City, 72-73, 78-80, 84-85, 89-90, 92-93, 95-96, 99-101

Wachusetts: U.S. naval vessel in Hawaii, 138-39

"Waikiki": Hawaiian poem composed by Daggett, 159

Ward, Artemus. *See* Browne, Charles Farrar

Warner, Adoniram J.: congressional colleague of Daggett, 106; free silver advocate, 114

Warren, Mrs.: Virginia City madam, 81

Washington, D.C.: Daggett's life there as congressman, 105-07, 120, 123, 124, 131, 173-74; Daggett and his wife visit, 161

"Watch on the Heights": poem by Daggett, 102-04

Weekly Occidental: pioneer Nevada literary magazine, 56, 185 note 15

Welsh: miners in Virginia City, 82

White, Luke (father-in-law of Rollin): 5, 7

Wiegand, Conrad: leading assayer of Virginia City, 57

Williams, Thomas: political candidate, attacked by *Enterprise*, 65

Wodehouse, James H.: Great Britain's diplomatic representative in Hawaii, 155; shares convivial moods with Daggett, 155

Woodhull, Victoria: unconventional lecturer and woman's rights leader, 91

Wright, William (Dan De Quille): editorial writer on *Enterprise*, 54-55, 58-59; summary of career, 58-59; author of *History of the Big Bonanza*, 59; theatre patron, 86; opinion of William Sharon, 96

Yellow Jacket mine, Virginia City: serious fire in, 78

Young, Thomas L.: congressman from Ohio, 106; Daggett's friendship with, 106; compared with Daggett, 106